THE POLITICS OF ARMENIAN MIGRATION TO NORTH AMERICA, 1885–1915

SOJOURNERS, SMUGGLERS AND DUBIOUS CITIZENS

David E. Gutman

EDINBURGH
University Press

Edinburgh University Press is one of the leading university presses in the UK. We publish academic books and journals in our selected subject areas across the humanities and social sciences, combining cutting-edge scholarship with high editorial and production values to produce academic works of lasting importance. For more information visit our website: edinburghuniversitypress.com

Edinburgh University Press Ltd
The Tun – Holyrood Road
12 (2f) Jackson's Entry
Edinburgh EH8 8PJ

First published in hardback by Edinburgh University Press 2019

Typeset in Jaghbuni by
Servis Filmsetting Ltd, Stockport, Cheshire,

A CIP record for this book is available from the British Library

ISBN 978 1 4744 4524 5 (hardback)
ISBN 978 1 4744 4525 2 (paperback)
ISBN 978 1 4744 4526 9 (webready PDF)
ISBN 978 1 4744 4527 6 (epub)

Contents

Acknowledgements

This book has benefitted enormously from the guidance and input of numerous people whom I have been fortunate enough to encounter as this project evolved. As an undergraduate at the University of Minnesota, I benefitted from the mentorship of a number of scholars who were very patient with a motivated but naïve student. I thank especially Gary Cohen, Theofanis Stavrou and the late Stephen Feinstein for helping to lay a foundation for my study of the past. In particular, however, I would like to thank Taner Akçam who helped to introduce me to the history of the Armenian genocide, an interest that served as my entrée into the history of the late-Ottoman world.

I am forever grateful to Donald Quataert for taking a chance on a young and very green aspiring Ottomanist. He took me on as a graduate student despite the fact that I had little training or background in the field. I imagine he could see my eyes bulge from across the table the first time he laid an Ottoman document in front of me. But he was infinitely patient. He introduced me to new ways of thinking about the dynamics that drive change over time. Despite my interest in topics long considered to be 'taboo' in the field of Ottoman history, he never once attempted to steer me in a different direction. Instead, he served as a generous – if sometimes tough – guide along a path less travelled. It was Donald who encouraged me to go to the National Archives in the summer of 2007 with an open mind to see if I might find something that could serve as the basis of a dissertation topic. It is there, in the consular reports from Harput, that the impressive story of these transhemispheric sojourners first caught my eye. I will always regret that Donald did not live to see this book, one that owes its very existence to his mentorship and guidance.

Jean Quataert stepped in after Donald's death and, at a very difficult time, saw me through to completion. Her influence has also been tremendous, and she encouraged me to read widely and to transcend boundaries of discipline and region. This work is infinitely stronger because of her mentorship. Likewise, Rifaʿat Abou-El-Haj pushed me to think comparatively, and to always interrogate my own motivations for intervening in the past. Kent Schull has been a tireless and unflagging supporter of this project. He read over and provided extensive comments on earlier drafts of this manuscript, and helped me to navigate the world of academic publishing. His mentorship and friendship in these early years of my scholarly career have been indispensible. This work also owes much to him.

I have been fortunate to meet many lifelong friends and comrades since first beginning my career as an Ottoman historian. Nilay Özok-Gündoğan, Can Nacar and Azat Gündoğan have become like siblings to me. It is true that you often learn the most from your peers. They have left an indelible mark on this project. Allison Bramlett, Nurcin Ileri, Dan Johnson, Irfan Kokdas and Fulya Ozkan made enduring the long and desolate winters of the Southern Tier all the more enjoyable. I have enjoyed the opportunity to meet numerous people in archives or at various conferences and workshops over the past several years. Whether informally through chats over bisküvi and çay, or through formal invitations to share my research, their thoughts and feedback are reflected in the pages of this book. Thank you especially to Will Smiley, Josh White, Matthew Ellis, Lale Can, Will Hanley, Stacy Fahrenthold, Marc Mamigonian, Ümit Kurt, Barlow Der Mugrdechian, Shant Mardirossian, Zeynep Gürsel, Chris Gratien, Michael Christopher Low, Susanna Ferguson, Akram Khater, Lucy Salyer, Bedross Der Matossian, Lerna Ekmekçioğlu, Devi Mays, Andrew Arsan, Ibrahim Kalkan, Michael Ferguson, Lily Ballofett, Mukaram Hhana, Vladimir Hamed-Troyansky, Ilham Khuri-Makdisi, John Chalcraft, Janet Klein and Cengiz Kırlı. At Manhattanville, I have been truly fortunate to find myself in the same department as Irene Whelan, Greg Swedberg, Colin Morris, Mohamed Mbodj and Lawson Bowling. I am deeply grateful to the support they have provided me as I worked to balance my teaching and my scholarship. I also enjoyed the friendship and camaraderie of my colleagues outside of History, including Caralyn Bialo, Elizabeth Cherry, Megan Cifarelli, Meghan Freeman, Chris Pappas, Nayma Qayum, Lisa Rafanelli, Patrick Redding and Chris Sarver.

This project would not have been possible without the support of several other institutions. My initial ten month research stay in Istanbul was funded by a generous Fulbright grant. Shorter research stints have been funded by two faculty research grants from Manhattanville College, a grant from the Institute of Turkish Studies and the Binghamton University History Department. The archival staff at the Prime Ministry Archives in

Istanbul were without fail extraordinarily prompt and efficient in helping me to amass the thousands of documents that serve as the foundation of this study. I sincerely hope that the Ottoman archives will remain as open and as accessible to future generations of Ottomanists as they were to me and to my cohort. The staff at the National Archives in College Park, Maryland, graciously helped to introduce a still wet-behind-the-ears graduate student to the world of archival research. Susan Majdak, interlibrary loan librarian and the rest of the staff at the Manhattanville College library have helped to ensure I had access to sources. I am very grateful for their help. Nicola Ramsey has provided crucial support for this project since our first meeting at MESA in 2014. Thank you to her and to the staff at Edinburgh University Press for seeing this book through to completion. I am also grateful to the very helpful suggestions of the two anonymous reviewers whose feedback helped immeasurably in improving this book.

My deepest gratitude is reserved for my family. My in-laws Kathy Peterson, Mike Peterson, Amelia Peterson and Aaron Haug have been incredibly generous with their time and have helped me to carve out time from an otherwise very busy family life to finish the book. My parents Victor Gutman, Catharine Fogarty, my brother Daniel Gutman and my stepmother Roberta Wilhelm have helped to make me the person and scholar that I am today. They have helped me to celebrate triumph and to cope with tribulation. Their support and their love have guided me every step of the way. In April 2012, I was preparing to defend the dissertation project on which this book is based when my eldest son Isaiah entered the world. Three years later, as I quietly wondered whether I would be able to balance the intense demands of parenting, teaching and writing, he was joined by Ezra. Gabriel was born as I was finishing the final touches on the manuscript; the best kind of bookend. Isaiah, Ezra and Gabriel fill me with a sense of joy and fulfilment in a way that teaching and writing never can. And lastly to Sarah. She has been with me every step of the way, enduring this project in every form; reading drafts; suffering my absences while I researched and wrote – even if I was just in the other room; and being the best mother that three little boys could ever hope for. It is to her that I dedicate this book.

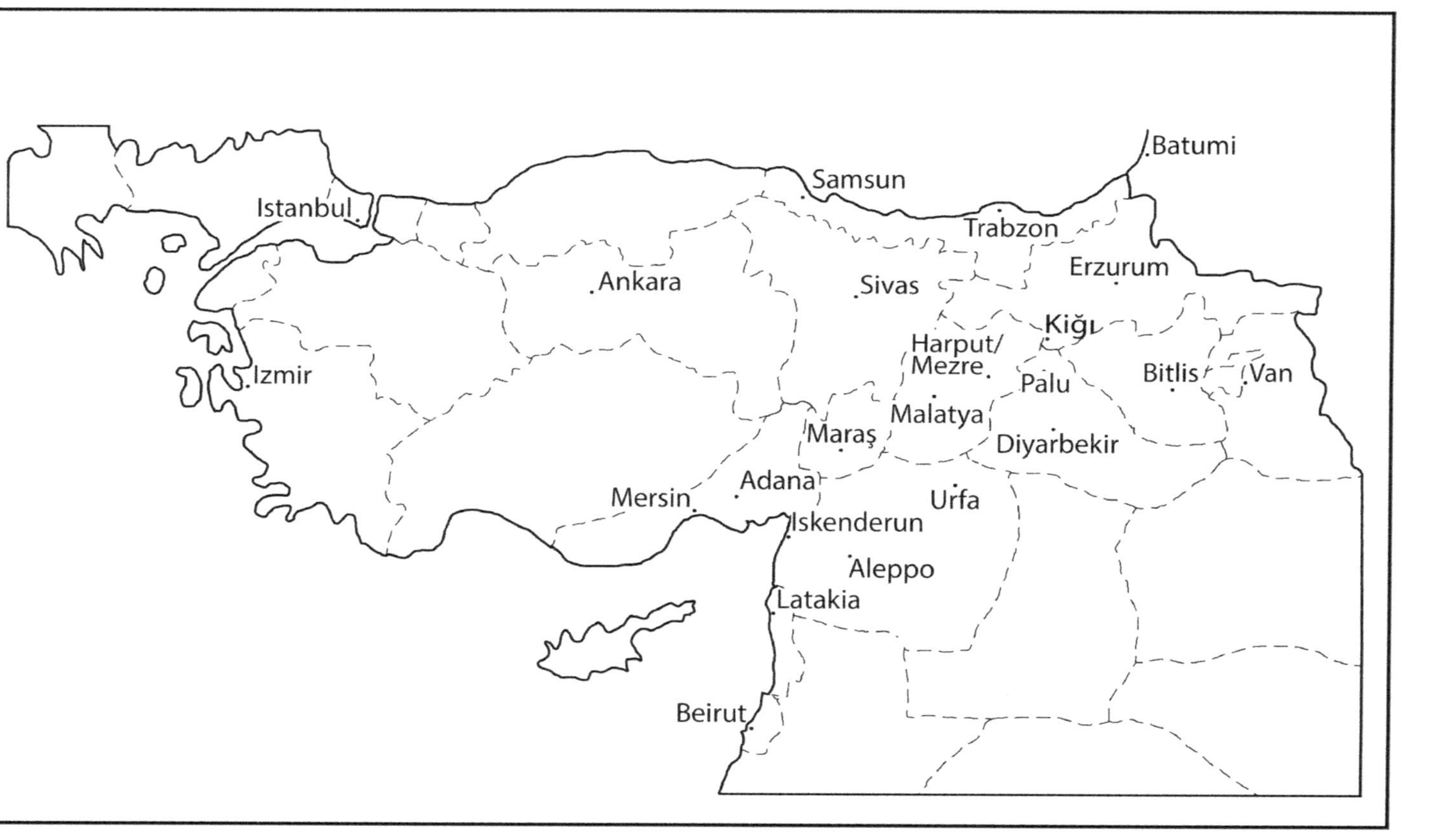

Map of the Ottoman Empire, ca 1900

Introduction

The migrant is, according to philosopher Thomas Nail, 'the political figure of our time.'[1] Perhaps nowhere is this more the case in the early twenty-first century than in the former lands of the Ottoman Empire. From Libya to Iraq, Yemen to Macedonia, the Middle East has become the epicentre of the greatest migrant and refugee crisis in generations. Countries throughout the region struggle to cope with swelling populations of displaced people, many of whom have been left to languish in squalid camps with little access to food, water, medical treatment or education. Exacerbating the situation are the efforts of many states, especially those located on the frontiers of the European Union, to close their borders, effectively stranding millions of migrants and refugees in transit. The militarisation of land and sea borders separating North Africa and the Middle East from the European Union has contributed to the emergence of a vast smuggling industry, particularly along the Mediterranean rim. Desperate migrants pay often exorbitant fees to smugglers who are eager to adopt ever-riskier strategies to assist their clients, while also avoiding capture. These dynamics have led one prominent scholar of migration to refer to the Mediterranean as 'the world's deadliest border.'[2] This deadliness is compounded by the fact that the European Union has poured vast resources into disrupting migrant smuggling operations despite the fact only a small fraction of the unauthorised migrants who arrive in Europe each year do so by crossing the Mediterranean or through other clandestine channels.[3] Meanwhile, the migrant and refugee crisis has emboldened and empowered xenophobic rightwing movements from Hungary to the United States, where the figure of the Middle Eastern migrant has been cast as a threat to political stability and to civilisation itself, helping to further influence policies that increase the dangers of the migration process.

The current situation in the Middle East and Mediterranean regions is not without precedent. In fact, at the turn of the twentieth century, Middle Eastern migrants and refugees were at the front and centre of several developments that would profoundly reshape how states throughout the world govern mobility, both across and within their own borders. In the Ottoman Empire's final decades, millions of Muslims fleeing persecution in the Balkans, the Caucasus and Crimea fled into the dwindling empire's Anatolian and Arab heartlands. Istanbul was left with the difficult task of settling these refugees and incorporating them into the Ottoman system, a process that triggered political and economic upheaval in many of the communities that received them.[4] Following World War I, Armenian and Assyrian survivors of the Ottoman state's wartime campaign of genocide were scattered throughout the former Arab provinces of the empire. The vast majority had been rendered stateless, without a home to return to and in a legally tenuous position in the societies that reluctantly harboured them. The international response to those displaced by genocide and ethnic cleansing in the former Ottoman Empire helped to lay the groundwork for the emergence of the refugee as a subject of international law.[5]

Refugees were not the only group whose mobility proved transformative at both the imperial and global levels in the late nineteenth and early twentieth centuries. Beginning in the mid-1880s, thousands of imperial subjects – Maronites from Mount Lebanon and Armenians from the empire's eastern provinces foremost among them – joined tens of millions of Eurasian migrants who left their home communities for destinations throughout the Americas. Large-scale migration from places as far afield as China and Italy was met with an increasingly restrictionist backlash in the United States and elsewhere in the Western Hemisphere; a response deeply rooted in racialised anxieties about the assimilability of these new arrivals. The Chinese Exclusion Act signed into law in the United States in 1882 inspired similar efforts by governments throughout the Americas to restrict Asian migration. By the first decade of the twentieth century, the United States government was experimenting with strategies to restrict immigration from Southern and Eastern Europe and the Middle East through the adoption of policies excluding migrants believed to pose a political, pathological, or moral danger or who risked becoming a 'public charge.'[6] The racist underpinnings of immigrant exclusion were on full display with the passage of legislation in 1924 introducing strict nationality-based quotas on immigration. Quotas were determined based on the percentage of the total US population each nationality group comprised in the 1890 census, taken when there were still relatively few immigrants in the United States from outside of Western Europe.[7]

The new law especially disadvantaged potential migrants from the former Ottoman Empire.[8] The empire's collapse had resulted in several independent states and colonial mandates being carved out of its erstwhile possessions. Many of the empire's former subjects were left without a legally recognised nationality. Those who did not fit easily within the national categories laid out in the 1924 law had virtually no chance of securing legal admission to the United States. Meanwhile, those already residing in the United States could face deportation to countries that did not exist when they had first migrated, the governments of which would not recognise them as citizens. The introduction of quotas and the deepening of restriction in the United States and elsewhere paralleled the widespread adoption of passport and visa requirements by governments, particularly in Europe and the Americas after World War I. The emergence of a global system of documents-based mobility control made it easier for states to bar people from entering their territory and provided an important mechanism for enforcing draconian restrictionist policies on immigration. By the end of the 1920s, an era that had been shaped by global mobility on a scale perhaps unprecedented in human history gave way to one increasingly defined by fences, border crossings and checkpoints. The ease with which these rapidly proliferating barriers to movement could be negotiated, meanwhile, was increasingly determined by the nationality emblazoned on one's passport.

Migration and mobility have played a role in shaping the contemporary global order, based on the primacy of the nation-state. Only in the past two decades, however, have scholars begun to study in earnest how migration intersects with other dynamics central to the modern nation-state such as citizenship, race, sovereignty and biopower. Historians of Latin American and East Asian migrations in particular have been pioneers in this regard.[9] Despite having been a major sender and recipient of migrants in the nineteenth and twentieth centuries, only recently have historians begun working to incorporate the Ottoman Empire and the broader Middle East region into this historiographical discussion. Newer studies have, for example, discussed the strategies adopted by the British, Russian and Ottoman states to both monitor and police the *hajj* and use their support for the pilgrimage as propaganda to win the hearts and minds of Muslims living under colonial rule.[10] Others have shed light on the transimperial linkages forged by Muslim pilgrims, migrants and refugees who regularly travelled between the Russian and Ottoman empires. These works have debunked earlier assumptions that Muslim mobility between the two empires was invariably unidirectional and have revealed the Tsarist empire's complicated and ambivalent relationship to the diverse

Muslim populations that lived under its rule.[11] Likewise, historians studying migration between the Middle East and the Americas, both before and after the collapse of the Ottoman Empire, have demonstrated the many connections migrants maintained with their home communities and regions, investigated the emergence of diaspora identities, and revealed the many challenges Middle Eastern migrants faced in navigating the politics of race and restriction.[12] Unlike studies on the *hajj* or Muslim migration between Russia and the Ottoman Empire, however, work on the overseas migration of primarily Middle Eastern Christians largely ignores the Ottoman state as an actor in the pre-World War I era. Indeed, even as scholars have worked over the past several decades to 'bring the state back in' as an important force shaping the migration process, the Ottoman state's migration policies have never been the subject of rigorous study.

This book contends that a focus on the Ottoman response to the emergence of large-scale overseas migration from the empire provides a new and unique angle on the much broader history of the rise of anti-migrant and restrictionist politics in the late nineteenth and early twentieth centuries. It was, after all, in this era (roughly 1880–1924), that modern practices and strategies of mobility control and immigration restriction were introduced, refined and reworked, eventually evolving into the internationalised system of passports, visas, rigid border controls and draconian immigration restrictions that exists today. Although the Ottoman Empire did not survive long into the post-World War I era, it was nonetheless a party to the historical processes that helped to give rise to this system, and it experimented with many of the strategies and methods of migration and mobility control that would later become integral to its function.

The Ottoman state did not respond uniformly to the overseas migration of its diverse subject populations. While by the late 1890s, Lebanese migrants faced few constraints on their ability to migrate, Armenians, whose global sojourning was deemed by Istanbul a threat to political and social order, faced draconian limitations on their ability to travel abroad. For this reason, this book focusses specifically on the Ottoman state's response to Armenian migration in the empire's final three decades. Between 1885 and 1915, at least sixty-five thousand Armenians left the Ottoman Empire for the United States. Several thousand also went to Canada in this same period.[13] At least half of the Armenians who migrated to North America left between 1888 and 1908, during which time the Ottoman state enforced a strict ban on Armenian overseas migration. This migration ban, introduced during the autocratic regime of Sultan Abdülhamid II (1876–1908), was motivated by Istanbul's belief that migration was directly related to the almost simultaneous emergence and rapid growth of political networks and organisations that sought greater autonomy or full independence for the empire's Armenian populations. Much like today, state efforts to limit and prohibit mobility led to the emergence of an underground economy based on helping migrants to overcome these obstacles. This study recreates the expansive smuggling networks that allowed Armenians to skirt Istanbul's migration ban. It also investigates the many methods and strategies employed by the Ottoman state to put a stop to clandestine migration. The complex interplay between migrants and smugglers on one side, and the central state and local officials on the other, provides a unique insight into the social and political dynamics that both shaped and frustrated the exercise of state power. Furthermore, tracing these ephemeral and constantly evolving smuggling networks reveals how Ottomans of many different ethnic, religious, class and geographic backgrounds could transcend seemingly insuperable barriers of time and space with surprising deftness and speed. Meanwhile, in the late 1890s, large numbers of Armenian migrants began returning to their home communities in the Ottoman interior even as Istanbul endeavoured to prevent them from reentering the empire. Armenian return migration forced the Ottoman state to reconsider its understanding of concepts such as territory, sovereignty and nationality in an increasingly interconnected world. Following the constitutional revolution of 1908, Hamidian-era prohibitions on migration and return were lifted, giving rise to a relatively liberal mobility control regime that faced an entirely new set of challenges. Contrasting the effects of the Hamidian regime's migration policies to those of the post-1908 constitutional government brings into sharper focus the integral role that policy and state power plays in shaping the migration process.

Migration Restriction, Mobility Control and the Ottoman Empire in Comparative Perspective

Prominent historian of migration Mae Ngai argues that the interstate system that emerged after World War I, one that 'aimed at achieving order and peace based on crustacean borders,' necessitated the imposition of 'rigid border controls, passports, and restrictions on entry and exit.'[14] The restrictionist policies and measures adopted by numerous states in the pre-war era laid the groundwork for the internationalisation of these practices beginning in the 1920s.[15] The historiography on anti-migrant politics and mobility control in the late nineteenth and early twentieth centuries is almost entirely focused on the Americas and Europe. Meanwhile, little work has been done on how non-Western states and societies responded to the global migrations of the steamship era. The ban on Armenian migration to North America was motivated by many of the same anxieties that animated restrictionist policies and discourses in the United States. By the turn of the twentieth century, migrants in the United States, especially those originating from outside of Western and Central Europe, were increasingly marked as inassimilable or as vectors of pathological and political contagion. For Istanbul, Armenians who travelled between eastern Anatolia and North America were dangerous troublemakers bent on spreading sedition throughout the empire's already politically unstable eastern provinces. In response to unwanted migration, the Ottoman Empire and the United States both adopted stricter border controls, increased their capacity to police mobility and ramped up deportations.

Juxtaposing the migration policies of the Ottoman and United States governments may appear on the surface to be a classic case of apples and oranges. The United States, a constitutional republic, was perhaps the single greatest recipient of migrants in the steamship age. The Ottoman Empire, meanwhile, was prior to 1908 an autocratic monarchy, and was an important source of overseas migration in this period. Despite the substantial differences between these two cases, scholars have advocated for an approach to studying migration that emphasises the inherent comparability of its many modalities. Although the United States was a net recipient of overseas migration while the Ottoman Empire was in many ways a sending society *par excellence*, as Thomas Nail has argued: 'the figure called an 'emigrant' from one point and an 'immigrant' from another is *the same figure: the migrant*. It is the same figure seen from two sides of the same Möbius strip.'[16] Nail's metaphor is useful here because it serves as a reminder not to let the direction of movement interfere with the comparison because at a fundamental level, the governments of the United States and the Ottoman Empire were responding to the same phenomenon.

Of course, this is not to say that the US and Ottoman cases are exactly alike. It would be disingenuous, for instance, to overlook the fact that while foreign nationals were the targets of restrictionist policies in the United States, the Ottoman state's ban on Armenian migration targeted its own subjects. Nonetheless, even on this point important parallels exist. In the Ottoman Empire and the United States, citizenship and nationality were still relatively ill-defined categories in the late nineteenth century. The explosive growth of overseas migration forced both states to redefine concepts such as nationality and citizenship. Chinese exclusion, the United States government's initial experiment in draconian immigration restriction, was premised on the conceit that Chinese migrants were ineligible to become US citizens on grounds of their purported racial inferiority. In this way, immigration restriction in the United States grew in part out of a desire to define and to limit the parameters of citizenship, particularly following the American Civil War in an era where previously excluded groups such as African Americans and Native Americans were (at least in law) guaranteed citizenship rights. Excluding migrants from acquiring citizenship solely because of their race helped to give rise to 'the modern American alien and an illegal counterpart.'[17]

Similarly, over the course of the nineteenth century, the Ottoman state endeavoured to create a sense of common imperial identity among the diverse populations over which it ruled. Accompanying this effort, in a series of reforms in the mid-nineteenth century, Istanbul guaranteed its subjects equal treatment under the law regardless of their religious identity. The belief shared by many within the Ottoman state that Ottoman Armenians posed a unique and immediate threat to the empire's survival, a supposition that undergirded the ban on their migration, reflects the challenges that beset the project of creating a singular Ottoman nationality. The failure of this effort explains in part why Armenians who returned to the Ottoman Empire after sojourns in North America were treated in a manner that resembled the United States government's treatment of Chinese migrants in the exclusion era. Comparing the Ottoman and American response to overseas migration also sheds important light on the truly global process of state building in the nineteenth and twentieth centuries.

In addition to the insight it provides on synchronic developments in the late nineteenth and early twentieth centuries, the Ottoman case is also useful for what it can tell us about the present. Sociologists and anthropologists working on contemporary global migrations have demonstrated a close relationship between the criminalisation of migration and the militarisation of borders and the phenomenon of people smuggling.[18] As Maurizio Albahari notes in his study of migration control efforts on the Mediterranean: 'The militarization of straits has . . . deterred people travelling shorter and safer distances on smaller boats, with or without the services of small-scale smugglers. Conversely, it has contributed to the profiteering success of larger organised criminal enterprises, better equipped to provide transport in the light of the more demanding circumstances.'[19] People smuggling has become so ubiquitous in the second decade of the twenty-first century that Mexican coyotes and Libyan boatmen have entered the global popular imagination, typically as villains profiting handsomely off of their migrant clients' vulnerability and desperation. At the same time, governments are rarely targets of similar popular opprobrium despite the role their policies play in setting the state for this situation.

A similar migrant smuggling industry also emerged in response to efforts by the Ottoman state to curtail the overseas mobility of its Armenian subjects. Each effort by the Ottoman state to prevent migrants from leaving or reentering the empire's borders encouraged smugglers to expand the scope and sophistication of their enterprises. Similar to the dynamics Albahari describes in the contemporary Mediterranean, by the end of the Hamidian period, Armenian migrants were travelling longer distances and paying greater sums of money to increasing numbers of intermediaries in order to escape detection by state authorities. Understanding the dynamics that drove the emergence and evolution of migrant smuggling networks in the late Ottoman context can provide insights into how similar clandestine channels function in the present. Strikingly, migrant smuggling is a far more deadly and exploitative business today than it was in the late nineteenth and early twentieth centuries. This is the case despite a century of technological advances in transportation and communication, and the existence of numerous government and non-governmental organisations ostensibly dedicated to advocating for the rights of migrants. As this study shows, even the efforts of a relatively weak state like the Ottoman Empire to enforce restrictions on migrations gave rise to an impressive migrant smuggling infrastructure. Meanwhile, the sophisticated technologies and strategies employed to police mobility and control borders in the contemporary period force smugglers and their clients to rely on ever more risky strategies of evasion. Irrespective of the time period involved, the emergence of migrant smuggling networks in response to the efforts of states to restrict mobility reveals the tremendous impact that state power can have on the migration process.

The Ottoman case also affords an opportunity to compare two radically different migration control regimes, and their respective impacts on the experience of migration. Following the 1908 revolution, also known as the 'Young Turk' or Second Constitutional Revolution, and the subsequent reintroduction of constitutional rule in the Ottoman Empire, most Hamidian-era restrictions on domestic and international mobility were lifted. The new regime's belief in the intrinsic right to freedom of mobility was inspired by the nineteenth century liberal thought that held that state restrictions on movement and commerce were both uncivilised and anathema to the rule of law.[20] Yet by the early twentieth century, this view appeared increasingly quaint. In the years immediately preceding World War I, the Ottoman Empire was one of few states advocating for fewer limitations on mobility at a time when the global turn towards restriction was beginning to crystallise. Unbeknownst to the constitutional government that took power in 1908, the international migration control regime that would emerge to full form by the middle part of the twentieth century would, in practice, more closely resemble that of their autocratic predecessors. Indeed, the government of the post-Ottoman Republic of Turkey looked to the mobility control strategies of the Hamidian era as they endeavoured to keep Armenian genocide survivors from returning and laying claim to property forcefully appropriated from them during the course of the war. The nation-state system, with its well-defended 'crustacean' borders, and draconian restrictions on mobility had fully arrived in the post-Ottoman Middle East.

Armenians and the Ottoman East in Late-Ottoman Historiography

Only very recently have Ottoman historians begun to approach the Armenian and Kurdish populations who predominated in the empire's eastern periphery as subjects of serious scholarly inquiry. In the second-half of the twentieth century, as Ottoman history emerged as an established field of inquiry, Ottomanists were discouraged from studying topics related to the empire's Kurdish and Armenian populations. The study of Armenians in the late-Ottoman period was almost entirely focused on the genocide and other episodes of anti-Armenian violence and persecution, and most scholars were divided between two irreconcilable 'Turkish' and 'Armenian' camps. In this environment, fruitful dialogue between the closely interrelated fields of Armenian and Ottoman studies was rendered nearly impossible.

The past two decades, however, have witnessed a sea change in the historiography on Kurds and Armenians in the Ottoman Empire, the Armenian genocide and the Ottoman east more broadly. A new generation of Ottomanists has begun to explore subjects and themes long considered taboo, and the partisan impasse concerning the fate of the empire's Armenians during World War I has slowly begun to lift.[21] In the past several years, scholarship relying on both Armenian and Ottoman language sources have broadened our understanding of the Armenian experience in the final decades of the Ottoman Empire, moving beyond overly simplistic and deterministic portrayals of violence and persecution.[22] Meanwhile, recent studies on the Ottoman east have provided insight into the tumultuous and often-violent process by which the region and its populations were incorporated into the imperial fold as part of the broader Ottoman modernisation project.[23]

This study is inspired by developments in these two interrelated fields of inquiry. In contrast to much of the recent work on Ottoman Armenians, much of which focuses on urban and church elites, this study is situated in the provincial Ottoman east and, to the extent that is possible with the available source material, seeks to give voice to the mostly non-elite migrants that populate it. Furthermore, it is the aim of this study to complicate our understanding of the Ottoman east as a historical and spatial unit of analysis. Despite the recent efflorescence of scholarship on the region, violence and immiseration continue to dominate our understanding of the factors driving change in the empire's eastern provinces in the nineteenth and early twentieth centuries. This picture is not entirely inaccurate. In parts of the region, settled agriculturalists were vulnerable to dispossession and depredation particularly as the state worked to pacify the region by encouraging Kurdish tribes and Circassian refugees to settle on lands often taken by force from their prior owners or stewards. This, coupled with the economic privation that resulted from soaring tax burdens, led some Armenian communities in the region to turn towards revolutionary politics and even armed resistance by the turn of the twentieth century.

Focusing too much attention on dispossession and over-taxation risks ignoring the fact that not all communities in the Ottoman east experienced the seismic transformations of the nineteenth and early twentieth centuries in the same way. The dual cities of Harput/Mezre and their hinterland, the epicentre of migration to North America in this period, were largely spared the violence and upheaval experienced elsewhere in the Ottoman east. The relative economic stability that Armenian communities in the Harput region enjoyed was a key factor in the eventual emergence of large-scale overseas migration. Furthermore, the existence of an influential Armenian elite in Harput/Mezre, capable of shaping local, regional and imperial politics to their advantage, became key to facilitating migration in the face of Istanbul's ban. Thus, the migration story does not fit easily into the dominant narrative about the Ottoman east during the empire's final century. It is by no means the goal of this book to minimise the very real suffering endured by Armenian communities in the region in this period. It is nevertheless important not to assume that migration to North America was just another response to persecution and violence. Instead, it reveals a much more complicated picture of this region and its history than currently exists in the literature.

At the same time, the migration ban was emblematic of the Hamidian regime's uniquely fraught relationship with the Armenian populations over which it governed, one dominated by suspicion and hostility. Migration to North America was not solely an Armenian phenomenon. Assyrian Christians and Muslims from the Harput region joined the exodus, albeit in smaller numbers. While Ottoman law forbade all subjects from leaving the empire without first securing government permission, these populations were exempt from the much stricter restrictions placed on Armenian overseas mobility after 1888. Istanbul's efforts to enforce the ban shaped how Armenians experienced the migration process, especially when they attempted to return to the empire after temporary stays in North America, in ways these other groups did not experience. For this reason, this book focuses exclusively on Armenian mobility. Ottoman historians long ago dispensed with the idea that the empire's population was comprised of internally homogenous communities neatly divided along impermeable lines of religion and ethnicity.[24] Sectarian and ethnic categories nonetheless played a pivotal role in shaping how the Ottoman state interacted with its subject populations. Just as Chinese and later Japanese and Mexican migrants experienced the migration policies of the United States government differently based on their ethnic and national identities, a migrant's 'Armenianness' shaped his or her mobility in ways not experienced by any other Ottoman community, particularly under the rule of Abdülhamid II.

Indeed, for the Hamidian regime, the Armenian migrant was synonymous with disloyalty, sedition and terrorism. While the aftermath of the 1908 revolution saw the demise of Abdülhamid's despotic system, the lifting of the migration ban and even the participation of some Armenian political parties in the imperial parliament, the association of Armenians with sedition and untrustworthiness persisted. Indeed, this view continues to colour the efforts of the Turkish government and its apologists to deny the Armenian genocide. In this rendering, the massacres and deportations of the World War I-era were justified on the basis that the empire's perfidious Armenian population was a threat to the war effort and to the survival of the dynasty itself.[25] Meanwhile, in present-day Turkey, 'Armenian' (*Ermeni*) is often invoked as a slur connoting disloyalty and sedition. In a 2014 television interview, then-Prime Minister Recep Tayyip Erdoğan when discussing his ancestral roots in the Black Sea town of Rize, a region that once boasted a sizeable Armenian population, stated: 'They have called me a Georgian, pardon me, but there are those who have said even uglier things, that I am an Armenian.'[26] Meanwhile, in 2017, an imprisoned high-ranking member of the People's Democratic Party, a left-leaning political organisation that draws most of its support from Turkey's Kurdish minority, was accosted by right-wing Turks shouting: 'Martyrs are interred here, we do not permit terrorists to be buried here. This is not an Armenian cemetery,' as she buried her mother.[27] It is my hope that this book sheds some light on the historical dynamics that helped to give rise to the almost mythological image of the 'Armenian traitor' in Turkey, a country built in part on the genocidal annihilation of the Ottoman Armenians.

Setting the Scene: Migration and the Harput Region

Most Armenians who left the Ottoman east for North America originated from in and around the dual city of Harput/Mezre, situated approximately one thousand kilometres to the southeast of the imperial capital of Istanbul and five hundred kilometres to the southwest of the Russian–Ottoman frontier. Harput/Mezre and its surrounding hinterland were located in Mamuretülaziz province. The districts of Palu in Diyarbekir province and Kiğı in Erzurum province also sent large numbers of Armenian migrants to North America. Together, these communities comprised a more or less coherent sub-region within the broader Ottoman east, anchored by the Harput/Mezre urban area and tied together by commerce, politics and environment. The rich alluvial soils deposited by tributaries of the Euphrates River fed the Harput region's lush plains, oasis-like among the towering mountain ranges and arid highlands that dominated much of the Ottoman east. The damming of the Euphrates in the mid-twentieth century has since flooded the region, but the reservoirs created by the Keban and Özlüce dams reveal on satellite imagery how the Euphrates River and its tributaries tied Harput/Mezre and its hinterlands to Palu in the east, Kiğı to the northeast and the district of Dersim to the north. The estimated sixty-five thousand who migrated to North America between the late 1880s and 1915 were a relatively small fraction of the Ottoman Empire's more than one and a half million Armenian subjects. Armenians comprised no more than one-third of the Harput region's total population of approximately five hundred thousand.[28] Considering that well in excess of fifty per cent of the total number of Armenians who migrated to North America originated from the Harput region, the volume of migration in many of the communities in and around Harput/Mezre was quite high. Indeed, Manoog Dzeron, village historian of Parchanj, located just to the south of Harput/Mezre, wrote that by the dawn of the twentieth century, nearly every household in the village had at least one member in the United States.'[29]

Armenians migrating between the Harput region and North America faced logistical challenges that most other transhemispheric migrants did not. Transportation infrastructure in the Ottoman east was underdeveloped, even when compared to other regions of the empire such as the Balkans and the Mediterranean coast. Railway lines were not extended to the region until the mid-1930s, well after the Ottoman Empire's demise and the establishment of the Turkish Republic.[30] The 645-kilometre long journey between Harput and the Black Sea port of Samsun, a route regularly used by migrants seeking to embark on the first leg of their long sea voyage to North America, took two weeks in even the best of conditions.[31]

The Hamidian regime's efforts to enforce its ban on Armenian migration further added to the challenges migrants faced just to get from their home communities in the interior to the Ottoman coast and onto ships bound for European transit ports. The willingness of these sojourners to migrate in the face of these obstacles speaks to the vitally important role migration to North America played in the social and economic life of the Harput region in the late nineteenth and early twentieth centuries. The fact that this phenomenon was largely restricted to Harput/Mezre and its hinterlands was a reflection of the region's unique historical trajectory compared to elsewhere in the Ottoman east in the empire's final century. Through the lens of overseas migration, this study examines the socio-economic and political dynamics that shaped the Harput region in this period. In doing so, it aims to deepen our understanding of the heterogeneous ways in which communities in the empire's eastern periphery experienced and responded to the seismic transformations of the Ottoman Empire's final century.

Outline of the Study

This book consists of six Chapters and is divided into three thematic sections. The first five Chapters focus on the Hamidian era, while the final chapter deals with the second constitutional period following the 1908 revolution. The first thematic section of the book, titled 'Migrants, Smugglers and the State,' explores the historical roots of overseas mobility from the Harput region, the role of migrant smuggling networks in facilitating migration from the empire, and the ways in which state power shaped the migration process. Chapter One situates large-scale Armenian migration between the Harput region and North America in a long durée historical context. It also locates the origins of the ban on Armenian overseas migration in the evolving relationship between the modernising Ottoman state and its Armenian populations in the nineteenth and early twentieth centuries. Chapter Two explores the emergence and evolution of the migrant smuggling networks that arose in response to the Ottoman state's efforts to prohibit Armenian migration. It shows how these networks emerged out of pre-existing ties of migration and commerce that linked migrant sending communities in the empire's eastern periphery to various port cities on the Mediterranean and Black Sea coasts. Over time, these increasingly sophisticated networks, which together comprised a veritable migration industry, grew to involve a surprisingly wide and diverse array of actors and middlemen including bankers, corrupt state officials, consular employees, boatmen and debt collectors, whose operations extended from Harput to Worcester, Massachusetts and everywhere in between.[32] Chapter Three examines the many challenges and contradictions that bedevilled the Ottoman state's efforts to prevent Armenian migration to North America. The failure of Ottoman policy reveals a great deal about the internal dynamics that propelled Ottoman state power in the final years of Abdulhamid II's reign. While the central state prioritised halting Armenian migration to North America, its efforts were frustrated by contradictions in policy, bureaucratic strife and the interests of local power players, whose political and economic interests were frequently at odds with Istanbul's.[33]

Whereas the chapters that comprise the first section of the book deal with outmigration, and the efforts of the Ottoman state to prevent Armenians from leaving the empire, the chapters in the second thematic section, 'Fortifying the Well-Protected Domains' focus on return migration and its relationship to themes of sovereignty and nationality/citizenship in the late Ottoman Empire. Chapter 4, 'Return,' uses statistical data from a variety of United States and Ottoman statistical sources to demonstrate a high volume of Armenian return migration between the late 1880s and 1908. This relatively high volume of return took place in spite of the Ottoman state's efforts to prohibit Armenian migrants from reentering the empire on the basis that they posed an intrinsic threat to political stability. This chapter examines the Ottoman state's efforts to prevent returning migrants from reentering the empire, comparing them to similar efforts at border control and immigration restriction adopted elsewhere in the world in this period. These efforts to 'secure the border,' while ultimately unsuccessful, reveal a great deal about late-Ottoman conceptions of sovereignty and territoriality. Chapter Five examines the fate of the many hundreds of migrants who successfully returned to their home communities in the Harput region. A significant proportion of these migrants had returned to the Ottoman Empire after naturalising as United States citizens. Ottoman state officials especially feared the return of such individuals, who they believed might claim extraterritorial privileges under the Capitulations, allowing them to engage in outlawed political activities without fear of prosecution. Efforts in the early and mid-1890s to detain and deport returnees who claimed American citizenship triggered a minor diplomatic row between the Ottoman Empire and the United States. Ottoman concerns about the threat these returned migrants posed to the political stability of the empire, however, resonated with American political elites who harboured their own anxieties about the effects of 'uncontrolled' mobility. Partly in response to pressure from the Ottoman state, the United States ceased to recognise the naturalised status of most Armenian returnees beginning in 1901, effectively stripping them of their United States citizenship. Unable to claim the protection of the United States government, returnees were left to the mercy of Ottoman state policy. Following the 1905 attempted assassination of Sultan Abdülhamid II by Armenian revolutionaries, the Ottoman state began deporting Armenians suspected of having illegally returned to the empire after sojourns in North America. In the end, as this chapter shows, the transhemipsheric mobility of these Armenian sojourners put them into direct conflict with the anti-migration policies of both states.

The book's third section, 'Genocide, Revolution and Migration's Legacies,' includes the book's sixth and final chapter. This chapter focuses on the period after the 1908 revolution and the reinstating of the Ottoman constitution. Shortly after the revolution, the new government introduced a policy guaranteeing freedom of both domestic and international mobility for all Ottoman citizens, a decision that effectively ended Hamidian-era prohibitions on Armenian migration and return. The liberalisation of state policy resulted in ever-larger numbers of Armenians migrating from and returning to the empire between 1908 and 1914. Meanwhile, as was the case in the Hamidian period, the constitutional government's liberal migration policies were hamstrung by a wide range of increasingly insuperable challenges including growing dissent among anti-immigration hardliners in the Ottoman bureaucracy; a growing crisis involving Ottoman migrants left stranded in European transit ports as a result of the tightening of restrictionist policies in the United States; and the increasing challenge of balancing a commitment to freedom of mobility with the military and economic concerns of the state. The chapter ends by discussing the fate of the Armenian sojourners of the Harput region following the 1915 Armenian genocide.

This study is based primarily on a meticulous reading of Ottoman language archival documents. Documents from the Commission for Expediting Initiative and Reforms (*Tesri'-i Muamelat ve Islahat Komisyonu*) created in the aftermath of the Armenian massacres of the mid-1890s and housed in the Ministry of Interior proved especially vital to this project. Consular records, most of which were collected over the course of a summer research excursion in the National Archives in College Park, Maryland, State Department documents and the Congressional Record, also proved valuable for examining the role of the United States government in this story. In addition to these state sources, this project relies on a wealth of Armenian language material in translation, including an assortment of village histories, memoirs and letters.

PART I. MIGRANTS, SMUGGLERS AND THE STATE

Hazar, Minas and Ahmed were like so many other enterprising Ottomans seeking to profit off of the rapidly expanding human traffic that circulated through the empire's port cities in the late nineteenth and early twentieth centuries. Based in the Black Sea city of Trabzon, each ran inns that catered to the thousands of primarily Armenian travellers from the Ottoman east that passed through the city each year, usually on their way to find work in Istanbul, Batumi, or destinations even farther afield. Like many natives of the Ottoman east, Hazar, Minas and Ahmed tailored their business to travellers from in and around their own home communities, using ties of compatriotism (hemşehrilik) to fuel their business. Travellers tended to favour a familiar (if not always friendly) face. After all, innkeepers did much more than simply provide temporary shelter to their road weary clientele. Firmly ensconced in the above and below ground economic life of the port city, they assisted their clients in everything from obtaining steamship tickets to arranging transportation from shore to ship. An innkeeper's reputation for performing these services efficiently could spread far and wide through the chains of migration that linked communities in the Ottoman east to Armenian migrant colonies throughout North America. So too could a reputation for being a swindler and a cheat.

As the twentieth century dawned, business was booming. In years past, most Armenian migrants en route to North America passed through Samsun, over three hundred kilometres to the west, or left through the Mediterranean ports of Mersin or Iskenderun. The Ottoman state, however, was doubling down on its efforts to enforce its draconian migration ban, which intended to keep Armenians from travelling overseas. As a result, it was becoming ever more difficult to travel clandestinely through these other ports, forcing growing numbers of North America-bound Armenian migrants to try their luck transiting through Trabzon. Where they had once helped clients procure steamship tickets for destinations such as Istanbul or Constanţa, Romania, Hazar, Minas and Ahmed were now helping their guests plan travel to more exotic and forbidden destinations such as Marseille and Liverpool. The innkeepers were getting increasingly bold in their efforts to assist their clients in evading the watchful eye of local authorities. This was a difficult proposition because the hilly topography that surrounded Trabzon forced all steamship passenger traffic to pass through the city's main port, unlike in many Mediterranean cities where smugglers and boatmen frequently conducted their business along desolate stretches of beach hidden from the coastal surveillance towers that were beginning to dot the coastline. Through their contacts among the city's constabulary, they arranged false travel documents for their guests indicating that they intended to travel for legitimate purposes to destinations within the empire. Their connections to the city's Armenian boatmen ensured their clients could travel from the shore to foreign steamers anchored in the harbour with little trouble or interference. For these services, they commanded a hefty price and could expect to get paid with little fuss.

The illicit migrant smuggling business was indeed profitable, but it came with its own set of challenges, including unwanted attention from local and provincial authorities who did not accept bribes to look the other way. Hazar, Minas and Ahmed occasionally found themselves under arrest, dragged before a judge and slapped with a small fine or short jail sentence. These penalties were usually no more than a nuisance and the profits from smuggling Armenian migrants through the port city made enduring such legal harassment more than worthwhile. For their part, high-ranking police officials in Trabzon felt their hands were tied. They were under constant pressure from Istanbul to put a stop to the smuggling rings operating in the city and more successfully enforce the state's ban on Armenian overseas migration. The punishments meted out to those they suspected of engaging in such activity proved to have little deterrence value. Furthermore, it was next to impossible to distinguish between Armenians transiting through the city on legitimate business, and those who sought to travel illegally to North America. More and more, it seemed to some, enforcing the migration ban was diverting much needed time and resources from issues of more pressing concern.[1]

The story of Hazar, Minas and Ahmed reflects many of the themes discussed in the three chapters that comprise the first part of this book. Armenian migration between the Harput region and North America did not emerge from a historical vacuum. Rather, it was a product of socio-economic and political dynamics specific to the region, including well-established ties to the many port cities along the Black Sea and Mediterranean coasts that would become key exit and entry points for Armenian sojourners seeking to leave and to reenter the empire. These connections between the interior and the coast would play a pivotal role in the emergence and evolution of the smuggling networks that would become pivotal to the ability of Armenians to travel abroad in the face of the migration ban. Finally, while the Hamidian regime was adamant about preventing Armenian migration to North America, as this story suggests, its efforts to enforce the ban were frustrated by a series of challenges and internal tensions that would prove difficult for it to overcome.

1

Migrants

In the early months of 1888, word reached the highest echelons of the Ottoman state that Armenians from the Harput region (*Harput ahalisinden*) were attempting to depart Istanbul for North America. By March Yıldız Palace, seat of Sultan Abdülhamid II's (1876–1909) personal bureaucracy, had been informed of at least seventy Armenians who had been denied permission to migrate or had otherwise been prevented from leaving. Over the previous several years, reports had been trickling in from Beirut about the exodus of mostly Christian peasants from the highlands surrounding the Mediterranean port city. The vast majority of migrants from that region, most of whom were also destined for North America, left without first obtaining permission from state officials to travel abroad. Now, it seemed, Armenians from the empire's much more remote eastern periphery were joining their Lebanese counterparts in seeking economic opportunity overseas.

This news came at an especially trying time for the embattled empire. The 1880s had so far been a decade of deepening political and economic instability throughout much of the empire's Kurdish and Armenian-populated eastern periphery. Of even more pressing concern, in 1887, an organisation calling itself the Hunchakian Revolutionary Party was founded by expatriate Armenians living in Geneva, Switzerland. Despite being only a year old, the organisation, which sought the overthrow of the Ottoman system and the creation of an independent Armenian state, had already established branches in several locations throughout the world, including at least one in the United States. There was already chatter in the Ottoman Foreign Ministry that some Armenians were migrating to the United States at the behest of members of the newly created party.

It was, according to the 1867 Passport Law, illegal for Ottoman subjects to leave the empire's borders without first obtaining the permission of the state.[1] Istanbul had been working to put a stop to unauthorised migration from Mount Lebanon to little avail. Given its specific concerns about the political ramifications of migration, however, the palace decided special action was needed to ensure that the trickle of Armenians leaving through Istanbul did not expand any further. In March 1888, it issued the following decree:

> The government takes no issue with our subjects travelling to America and other places for legitimate commercial purposes. Nevertheless, it is suspected that some Armenians are migrating to find work or for other purposes to 'completely and utterly free' countries such as the United States. Furthermore, it should be assumed that some Armenians who migrate purportedly for educational purposes have instead been encouraged by seditious political organizations to go to America so that they may benefit from the freedom of expression that exists there in order to spread their well-known agenda among the Armenians of the Ottoman Empire. And when these individuals return (to the empire) they will spare no expense to poison minds wherever they go. From now on, migrants intending to go to America and similar locations ostensibly to find work, but with the real intent of devoting themselves to the service of such pernicious objectives must not be granted passports, and they must be fully prohibited from departing the empire.[2]

The decree introduced a ban on Armenian migration to North America that would remain in effect until the constitutional revolution of 1908. The text makes clear why Istanbul especially feared Armenians travelling to the United States, a country where it believed a political movement that contested the legitimacy of the Ottoman system would be uniquely positioned to take root and to flourish. The purpose of this chapter is to address two interrelated questions, the answers to which are central to understanding the themes and dynamics explored throughout the remainder of this book, namely:

1. What drove tens of thousands of Armenians to leave the Harput region for North America in the late nineteenth and early twentieth centuries?
2. Why did the regime of Sultan Abdülhamid II see Armenian migration to North America as particularly threatening to the extent that it was willing to expend a great deal of time and resources on putting a stop to it?

Answering these questions requires the investigating numerous historical dynamics, which are at play on several temporal and spatial scales. This is at once a story of the contradictions and paradoxes of Ottoman reform; the transformation of a regional economy and society; the birth of new political discourses intended to either strengthen or challenge the power of the state; and the proliferation of powerful new technologies of transportation, communication and social control.

Paradoxes of Ottoman Reform in the Nineteenth Century

The Ottoman state's response to the overseas migration of its Armenian subjects stemmed in part from a fundamental contradiction that emerged over the course of the nineteenth century between the effort to mandate equality and promote unity among the empire's diverse populations and the simultaneous strengthening of sectarian institutions and identities. Two documents issued in 1839 and 1856 respectively served as blueprints for an ambitious project of reform and modernisation that fundamentally transformed the relationship between the Ottoman state and its subjects in this period. The first, the Gülhane Rescript (*Gülhane Hatt-i Şerif*), inaugurated the era of the Tanzimat reforms (1839–1876). Alongside proposing dramatic reforms to the military and taxation, the edict called for the creation of a new legal regime that applied equally to all subjects regardless of religion. As Şükrü Hanioğlu argues, the issuing of the rescript marked 'a significant first step toward the transformation of hitherto Muslim, Christian, and Jewish subjects into Ottomans'.[3] Seventeen years later, an even more ambitiously worded document, the 1856 Reform Decree (*Islahat Fermanı*), heralded the end of the legal supremacy of Sunni Muslims by declaring all Ottoman subjects equal under the law.[4] The rise of nationalism among Christians in the empire's Balkan provinces in the early nineteenth century impelled this rhetorical commitment to legal equality. By the early 1830s, as a result of the emergence of these nationalist movements and the support they received from a variety of European powers, the empire had been forced to cede territory to the creation of an autonomous Serbia in 1817 and a fully independent Greek kingdom in 1832. Proponents of the Tanzimat reforms hoped that fostering a sense of common Ottoman identity would help to limit the spread of nationalism among the empire's non-Muslims and prevent further territorial losses.[5]

In addition to promising equal treatment under the law, bowing to pressure from Britain and France, the Reform Decree also devolved greater powers of self-governance to the various non-Muslim confessional communities. As part of this process, in 1863, the Armenian Apostolic community in the empire promulgated a set of regulations intended to reform its communal institutions, commonly known as the Armenian National Constitution (*Hay azkayin sahmanadrutyun*). The constitution mandated the creation of provincial councils throughout the Ottoman east where the majority of the empire's Armenians resided. These councils would then elect members to serve in the Armenian general assembly based in Istanbul. The constitution endeavoured to strike a delicate balance between the sacred and the secular by creating a religious assembly responsible for governing the community's spiritual affairs, and a civil assembly responsible for more secular matters including representing Armenian interests before the Ottoman state.[6] As one historian notes, by placing the empire's Armenian community more firmly under control of the Istanbul patriarchate, an institution with close ties to the Ottoman state, the Armenian National Constitution was 'a quintessential Tanzimat document.'[7] The document would later serve as an inspiration for the Ottoman constitution introduced thirteen years later, with many of its authors also participating in the drafting the latter document.[8] Nonetheless, from the perspective of many within the imperial bureaucracy, the Armenian National Constitution and the robust governing structure it created, which paralleled similar developments among other non-Muslim communities, threatened to undermine the Tanzimat reform project founded on the principles of centralised rule and a shared Ottoman identity.[9]

The Tanzimat era ended with the introduction of an imperial constitution (*Kanun-i Esasi*) in 1876, a document that further enshrined the guarantees of legal equality and mandated the creation of an elected parliament. Although intended to serve as a blueprint for a more democratic and less centralised imperial system, in its final form the constitution gave the sultan the power to dissolve parliament and suspend constitutional rule. Introduced in a failed effort to secure British and French support in a looming war with Russia, the constitutional experiment was to be short lived. The ensuing war proved catastrophic, with the empire losing even more territory, its military in utter disarray and its economy in shambles. When the guns fell silent in early 1878, Sultan Abdülhamid II, who had been installed two years earlier in hopes that he would defend the new order, exercised his power to disband parliament and suspended the constitution.[10] He would rule as an autocrat for the next three decades, a period during which he would oversee the further centralisation and bureaucratisation of state power inaugurated by the Tanzimat. Meanwhile, in contrast to his reform-minded predecessors, Abdülhamid II emphasised the empire's Islamic identity as he endeavoured to cement the legitimacy of his rule in the eyes of the empire's Sunni Muslim majority.[11]

Abdülhamid II's autocratic rule, and his vaunting of the empire's identity as an Islamic state, was partly a reaction to the contradictions of the Tanzimat reforms. The effort to mandate equality and to create a common Ottoman identity occurred at the same time that non-Muslim ethno-religious communities enjoyed greater power and autonomy within the Ottoman system. This situation was also partly driven by the increasing intervention of European Great Powers in the internal affairs of the empire, ostensibly to protect the interests of its non-Muslim populations. This dynamic, which began in earnest in the late eighteenth century, was on full-display with the issuing of the 1856 Reform Decree.

The Russo-Ottoman War (1877–1878) and its aftermath only further heightened the contradictions embedded in the Ottoman reform project. In 1876, Istanbul found itself embroiled in an international controversy over allegations that irregular forces carrying the Ottoman flag had carried out atrocities against civilians in the process of quelling a revolt among its Bulgarian subjects. Russia used the allegations as a pretext to go to war, invading much of the empire's Balkan territories, sacking several cities in the Ottoman far east and preparing to march on the imperial capital. Only the intervention of Britain and France prevented all-out catastrophe. The subsequent Treaty of Berlin (1878) stripped the empire of much of its remaining territory in the Balkans, and permitted Russia to maintain control over the cities of Batumi and Kars in the Caucasus region. Meanwhile, Article 61 of the treaty, included at Russia's insistence, required Istanbul to enact a series of Armenian reforms, and mandated that it take special action to protect Armenian civilians from mistreatment at the hands of Kurdish tribesmen and Circassian refugees in the empire's eastern provinces. The treaty replaced the much more punitive Treaty of San Stefano that Russia unilaterally imposed on the Ottoman Empire immediately following the cessation of hostilities. The Treaty of San Stefano included concrete measures for enforcing these reforms. These measures were absent in the final text of the Treaty of Berlin, giving Istanbul little reason to carry out the reforms mandated by it. Regardless, as Ronald Suny argues, the treaty transformed Armenians in the Ottoman Empire into 'an instrument that could be used by European states to intervene in the affairs of the sultan's realm.' For Abdülhamid II, already reeling from fresh territorial losses stemming from the rise of nationalism among non-Muslims in the Balkans, the treaty further raised the spectre of Armenian nationalists securing the support of the Great Powers to create an independent state in the empire's eastern periphery. Over the course of the Hamidian era, these anxieties would fuel increasingly repressive and discriminatory policies specifically targeting the empire's Armenians, including special measures intended to limit their ability to travel both within and outside the empire's borders. At the same time, the Tanzimat-era principles of legal equality and the rule of law would continue to shape and also frustrate the implementation of these policies.

Migrants, Missionaries and Steamships

The emergence of large-scale Armenian migration from the Harput region to North America in the late 1880s was also heavily influenced by the twin dynamics of reform and modernisation. Istanbul's uneven efforts to bring the empire's eastern periphery more firmly under central state control over the course of the nineteenth century deepened already existing variations in the region's political and economic structures. The important role played by Harput in the implementation of the Tanzimat reforms in the Ottoman east helped to ensure that it would experience the jolting transformations of the empire's final century in a much different way than other communities in the region. Additionally, the establishment of a significant American missionary presence in Harput beginning in the middle of the nineteenth century, coupled with its strengthening economic connections to other regions in the empire and the outside world, only helped to set it further apart. Outlining the Harput region's unique historical trajectory in this period, shaped in large part by the convergence of these interrelated historical dynamics in the final decades of the nineteenth century, sheds light on why its residents migrated overseas to a much greater degree than their compatriots did elsewhere in the Ottoman east.

The eastern periphery of the Ottoman Empire, where the majority of its Armenian and Kurdish speaking populations resided, was incorporated into the sultan's realm in piecemeal fashion over the course of the sixteenth century. Sultan Selim I (1512–1520) secured the support of several independent Sunni Muslim Kurdish feudal grandees in his campaign against the empire's Shi'a rival, Safavid Persia. In the process, these grandees accepted Istanbul's suzerainty in order to protect their power and prestige from the Safavid threat.[12] Selim's successor Süleyman I (1520–1566) strengthened Ottoman control over the region by conferring on to the grandees the legal rights of proprietorship over their lands and guaranteeing the protection of the imperial military.[13] Until the early nineteenth century, a patchwork of autonomous Kurdish principalities governed much of the Ottoman east, with Istanbul retaining a limited but influential presence.[14] Little is known about Harput's historical trajectory in the sixteenth and seventeenth centuries. Beginning in the early eighteenth century, the commencement of mining at Keban helped strengthen the Harput region's economic and political ties to Istanbul, and by the end of the century, central state authority was much stronger there than in much of the rest of the Ottoman east.[15]

With the dawn of the nineteenth century, the reform-minded Ottoman state increasingly viewed the decentralised system of rule that existed in its eastern periphery as inimical to its efforts to build a modern empire.[16] As part of its nineteenth century reform and modernisation effort, the Ottoman state sought to bring the entirety of the region more firmly under its control. For the next several decades, Istanbul employed a number of strategies to realise this goal. These included breaking the power of the autonomous Kurdish feudal grandees, often through the use of military force; encouraging or compelling the sedentarisation of nomadic populations; settling refugees on land often expropriated from local agriculturalists; and introducing new forms of land tenure. Beginning in the 1830s, the Harput region played an increasingly important role in this process as a node of central state authority. A few years following the promulgation of the Tanzimat reforms, the regional governor – along with several other prominent local families – moved from the tightly packed neighbourhoods that surrounded Harput's ancient citadel to a new lowland settlement called Mezre, which developed over the course of the century into a modern provincial administrative centre. The dual city of Harput/Mezre would serve as a staging point for Istanbul's efforts to pacify the Ottoman east and to strengthen its authority over the region.[17]

Scholars have generally argued that the extension of the Tanzimat reforms into the empire's eastern periphery was a traumatic process for the region's Armenian populations in particular.[18] Istanbul's efforts to strengthen its authority by breaking the power of the ruling Kurdish grandees resulted in a political vacuum in many places. Elsewhere, settled agriculturalists, non-Muslims and Muslims alike, found themselves stuck in the middle of a conflict between state forces and those seeking to defend the existing power structure. Meanwhile, many of the region's peasants were subject to double taxation: compelled to pay the taxman sent from Istanbul alongside furnishing tribute to the local Kurdish tribal elites who continued to exercise extensive authority over their communities and lands.[19] In many areas of the Ottoman east by the second half of the nineteenth century, these dynamics contributed to widespread dispossession and economic immiseration among Armenian communities in certain areas of the Ottoman east, eventually helping to strengthen support for those voices calling for organised armed resistance against both Istanbul and Kurdish elites.

Armenian communities in the Ottoman east did not universally experience disempowerment and economic immiseration during the Tanzimat period. For some, the increasing consolidation of central state authority over the region proved to be a boon. As Masayuki Ueno shows, Armenians used the promise of reform as leverage to challenge practices they deemed unfair, took advantage of the creation of provincial councils to bolster their political influence at the local and regional levels and otherwise 'equipped themselves with knowledge of the language and principles of the Tanzimat . . . for their own purposes.'[20] Meanwhile, as Nilay Özok-Gündoğan demonstrates, as part of the effort to extend the Tanzimat reforms to the region, in 1848 the Ottoman state vanquished the Kurdish grandee, Abdullah, who controlled much of the lands in Palu, located roughly eighty kilometres to the east of Harput/Mezre. Istanbul took action against Abdullah after he and his henchman were accused of viciously attacking a local village populated by Kurdish and Armenian peasants, and sent him into internal exile following his defeat. The state confiscated and subdivided Abdullah's lands upon his death, using the parcels of land created in the process to introduce a system of private landownership to the region based on possession of transferable deeds issued by the central state treasury. The state subsequently issued the deeds for the newly subdivided parcels to local Kurdish and Armenian agriculturalists, many of whom had been victims of Abdullah's depredations.[21] Özok-Gündoğan speculates that this may have eventually helped to foster the emergence of a landholding middle peasantry with the combined economic and political influence to rival that of Palu's remaining feudal elites.[22] The comparatively peaceful conclusion to the episode was probably aided by Palu's proximity to Harput/Mezre, with the provincial council becoming the primary forum in which Abdullah's victims sought redress from the central state, earning the support of the province's governor.[23] Palu would become a major source of Armenian migrants to North America by the end of the nineteenth century.

While more work is needed to determine how representative the case Özok-Gündoğan describes was, circumstantial evidence suggests that rates of Armenian landownership in the Harput region increased dramatically in the mid-nineteenth century. For example, in 1876, the Archpriest Boghos Natanyan, prelate of the Palu Armenian Apostolic diocese, noted that Armenians in Harput:

> (u)ntil thirty years ago did not own a single piece of land . . . today, Armenians in the city as well as those in the villages have become landowners. One eighth of all land belongs to Armenians. Turks sell while Armenians buy. Trade is also in Armenian hands. Although they are subjects politically, economically they are in the dominant position.[24]

Armenians in the Harput region enjoyed the political stability that came along with Harput/Mezre's status as a bulwark of central state power in the Ottoman east. As hinted at by Natanyan, the mid-nineteenth century witnessed the emergence of a powerful Armenian merchant bourgeoisie in the

Harput region, whose wealth was tied to the region's increasingly vibrant agricultural economy.[25] The several Armenian families soon rivalled their more established Muslim counterparts in terms of political and economic influence.[26] Meanwhile, less well-to-do Armenian households increasingly employed a wide variety of strategies, from experimenting with the growth of cash crops such as opium, cotton and silk, to small-scale textile manufacturing to ensure their own economic survival and well-being. The success of these efforts likely also contributed to the increasing rates of Armenian land ownership. They also contributed to the emergence of what was, by the end of the nineteenth century, a vibrant regional economy based in and around the dual cities of Harput/Mezre.[27]

In addition to the growth of cash crops and textile manufacturing, labour migration also became an increasingly important economic strategy for Armenian households in the Harput region and throughout the Ottoman east in the nineteenth century.[28] In 1867, for example, more than 75,000 labour migrants travelled from the empire's eastern provinces to the imperial capital, and together remitted more than one-and-a-half million liras to the families they left behind.[29] By the second half of the nineteenth century, whole neighbourhoods in Istanbul were populated almost entirely by migrant labourers from the Ottoman east.[30] In addition to Istanbul, migrants from the Harput region also flocked to coastal boomtowns such as Adana and Izmir, and more established inland hubs such as Aleppo. Many of the same dynamics that led thousands of primarily young male sojourners, known as *pandukht* in Armenian, to leave their homes and seek work elsewhere within the empire would later compel some to embark on the much longer and more perilous journey to North America. However, whereas domestic labour migration was a widespread practice throughout the Ottoman east, large-scale overseas migration was a phenomenon largely restricted to the Harput region. The transition from brief stints in Istanbul or Aleppo to longer (and riskier) sojourns in Worcester, Providence or Brantford, thus involved a series of factors unique to Harput. The relative political and economic stability enjoyed by Armenian communities in the region, especially when compared to conditions prevailing elsewhere in the Ottoman east, was probably the single most important of these factors. Put simply, those who made the decision to embark on such a costly and sometimes dangerous journey, especially in the context of the Hamidian regime's efforts to enforce the ban on migration, only did so because the benefits outweighed the many risks. Wages in North America were far higher than what migrants could hope to earn by remaining in the Ottoman Empire. The money earned during a years-long sojourn abroad was indispensable to those households that hoped to expand their landholdings or otherwise improve their economic position. Indeed, the available evidence suggests that migrant dollars fuelled a sharp increase in Armenian landownership in the Harput region following the onset of large-scale migration to North America.[31] Further east and south, where the economic and political conditions for Armenians were far more precarious, particularly during the final decades of the Hamidian era, the time, expense and risk involved in overseas migration put it out of reach for most as a viable economic strategy.

Two other important factors, both originating outside of the Ottoman Empire, also help to explain why the Harput region emerged as the epicentre of Armenian migration to North America at the end of the nineteenth century: the arrival of American missionaries and the advent of cheap steam travel. In 1810, in the midst of a period of intense religious revivalism in the United States, a pious group of Massachusetts Protestants founded the American Board of Christian Foreign Missions (ABCFM).[32] When the first ABCFM missionaries arrived in the Ottoman Levant in the early 1820s, they hoped to convert Ottoman subjects, regardless of their religious background, to their unique brand of Christianity and remake the Ottoman Empire in the image of the United States.[33] When it was clear that this ambitious endeavour was doomed to fail, falling victim to a mixture of state opposition and Muslim and Jewish indifference to their evangelising efforts, they turned their focus almost entirely to the native Christian populations of the Middle East.[34] To echo Ussama Makdisi, their efforts to convince the Maronites of Mount Lebanon to buy into their vision of 'evangelical modernity' largely failed. Following the 1860 outbreak of sectarian violence in Mount Lebanon, American missionaries in the region abandoned some of their evangelical zeal, instead finding greater success meeting the significant local demand for the secular education they offered in their increasingly expanding network of missionary schools.[35] As Selim Deringil notes, the concomitant effort of the Hamidian regime to counter missionary education efforts by expanding its own system of schools in far-flung parts of the empire geared largely to Muslims had the effect of only deepening the politics of sectarianism that was already a hallmark of Abdülhamid's rule.[36]

This dynamic was certainly at play in the Harput region in the late nineteenth and early twentieth century.[37] Beginning in the middle of the nineteenth century, missionaries under the ABCFM umbrella set up shop in communities throughout regions of the Ottoman east with large Armenian and Assyrian populations. Their efforts at conversion were somewhat more successful than they had been in the eastern Mediterranean, and a sizeable and organised community of Armenian Protestants quickly emerged to the consternation of both the Ottoman state and many non-Protestant Armenians alike.[38] As was the case in the Levant, however, American missionary efforts were most visible in the realm of secular education (for both boys and girls), and perhaps nowhere were these efforts more visible in the Ottoman east than in the Harput region. By the final decades of the nineteenth century, the region boasted a dense network of ABCFM-run missionary schools catering to boys and girls alike. Most notable among these schools was Euphrates College, the campus of which was perched in the hilltop neighbourhoods of the old city of Harput.[39] Some of the first Armenians to travel to North America from the Harput region were graduates of Euphrates College who went on to study in prestigious universities in the United States, or opened businesses in communities throughout the American Northeast, becoming pioneers in the Oriental rug trade. These early immigrants, along with the missionaries themselves, proved to be an important conduit for information about the economic opportunities that existed in the United States.[40] It is thus no coincidence that New England factory towns in and around Boston, the headquarters of the ABCFM and the initial destination for many of these early immigrants, would become the primary destination of labour migrants arriving from the Harput region. It is nonetheless important not to overstate the role missionaries played in this story. Missionaries largely opposed emigration and actively sought to dissuade their Armenian acolytes from leaving the region, fearing they may not return to fulfil their duty to spread the American Protestant gospel among their compatriots.[41] Nevertheless, the links they helped to establish between the relatively prosperous but otherwise isolated and remote Harput region and North America were critical in bringing large-scale overseas migration more firmly into the realm of the possible. Furthermore, given the socio-economic and political dynamics in the region, the image these missionaries helped to introduce of a dynamic and modern America, rich with opportunity, found fertile ground in which to take root.

The steamships that brought the ABCFM to Ottoman shores were at least as important to the emergence of large-scale migration to North America as the missionaries themselves. The evolution of steamship transportation in the empire's Mediterranean and Black Sea ports parallels the broader history of the empire's uneven incorporation into the European-dominated global capitalist economy. In 1838, Sultan Mahmud II was compelled by his British rivals to sign the Treaty of Balta Limanı. The treaty opened the empire's markets to British goods, and extended a slew of extraterritorial privileges to its merchants operating in the sultan's realms. Its signing was the clearest indication to date that the Ottoman economy was being rapidly incorporated into networks of global trade that were increasingly dominated by Great Britain and the United States. This process would prove to be deeply uneven.[42] By the late nineteenth century, economic production along the Ottoman Black Sea and Mediterranean coasts was increasingly oriented towards the export of primary commodities such as tobacco, cotton and silk to markets in Europe and North America. Meanwhile, regional economies primarily centred on production for domestic consumption continued to thrive throughout much of the Ottoman interior.[43] As indicated by the large flow of migrant labourers between the Ottoman east and port cities along the Mediterranean and Black Seas, the vastly different trajectories of the empire's coastal and interior economies did not preclude the forging of close linkages between the two.

The geography and economics of steam transportation, both shipping and the railroad, were key factors shaping this uneven economic development. The Ottoman rail and steamship sectors were dominated largely by foreign capital, meaning that the development of rail lines and the extension of steam service were concentrated primarily in regions of the empire already well integrated into the western-dominated global economy. The railroad was not extended into eastern Turkey until the 1930s, well after the empire's collapse. The overland trip from the Harput region to the nearest port cities, either Samsun on the Black Sea or Mersin on the Mediterranean, could easily take two weeks, even in the best of weather.[44] This isolation was key to preserving the dynamic regional economy centred on Harput/Mezre, but also contributed to the challenges faced by North America-bound migrants in their efforts to depart the empire. In the middle decades of the nineteenth century, steamship traffic was largely restricted to Istanbul and a handful of other large ports such as Izmir and Salonica.[45] By the century's end, however, as the Ottoman economy fell further under the influence of European capital, companies such as Austrian Lloyd, the British Cunard Line and the French Messageries Maritimes began operating out of several secondary ports along the empire's Black Sea and Mediterranean coasts. Despite lacking the facilities and infrastructure of most modern ports, by the late 1880s cities such as Samsun and Trabzon on the Black Sea coast, and Mersin, Iskenderun and Latakia on the Mediterranean saw their cargo and human traffic grow exponentially. As the number of lines servicing Ottoman ports increased, the cost of steamship travel plummeted.[46] As was the case all over the world in this period, the increasing accessibility of steamship travel was key to making large-scale overseas migration from the Harput region possible.

The peculiarities of the Ottoman steamship sector played a key role in shaping the migration process, becoming a crucial factor in allowing

Armenians to depart the empire in the face of the migration ban. For one, the Ottoman state found it difficult to restrict the ability of its subjects to travel aboard vessels owned and operated by foreign companies, which comprised the vast majority of steamships that transited through the empire's ports. Meanwhile, the underdeveloped infrastructure commonplace in most of the empire's secondary ports, many lacking formal piers for loading and offloading passengers and goods, contributed to a vibrant underground economy. This was dominated by boatmen who specialised in smuggling, moving everything from tobacco and weapons to human beings onto and off of foreign steamers anchored just off shore.[47] These boatmen would become critical players in assisting the clandestine travel of North America-bound Armenian migrants. While the Harput region was located far from the coasts and was somewhat isolated from the economic transformations that shaped the development of the empire's rail and steamship sectors, steam is nevertheless pivotal to our story.

The convergence of Ottoman reforms and the social and political transformations they helped to spark, the arrival of American missionaries and the increasing availability of steamship transportation were not unique to the Harput region. A similar conjuncture of factors also helped to fuel overseas migration of (mostly) Maronite Christians from Mount Lebanon on an even larger scale. The economy of Mount Lebanon was closely tied to the bustling port city of Beirut, one of the earliest Ottoman steamship ports; the region was also home to a vast network of American missionary schools. According to Akram Khater, the emergence of large-scale overseas migration from the region coincided with the decline of the region's export-oriented silk economy in the 1880s. The commercialisation of silk production triggered a significant increase in living standards in Mount Lebanon, driven in large part by young women, workers who flocked to Beirut to find work in the city's silk factories, sending much of what they earned to their families back on the Mount. The sudden decline of the Lebanese silk industry compelled many women and men to migrate abroad in hopes of replacing the income they had once earned through sericulture and factory work. As Khater argues, the economic dynamics at play in Mount Lebanon shaped the gendered dimensions of overseas migration from the region where women were as likely as men to travel abroad in search of work. In contrast, Armenian migration from Harput was a much more male phenomenon, and closely paralleled the gendered dimensions of migration from the southern Italian regions of Abruzzi and Calabria in the late nineteenth century where, as Donna Gabaccia and Franca Iacovetta argue, because of the continued survival of cottage textile manufacturing, dominated largely by female labour, male workers were much more likely to travel abroad.[48] Between the 1880s and the onset of World War I, well over one-hundred thousand migrants left Mount Lebanon for a wide variety of overseas destinations, with many thousands eventually returning to their home communities over the course of the same period.[49] Despite differences in the volume and gender composition of migration from the Harput region and Mount Lebanon, these were parallel movements driven by many of the same overlapping factors. Nevertheless, the Ottoman state responded more harshly and with much greater to alarm to the emergence of Armenian overseas migration than it did to Lebanese migration. This very different reaction was shaped by the Hamidian regime's increasingly turbulent and sometimes violent relationship with the empire's increasingly organised and assertive Armenian population.

The Politics of Restriction

Istanbul's decision to ban Armenian migration to North America in 1888 reflects the many contradictions of the Ottoman reform project of the nineteenth century. The architects of the Tanzimat had endeavoured to create a singular Ottoman identity, backed by a commitment to equality under the law, that could bridge the many divides that existed among the empire's heterogeneous population. Targeting Armenians with discriminatory treatment seemed to contradict the spirit of nineteenth century Ottoman reform. By the century's closing decades, these transformations paradoxically strengthened the importance of sectarian and ethnic differences within the Ottoman system. In some regions of the Ottoman east, the reform process helped to give rise to an increasingly prosperous Armenian population, one that was becoming more educated and worldly thanks in part to the work of American missionaries and their local acolytes. In other parts of the region, the increasing vulnerability and immeseration of Armenian communities augured by the destruction of the old feudal order and the resultant political instability had helped to generate international interest in the plight of Ottoman Armenians and was a major factor leading to the inclusion of Article 61 in the Treaty of Berlin. By the 1880s, the dire conditions of Armenians, especially those who resided in the empire's far eastern periphery, helped fuel the rise of political organisations calling for autonomy or even independence for the empire's Armenian population. At the same time, and partially in response to these developments, imperial politics became increasingly sectarian in nature as Abdülhamid II sought to emphasise the empire's Sunni Islamic identity. The migration ban was thus inspired by the uniquely problematic relationship between the Hamidian regime and the empire's Armenian population.

In 1879, an uprising led by a local Kurdish sheikh broke out in the province of Van, located at the empire's far eastern periphery. The uprising was motivated in part by fears that the Treaty of Berlin would confer special privileges on the province's minority Armenian population, and perhaps even result in the creation of an independent Armenian state in the region.[50] Although the uprising was eventually quelled, the situation in the Ottoman east worsened a year later with the outbreak of famine that only further strained the relationship between Kurdish pastoralists and (mostly) Armenian agriculturalists. While resource scarcity was the primary driver of social and political unrest during the famine years, conflict in communities throughout the Ottoman east increasingly took on an ethno-religious dimension, a fact that foreign observers and Ottoman state officials stationed in the region were quick to highlight.[51]

Within this context of growing political upheaval and social strife, the 1880s was a transformative period for Ottoman Armenians – characterised by the emergence of several Armenian nationalist political parties. The birth and meteoric rise of these organisations was driven by the failed promise of reform in the aftermath of the Treaty of Berlin, and inspired by the global rise of nationalist, socialist and anarchist politics in this era. As Gerard Libaridian notes, these parties sought to 'redefine the Armenian population as a political rather than a religious community,' thus challenging the primacy of the Armenian Apostolic Church in the communal life of Ottoman Armenians.[52] The Armenakan Party, founded in 1885 by Mekertich Portukalian, an Istanbul-born Armenian schoolteacher and publisher based in the far-eastern city of Van, is generally recognised as the first modern Armenian political party. The Armenakan's platform was built around demands for greater Armenian autonomy and self-protection. The Hunchakian Revolutionary Party, founded in Geneva in 1887 by Armenian expatriates from the Ottoman, Russian and Persian empires, quickly supplanted Portukalian's small organisation in both size and importance. The Armenian Revolutionary Federation (ARF), founded two years later in Tblisi, also quickly emerged as a major player in Armenian politics. The founders of both the Hunchakian Revolutionary Party and the ARF were heavily influenced by radical underground political organisations operating in the Russian Empire, and both combined calls for Armenian autonomy or independence with a platform advocating broader revolutionary change.[53]

These parties took advantage of the political and social unrest gripping parts of the Ottoman east as they worked to expand their respective bases of support both inside and outside of the empire. For example, in 1889, Musa Bey, a powerful Kurdish grandee from the remote mountain district of Muş in far eastern Anatolia, stood accused of kidnapping and raping a local Armenian girl. The case generated great interest among Armenian migrant labourers in Istanbul who demanded that Musa be prosecuted. Although he was eventually tried, he was acquitted on all charges. The Hunchakian Revolutionary Party used this perceived miscarriage of justice as an opportunity to organise Armenian labourers in the capital city. In 1890, shortly after Musa's acquittal, the party helped to stage a large protest outside of the Armenian Patriarchate in the neighbourhood of Kumkapı that quickly escalated into violence, resulting in the deaths of several protestors and police. This was followed by a massive and brutal crackdown on suspected agitators in Istanbul, forcing many Armenians to flee the capital.[54]

Already concerned about the explosive growth of Armenian political organisations, the events in Kumkapı in the summer of 1890 left the Hamidian regime panicked. Deeply scarred by its experience with nationalism in the Balkans earlier in the century, Istanbul was especially concerned that the parties would help to engineer an armed separatist movement among Armenians in the Ottoman east, one that could possibly earn the support of Russia and other Great Powers. In reality, the influence of these political parties was still quite limited among Ottoman Armenians in the early 1890s, with the bulk of their leadership residing outside of the empire. This fact, however, did not stop the Hamidian regime from taking drastic action to curtail the threat of Armenian separatism in the bud. In 1890, the same year as the Kumkapı demonstrations, the Ottoman state began arming and equipping various Kurdish tribal groups in the empire's far east, organising them into a several military regiments together known as the Hamidiye Light Cavalry (*Hamidiye Hafif Süvari Alayları*). As Janet Klein argues, the cavalry's creation was part and parcel of the broader effort to 'bring the region into the Ottoman fold and to ensure, by almost any means necessary, that it remained there.'[55] A central component of its 'manifold mission' was to protect the frontier zones abutting Russian territory against incursions by suspected Armenian revolutionaries.[56] The tribal groups that comprised the cavalry took advantage of their connection to the central state to enhance their own economic and political power in the empire's eastern periphery. Some Hamidiye chiefs deftly exploited Istanbul's fear of separatism to carry out attacks on Armenian agriculturalists in the region, forcefully dispossessing them of their lands.[57] The cavalry's creation only further added to the increasingly sectarian dimensions of political and social unrest that gripped the Ottoman east in the final two decades of the nineteenth century.

These developments reached a violent crescendo in the mid-1890s. In the summer of 1894, violence broke out between Armenian villagers and

Kurdish tribesmen in the remote district of Sasun, located in Bitlis. The violence appears to have been triggered in part by the refusal of Armenian agriculturalists in the district to pay tribute to local tribal chiefs. Acting on reports that militants associated with the Hunchakian Revolutionary Party were involved in the violence, Istanbul responded swiftly. On the pretext of quelling a revolt led by a seditious organisation, Ottoman forces, aided by local Kurdish tribesmen, massacred Armenian civilians and raised several villages in Sasun.[58]

Accounts of the violence in Sasun produced both by foreign missionaries stationed in the region and the propaganda efforts of the major Armenian political parties helped to generate a fierce international outcry. News of anti-Armenian atrocities in the Ottoman Empire quickly dominated headlines in Paris, London and New York.[59] The Hamidian regime was convinced the Sasun uprising was part of a broader revolutionary plot to undermine the empire's political stability, and tacitly sanctioned a series of massacres and pogroms targeting Armenian communities throughout eastern Anatolia in the ensuing months. The extent of Istanbul's role remains murky, partly owing to the continued controversy surrounding the anti-Armenian violence that marred the empire's final decades and the resulting dearth of high quality scholarship. Selim Deringil describes the massacres as an effort on the part of the Hamidian regime to 'cow, decimate, and humble the Armenians, but not to destroy them.'[60] Janet Klein, meanwhile, contends that, at a minimum, the Ottoman general Zeki Pasha, who had cut his teeth as the architect and commander of the Hamidiye Light Cavalry, bore some responsibility for the violence.[61] For nearly two years between 1894 and 1896, looting and massacres carried out by local mobs and cheered on by government officials and clergymen, ravaged communities from Van in the east to Sivas in the west. In some areas, whole villages converted to Islam in the hopes of being spared from violence.[62] The violence was met by several instances of organised resistance by Armenians in the empire. Notably in 1895, Armenians in Zeytun near the city of Maraş in southeastern Anatolia took up arms against Ottoman forces that had surrounded the district in an attempt to starve it of food and other provisions.[63] The following year, members of the ARF occupied the Ottoman Bank in Istanbul in the hope of convincing the Great Powers to intervene directly on behalf of Armenians in the Ottoman east, an event that triggered a wave of violent reprisals against Armenians living in the imperial capital. As the situation began to settle in late 1896, thousands of Armenian civilians had been murdered, and many more displaced from their homes or compelled to convert to Islam.[64] The Ottoman state was roundly condemned in the international press and by various western powers for its role in fomenting the violence.

The Harput region was not spared from the wave of terror that gripped the Ottoman east in the mid-1890s. In November 1895, a mob attacked and burned several buildings on the campus of Euphrates College, while several surrounding villages were ransacked. At minimum, several hundred Armenians were killed or injured as a result of the violence.[65] The scale of destruction, however, does not appear to have approached that wrought upon regions further to the east and the south. Located far from the Russian frontier, and already a bastion of central state power, the Harput region was largely spared from the instability elsewhere in the Ottoman east resulting from the creation of the Hamidiye Light Cavalry and other efforts by the Hamidian regime to pacify the region.[66] Nor was Harput a site of organised Armenian resistance to the Ottoman state or local power brokers as was the case further south and east in Sasun, Zeytun and Van. Armenian political parties such as the Hunchakian Revolutionary Party and the ARF certainly attracted support among Armenians in Harput, but much of the region's Armenian elite preferred a much more collaborative relationship with Istanbul, and wielded extensive power and influence over local and provincial politics.[67]

Harput's relative political stability, and the fact that its Armenian population was better integrated into the Ottoman system than their counterparts elsewhere in the east had little bearing on the Hamidian regime's response to large-scale overseas migration from the region. Istanbul's policies were motivated almost entirely by the belief that both migration and support for 'seditious' politics among the empire's Armenian populations were intrinsically linked. This is on full display in the 1888 order from Yıldız Palace introducing the migration ban, the text of which is reproduced in the introduction to this chapter. A mere year after the creation of the Hunchakian Revolutionary Party and more than two years before the Kumkapı protest first demonstrated the party's capacity to organise within the empire, Istanbul already feared the prospect of Armenians migrating overseas, radicalising under the influence of these organisations, and then returning to sow dissent in the political tinderbox of the Ottoman east.

It is beyond the scope of this study to determine the degree to which Armenian migrants supported the major Armenian political parties. Robert Mirak's now classic work on Armenians in the United States in the pre-World War I era addresses this question to some extent. The Hunchakian party had a presence in the US as early as 1888, less than one year after it was formed in Geneva.[68] By 1890, they had established several branches in Armenian migrant communities throughout the Northeast, where they organised regular meetings and rallies, and encouraged migrants to advocate on behalf of the interests of Armenians in the Ottoman east. By the late 1890s, the influence of the Hunchaks had been displaced by the ARF and other organisations that nonetheless followed a similar organisational model.[69]

Meanwhile, in the mid-1890s, as the controversy was brewing over the anti-Armenian violence in Sasun, the Ottoman ambassador to the United States, Alexandros Mavroyeni, sought assistance from a Boston-area Armenian–American rug merchant in monitoring Armenian political activity in the city and its surrounding areas. The merchant, Hagop Bogigian, was originally from the Harput area, having migrated to the United States in the late 1870s. As a wealthy and assimilated American businessman, he was a vociferous opponent of the Hunchak's revolutionary platform. Mavroyeni also contracted by the Pinkerton Detective Agency to spy on suspected Hunchak leaders. If anything, the information he gathered through these efforts seemed to belie Istanbul's anxieties about the threat posed by Hunchak efforts to organise Armenian migrants.[70] By the turn of the twentieth century, Mirak suggests that the parties found much greater success in their efforts at fostering a sense of community among migrants sojourning thousands of miles from home, than they did in encouraging them to fight against the Ottoman state.[71] Meanwhile, I have found little evidence to suggest that migrants who returned to the Harput region from the United States actively engaged in political actions against the state, although it is certainly conceivable that many – if not most – sympathised with the efforts of the Armenian parties.

The order introducing the migration ban reflects a keen awareness on the part of the Ottoman state very early on that for many Armenians, migration to North America was not intended as a permanent move. The Hamidian regime's fear was driven by an anxiety around migrants *returning* to the empire, not their going abroad in the first place. For Istanbul, the United States government's liberal approach to governing political speech and assembly was especially dangerous, fuelling its belief that migrants would radicalise while there and return to spread sedition in their home communities. The constant circulation of people between the politically restive Ottoman east and North America threatened to become a conduit for the circulation of ideas and individuals the Hamidian regime deemed dangerous or subversive. The Ottoman state was also deeply concerned about the ease with which migrants could naturalize as citizens of the United States while abroad. As is discussed in greater depth in Chapter five, nationals of several foreign states, including the United States following an 1837 agreement between Washington and Istanbul, enjoyed extensive extraterritorial privileges within the Ottoman Empire including immunity from prosecution under imperial law under a set of agreements known as 'The Capitulations'. For the remainder of the Hamidian era, the prospect of Armenian returnees 'poisoning the minds' of their fellow compatriots, all while enjoying diplomatic protection as nationals of a capitulatory power, motivated the regime's efforts to prevent Armenians from migrating to and returning from North America.

At least initially, these anxieties did more than just animate Ottoman policy towards Armenian migration. Until the late 1890s, Istanbul also worked to prevent overseas migration from Mount Lebanon and surrounding areas, motivated by fears that migration could negatively impact the region's delicate sectarian politics and concerns about the return of Lebanese migrants claiming US citizenship. In November 1898, a policy was introduced permitting migrants from Mount Lebanon and surrounding regions to travel abroad and to return as long as they promised to refrain from 'suspicious' political activity and retain their Ottoman nationality. This policy change was made in response to the failure of Ottoman efforts to prevent migration from the region, especially in the face of the massive and well-coordinated smuggling infrastructure that emerged to assist Lebanese migrants in clandestinely departing the empire. By conditionally allowing migration from Mount Lebanon, a process regulated through the issuing of special mobility documents to individuals granted permission to leave, Istanbul was able to clamp down on the illegal migration business while also limiting what it perceived as the possible negative political ramifications resulting from the continued exodus.[72]

The Hamidian regime would encounter many of the same obstacles in its effort to enforce the ban on Armenian migration, as is addressed in Chapters two and three. Nevertheless, there was to be no equivalent relaxation of the ban on Armenian travel to North America. Instead, on the heels of the anti-Armenian violence of the mid-1890s, the Ottoman state introduced a policy that permitted Armenians to migrate to the United States in return for renouncing their Ottoman nationality (*terk-i tabiiyet*) and vowing never to return (*bir daha avdet etmemek*). The policy reflected the extent to which the Hamidian regime viewed Armenian mobility as uniquely menacing. Until 1908, the Ottoman state generally allowed Armenians to travel to North America if any possibility of their return was foreclosed. Additionally, the state sought to curtail the ability of those Armenians it permitted to leave to retain connections with their home communities.[73] The policy allowed wives and dependent children to join their husbands and fathers already residing in the United States. By the beginning of the twentieth century, the newly created American consulate in Harput devoted much of its time and resources to assisting local Armenian families of naturalised US citizens with obtaining permission from Istanbul to depart the empire.[74] The creation of an authorised stream of Armenian migration to North America alongside the much larger flow of unauthorised departures was reflected in the terminology the state employed to distinguish between the two, with *hicret*, derived from the Arabic term for migration or flight, used to refer to the former, and *firar*, meaning desertion or escape, used in reference to the latter.

The Hamidian regime's policies towards Lebanese and Armenian overseas migration, respectively, existed at two extremes of a broad spectrum. Imperial law only permitted Ottoman subjects to travel abroad if they possessed a valid passport, a document that was both expensive and difficult to obtain, and was generally reserved for prominent individuals and men of commerce.[75] Both the 1888 ban on Armenian migration and the 1898 policy lifting many of the restrictions on Lebanese migration, however, demonstrated a willingness on Istanbul's part to selectively modify the law depending on region and population. Muslims and Assyrian Christians also migrated from the Harput region in some numbers in the late nineteenth and early twentieth centuries.[76] While Assyrians and Muslims were not granted the same privileges to migrate enjoyed by their counterparts in Mount Lebanon, neither did the Ottoman state view their international travel with nearly the same degree of suspicion as it did that of their Armenian compatriots. Because it was forbidden for Muslims and Assyrians to leave the empire without first obtaining a passport, a document out of reach for most, they largely departed the empire through the same clandestine channels used by Armenian migrants. As a result, and because many (especially) Muslim migrants worked side-by-side with Armenian labourers in the United States, in 1894 the foreign minister issued a warning that they risked being exposed to anti-Ottoman propaganda. He recommended that local authorities closely monitor Muslims who returned to the empire to ensure they did not cause trouble.[77] Meanwhile, in 1893, the grand vizier demanded more be done to prevent Muslims from the Harput region from illegally travelling overseas, as he was concerned that they were leaving to escape military service, and risked becoming an embarrassment to the empire while abroad owing to their poverty and their ignorance of American cultural mores.[78] Despite such concerns, the Hamidian regime did not view either Assyrian or Muslim migration as posing an intrinsic threat to the empire's political stability. While most left without proper documents and in contravention of Ottoman law, they were not the targets of a concerted effort by the state to prevent their departure, unlike Armenians, nor did Istanbul bar them from returning as it would do to Armenian migrants in 1893.[79]

Conclusion

Armenian migration from the Harput region to North America and the Hamidian regime's response are both firmly embedded in the broader story of Ottoman reform and modernisation in the nineteenth and early twentieth centuries. It is therefore tempting to assume that Armenians left the Ottoman Empire to escape the political instability and increasing violence that had come to define Istanbul's efforts to bring its eastern peripheries more firmly into the imperial fold. There is no question that life became increasingly precarious for most Armenian communities in the Ottoman east as a result of this process, as many other scholars have demonstrated. But the story of Armenian migration from the Harput region is not only, or even *primarily*, one of escape from persecution. Even after the massacres of the mid-1890s, the young men that made up the bulk of those who migrated in this period continued to leave their families, often for years at a time, remitting money back to their home communities and even making the perilous return trip. That these sojourners were willing to risk leaving their families behind and bearing the cost of the risky journey was a testament to the relative stability of the Harput region, where unlike much of the rest of the Ottoman east, the Armenian population was economically and even politically ascendant. By the first decade of the twentieth century, the money flowing into Harput from migrants toiling in North America placed it even more firmly on its own unique historical trajectory.

The Hamidian regime's response to Armenian migration reflected many of the fundamental contradictions of the Tanzimat and post-Tanzimat reform process. The strategies Istanbul employed to enforce the migration emerged out of its efforts throughout the nineteenth century to create a powerful, bureaucratic state apparatus that could make its presence felt throughout the empire's vast realm. At the same time, the Tanzimat reforms were impelled by an ethos that emphasised equality under the law and common Ottoman identity. The Hamidian regime's dogged suspicion of Armenian mobility, and its willingness to enact and enforce numerous discriminatory measures in order to put a stop to this, stemmed from a central paradox of the Ottoman modernisation effort: the reinforcement and entrenchment of sectarian and ethnic difference. With this complex historical canvas as a backdrop, subsequent Chapters tell the story of how Armenian migrants both departed and reentered the empire in the face of the migration ban, and the increasingly draconian measures that were employed to put a stop to their transhempisheric sojourning. In the process, many of the tensions that existed between the Ottoman state and the Armenian populations over which it ruled were further magnified.

2

Smugglers

In the mid-1930s, Israel Safarian sat down to write an account of his journey from his home village in the district of Kiğı (Keghi) in Erzurum province to the Black Sea port of Batumi, then under the control of the Russian Empire. His trip began in the early fall of 1907, and was but one leg of a longer journey that would eventually end in the small Canadian factory town of Brantford, Ontario. Safarian recounted his perilous travel as he and a small group of fellow migrants, accompanied by two experienced Kurdish guides, traversed the rugged terrain of the Russo–Ottoman frontier. His group only narrowly escaped detection and arrest by Ottoman authorities, and was compelled to bribe Russian border guards as they crossed the frontier. Upon their arrival in Batumi, Safarian described the poor treatment he and his fellow migrants experienced at the hands of two innkeepers, natives of his hometown, while they awaited the beginning of their overseas voyage for several months. This arduous trip out of the Ottoman Empire and to a port city where he could embark on his long oceanic voyage left such an indelible mark in Safarian's mind that the remainder of his journey to Canada warranted only two sentences in a brief postscript to his account.

Safarian's story would no doubt resonate with many global migrants of the early twenty-first century. The mechanics of mobility control, the machinery of border security and the anti-immigrant politics that fuel them have created a world of walls, both literal and figurative, over the past century. In response, ever more creative, expansive and often exploitative clandestine networks have emerged, promising to assist their clients in crossing borders and traversing frontiers that every day become more militarised and more dangerous.

The migration and refugee crisis of the past decade has awakened a great deal of scholarly and journalistic fascination with the topic of migrant smuggling.[1] This parallels a growing interest in the history of this phenomenon. For example, historians of Chinese exclusion in particular have reconstructed the dense transnational networks, crisscrossing the Pacific, which helped Asian migrants to evade incipient efforts by governments throughout the Western Hemisphere to enforce racial restriction.[2] Scholars writing on clandestine migration in the contemporary period, however, are rarely in conversation with historians. In the Mediterranean context, for example, migrant smuggling is commonly portrayed as a modern development *par excellence*. In this rendering, consummately twenty-first century technologies such as mobile phones, the Internet, lorries and rubber dinghies allow smugglers to build highly coordinated networks over vast stretches of space and time as they work to outsmart the increasingly sophisticated methods that states employ to combat unauthorised migration.[3] This dynamic is certainly present and is a major reason the past decade has been so especially dangerous for migrants traversing the Mediterranean. Nevertheless, migrant smuggling in the Middle East and North African region has a much longer history – and like their contemporary counterparts, the smuggling networks that existed more than a century ago employed creative strategies, negotiated vast stretches of space and time and brought together diverse and disparate sets of intermediaries to assist migrants in evading state efforts to limit their mobility. It is thus important to consider how an understanding of how these operations functioned in the past might shed light on contemporary developments.

This Chapter traces the smuggling networks that emerged in the final decades of the nineteenth century to assist Armenian migrants in leaving the Ottoman Empire for North America in the face of the Hamidian regime's migration ban. Tracing these networks requires piecing together evidence that is at times fragmentary and ephemeral. Most of the surviving documents on these networks are state records that were only produced on those occasions when smugglers failed to fully conceal their activities from the authorities. Nonetheless, these documents reveal a story of powerful migration agents based in the Harput region who were connected to diverse intermediaries in several exit points on the Black and Mediterranean Sea coasts and beyond to European transit ports and Armenian migrant colonies in North America. As in the present moment, these networks regularly evolved in both scale and sophistication in response to the state's shifting efforts to crackdown on unauthorised migration. With the ban on Armenian migration to North America in place from the late 1880s until the 1908 constitutional revolution, these migrant smuggling networks were essential for maintaining the continuous flow of overseas migration from the Harput region.

Migration Intermediaries in the Harput Region

On a June afternoon in 1893, employees of a steamship company brought six Armenian migrants bound for North America to the Ottoman consulate in Liverpool. The migrants, all natives of the Harput region, had encountered a problem with their steamer tickets for the transatlantic arm of their journey. With no translator available to bridge the language divide, the shipping company officials sought the assistance of the city's Ottoman consul. It was not unusual for Armenian migrants to be brought before the consul under such circumstances. He would use these encounters to supply his superiors in Istanbul with information about the steadily increasing numbers of Armenian subjects of the empire travelling overseas in contravention of Ottoman state policy. In this instance he demanded that the group reveal how they had managed to get from their remote home communities in the Ottoman interior to the industrial seaport on the west coast of England. Their response was a familiar one. The group had sought the assistance of one of the many 'merchants' (*tüccarlar*) located in and around Harput who profited handsomely from the business of facilitating clandestine migration. After enduring the long overland trip to the Mediterranean port city of Mersin, the six were met by contacts of the Harput-based merchant who helped them arrange their steamship travel. When the day came for them to embark on their transhemispheric voyage, the six were loaded on to a small boat under the cover of darkness and shuttled to a steamship bound for Liverpool. Hidden deep in the bowel of the ship to avoid detection by Ottoman authorities, they finally set sail.[4]

The consul's report on the encounter demonstrates just how quickly highly coordinated and geographically expansive migrant smuggling networks emerged following the introduction of the ban on Armenian overseas migration in the late-1880s. Powerful migration agents, such as the 'merchant' mentioned in the report, connected would-be migrants to a vast underground web of intermediaries all involved in shepherding Armenian migrants from the interior to the coast and from shore to ship out of view of state authorities. For those individuals seeking assistance in leaving the empire, access to these networks did not come cheap. Furthermore, these migration agents, some of whom wielded tremendous economic and political power in the Harput region and beyond, developed elaborate strategies to ensure that their clients paid their debts, even while they were labouring half a world away. The examples given by the reports of two such agents, whose sizeable operations left paper trails sufficient enough to reconstruct their inner-workings, hint at the degree of economic and political power that was necessary to maintain a successful migrant smuggling network.

In the early 1890s, around the same time the Ottoman consul in Liverpool penned his report, Gaspar Nahigian was heading a large migrant smuggling network based out of the village of Husseinig, located a few kilometres outside of the Harput city centre.[5] In 1892, provincial officials in Mamuretülaziz identified Nahigian as a 'merchant and moneylender' (*tüccar ve sarrafından idüğü*) who lent money at high interest rates to migrants who sought out his smuggling services.[6] That same year, a report from the Ottoman Embassy in Washington DC claimed that Nahigian's 'son', Mardiros, who was based in Worcester, Massachusetts, was responsible for collecting debts from his father's clients living and working in the United States.[7] Mardiros sent the money to a contact in Istanbul where it was processed and then forwarded to Husseinig. One document names a member of a prominent banking family in the Harput region, the Harputlians, as an important intermediary in the chain of transactions that linked Worcester to Husseinig.[8] By the first decade of the twentieth century members of the Harputlian family would also be dominant players in the migrant smuggling business.

The state's interest in Nahigian's operation was driven, at least in part, by concerns about both Gaspar and Mardiros' alleged links to Armenian political organisations. Indeed, the first mention of the Nahigians' smuggling operation in Ottoman source material, a February 1891 report from the Ottoman Ambassador in Washington, cited information gleaned from a letter an Armenian migrant in the United States had sent to the ambassador naming Gaspar Nahigian as the chief migration agent in the Harput region and characterising his home village of Husseinig as 'a hotbed of revolutionary intrigue.'[9] More than two years later, the Ottoman consul in New York claimed that Gaspar's network was smuggling suspected revolutionaries returning from the United States back into the empire, as well as serving as a conduit for communication between Armenian political activists in the United States and the Ottoman east.[10] In January 1895, an employee of the Pinkerton Detective Agency – hired by Ottoman consular authorities to spy on Armenian political activities in Boston and Worcester – identified Mardiros Nahigian as a powerful 'broker' in the local Armenian migrant colony and a vocal anti-Ottoman 'agitator.' His report went on to quote a lawyer in Worcester who accused Mardiros of 'robbing the Armenians', likely a reference to his work collecting the debts of Gaspar's clients.[11] Such reports could only have deepened the Ottoman state's concerns regarding an intrinsic link between overseas migration and Armenian political activity.[12]

For reasons that are not entirely clear, after the mid-1890s, the document trail on Gaspar and Mardiros' smuggling operation ends abruptly. By the first decade of the twentieth century, however, state officials were directing their attention to another smuggling kingpin whose operation appears to have been much larger than that of the Nahigians. Artin Harputlian, scion of a prominent and powerful banking family in the Harput region, was a notorious local power broker, consummate wheeler-dealer and a prominent member of the Mamuretülaziz provincial council. If anyone could command the resources and marshal the connections necessary to run a large smuggling operation without much interference from the authorities, it was he. Artin Harputlian's clandestine activities captured the interest of Ottoman officials beginning in the first years of the twentieth century. For example, in September of 1905, a large group of twenty to thirty Armenian migrants from the Harput region was caught and arrested while en route to the Mediterranean coast. The group was accompanied by a guide with a long rap sheet connected to his smuggling work. The guide was found to be in possession of numerous promissory notes bearing the signatures of migrants he had already guided to the coast. The documents indicated that this earlier group of migrants had agreed to pay over four hundred gold liras, a substantial sum of money, to be smuggled out of the Ottoman Empire and that at least some of this money had already been paid.[13] The report identified the guide as a probable associate of Artin Harputlian, claiming that the prominent banker's large smuggling operation involved the close cooperation of several high-ranking provincial officials in Mamuretülaziz.[14] According to one source, by 1907, Harputlian's network was smuggling between five and six hundred Armenian migrants out of the empire each year, a number that constitutes a very substantial percentage of the annual volume of Armenian migration from the Ottoman Empire to North America during this period.[15]

Like Gaspar Nahigian's smuggling network, Harputlian's operation was truly global in its scale. His brother Mihran, who was based in New York, served as Artin's contact in the United States and, like Mardiros Nahigian, appears to have played an important role in ensuring that his brother's clients paid their smuggling debts. Despite the great distances involved, the Harputlians (and the Nahigians before them) took advantage of the intimate and close-knit nature of most Armenian migrant communities in North America. Labouring on the other side of the world in a society very different from the one they left behind, Armenian migrants relied on more established and well-connected community members for assistance in navigating this alien environment and in remaining connected to their home communities.[16] In addition to their smuggling services, the Harputlian brothers may have served as the primary conduit through which Armenian migrants in the United States sent letters and remittances to the Harput region, giving Mihran Harputlian the leverage necessary to collect on outstanding debts.[17] Although the evidence is somewhat thin, if this was indeed the case, the Harputlians were employing a strategy common to labour recruiters and other intermediaries embedded in migrant communities throughout the world for keeping their clients in line.[18] Artin Harputlian appears to have been directly connected to at least one innkeeper in the city of Liverpool who was tasked with housing the banker's clients as they waited to embark on the transatlantic leg of their journey.[19] Thus Harputlian's vast network was present at every level of a migrant's voyage from the Harput region to North America. Indeed, as both the Nahigian and Harputlian operations demonstrate, successful migrant smuggling operations necessarily extended beyond the borders of the Ottoman Empire, connecting sending communities in the Anatolian interior across vast stretches of space to migrant colonies sprouting up throughout North America.

Gaspar Nahigian and Artin Harputlian were by far the most visible migration agents in the Harput region in this period. Both possessed a wide range of connections that stretched across both sides of the planet. They were powerbrokers of the first order and leveraged their tremendous economic and political capital to maintain and grow their respective operations. Nevertheless, smuggling migrants out of the Ottoman Empire was not the sole province of powerful Armenians such as Nahigian and Harputlian. In 1908, the Ministry of Police identified two Muslim artisans operating out of a small town outside of Harput/Mezre who had 'through deception and in exchange for money' (*biliğfal para mukabilinde*) helped between three hundred and four hundred people migrate to North America. The ministry's brief report was based on information supplied to it by a Muslim migrant living in the United States and unfortunately provides few details concerning the inner-workings of this alleged smuggling operation.[20] A more detailed investigation conducted nearly six years earlier by local officials in the province of Mamuretülaziz revealed that several powerful Muslim landlords were working in conjunction with skilled muleteer guides to smuggle migrants from the interior to the coast.[21] Travel from the interior to port cities on the Mediterranean or Black Sea coasts was a dangerous undertaking that entailed long journeys on foot over roads that even today are frequently impassable in inclement weather. Migrant parties were generally large, frequently more than twenty people. Safely transporting such groups to distant port cities necessitated the use of a guide with intimate knowledge of the roads that linked the interior to the coast.[22] Connections to skilled guides, often members of local Kurdish tribes with a long tradition of aiding travellers along the treacherous roads of the Anatolian interior, were critical to the successful operation of a migrant smuggling network, and thus unsurprisingly they frequently appear in the source material.[23] These guides probably also served as crucial bridges between migration agents in the interior and the networks of intermediaries in port cities that housed migrants, arranged their passage to North America and smuggled them onto waiting steamships. For individuals such as the wealthy landlords named in the report, leveraging such connections in order to profit from the lucrative migrant smuggling business must have been an enticing proposition.

Smuggling Armenian migrants was indeed a highly remunerative business. In January 1901, the American consul in Harput reported that smugglers were charging '$40.00 a head' for travel from the Ottoman interior to Marseille. Travel to the coast, according to Norton, cost eighteen dollars, a price that did not include falsified travel documents, food and drink and other necessities.[24] A year later, Ottoman officials cited a much higher cost for travel between the interior and the coast of between nineteen and twenty gold liras. As the value of the lira was worth four times that of the United States dollar, this was nearly double the amount given by Norton.[25] Meanwhile, a detailed investigation of Artin Harputlian's smuggling operation conducted in 1907 revealed that he charged migrants eighteen liras for his services.[26] Whether forty dollars or twenty liras, these were significant sums of money considering that daily wages in the Ottoman east often amounted to little more than a few kuruş.[27] Payment of large sums of money to smugglers has become a common experience for migrants in the contemporary period as mobility has become increasingly criminalised and states continue to militarise their borders, making evasion more difficult and more expensive.[28] It is likely that few Armenian migrants could cover the cost of migration up front, and indebtedness to smugglers was common.[29] Migrants nevertheless appear to have enjoyed at least some protection from fraud and other abuses at the hands of agents. According to the US consul in Harput, agents guaranteed full refunds to those who were not successfully able to depart the empire, a practice that Ottoman officials were also aware of.[30] Despite the unequal power relationships that existed between migration agents and their clients, it was likely in the agent's interest to honour such agreements. Information about flagrantly abusive practices could easily spread through the same networks of communication and exchange that sustained these smuggling enterprises over the vast distances, and thus a certain moral economy may have provided some degree of protection from the worst forms of exploitation during the long journey to North America.[31]

The Shifting Geography of Clandestine Migration

Successfully smuggling North America-bound Armenian migrants from the Harput region, deep in the Anatolian interior, to the coast and eventually out of the Ottoman Empire was contingent on avoiding detection by the state. The ever-shifting geography of these migrant smuggling networks was driven first-and-foremost by the dynamics of evasion. Thus, after contracting with a migration agent, where and how an Armenian migrant departed the empire was not simply a matter of travelling to whichever coastal port was closest. Instead, between 1888 and 1908, the geography of migration expanded to include a wide array of port cities from Mersin to Beirut on the Mediterranean Sea and Samsun to Batumi on the Black Sea. At any given time, a wide range of political, economic and geographic factors led smugglers and their clients to prefer certain ports of exit to others. This use of geography and space as a strategy is a reflection of the creativity and versatility that sustained these networks and allowed them to flourish in the final decades of the Hamidian regime.

In the immediate aftermath of the ban imposed on Armenian migration to North America, most migrants appear to have preferred Istanbul as a port of exit. Some acquired travel documents permitting travel to the imperial capital. Upon arrival, they would clandestinely board steamers bound for European transit ports with the aid of local boatmen.[32] Others sought passage on British and French steamers at the Black Sea port of Samsun ostensibly for travel to Istanbul. Instead of disembarking at their stated destination, they stowed away as the ships sailed on to their home ports.[33] Generations of young men from communities throughout the Ottoman east had migrated to Istanbul looking for work so that they could support their families back home. Thus for many of these early migrants seeking to travel clandestinely to North America, procuring the necessary documents for travel to Istanbul was likely not difficult.[34] As the 1890s dawned, however, the Ottoman state began curtailing the ability of Armenians from the empire's eastern provinces to travel to Istanbul. The Hamidian regime's concerns about the growing visibility of Armenian political activism both within and outside the empire's borders, coupled with a spate of violent incidents involving migrant labourers in the city, helped to fuel the crackdown.[35]

Following the occupation of the Ottoman Bank in August 1896 by members of the Armenian Revolutionary Federation, an event that was followed by waves of anti-Armenian violence in the imperial capital, the Ottoman state decided to expel much of the city's Armenian migrant population. This action was followed by an order that banned most Armenians from travelling to the imperial capital.[36] At the same time, state officials also sought to make travel through Samsun, long the preferred transit port for labour migrants from the Ottoman east en route to Istanbul, more difficult. In 1890, the growing practice of boatmen smuggling Armenian migrants to waiting foreign steamers anchored just off shore led officials in Samsun to call for the construction of a passenger pier that would allow for better surveillance of traffic in and out of the city's port.[37] Given the chronically woeful state of imperial finances, funds for such a project were not forthcoming. Nevertheless in 1893, in an effort to bar Armenian travellers from accessing foreign steamers, Ottoman officials proposed mandating that they only be allowed to travel on ships bearing the Ottoman standard.[38]

While neither initiative was immediately successful, they signalled a concerted effort by the state to enforce the migration ban by making it more difficult for Armenians suspected to be attempting to migrate to North America to transit through the empire's port cities. These efforts had the effect of pushing smuggling networks and their clients southward to the Mediterranean coast where both the social and geographic conditions were better suited to evade state efforts to prevent unauthorised migration. For example, Mersin, a city on the northeastern coast of the Mediterranean, was increasingly favoured as a port of exit. In early 1892, officials in Mamuretülaziz complained that local Armenians were obtaining permission to travel to Adana ostensibly to find work, only to surreptitiously board steamships in Mersin bound for European transit ports.[39] Mersin in the final decade of the nineteenth century was just completing a rapid transformation from a sleepy fishing village to a major port city, a metamorphosis driven primarily by its proximity to the inland boomtown of Adana, the epicentre of the empire's rapidly growing cotton export economy.[40] Beginning in the late 1880s, major European shipping lines such as the French Messageries Maritimes and Austrian Lloyd began offering regular steamship service out of the city. Additionally, the Adana region's rapidly growing population of migrant labourers and merchants with ties to communities in the Harput region made it much easier for migration agents in the interior to develop networks of support for their North America-bound clients transiting through the port of Mersin. Likewise, Iskenderun, located approximately two hundred kilometres south and east of Mersin on the eastern Mediterranean coast, was also emerging as a favoured exit port for Armenian migrants bound for North America. Like Mersin, Iskenderun was the primary entrepôt for Aleppo, a city with long-standing economic ties to the Harput region, and it too was becoming a favoured port for European shipping companies in the late nineteenth century. Both factors are critical to explaining their incorporation into the geography of migration.

For smugglers and their clients, Mersin, Iskenderun and other port cities along the Mediterranean coast also possessed a significant advantage over their Black Sea counterparts: their coastal geography. The northeastern Mediterranean is abutted by the Çukorova plain, a vast swath of flat land separating the coastline from the Taurus Mountains. At its widest point between the coastal town of Karataş and the city of Adana, the plain stretches fifty kilometres from north to south. The region, frequently blanketed by hot, humid air and fertilised by numerous creeks and rivers, was perfectly suited to plantation agriculture. In the 1860s, the Ottoman state encouraged the mass cultivation of cotton for international export, a development that drove the region's rapid economic expansion in the final decades of the nineteenth century. Swaths of coastline immediately outside of both Mersin and Iskenderun, meanwhile, where rugged terrain quite suddenly gives way to coastal plain, were thickly forested, thus providing perfect cover for smugglers involved in trafficking everything from weapons to drugs.[41] Furthermore, the calm and shallow waters provided ideal conditions for boatmen to establish informal launch sites from which they could ferry North America-bound migrants onto waiting foreign ships, avoiding the watchful eyes of state authorities stationed in the central ports.[42] Major Black Sea ports such as Samsun and Trabzon, on the other hand, were hemmed in on three sides by steep rises in elevation, and on the fourth by choppy, storm-prone waters. These conditions all but required Armenian migrants bound for North America to transit directly through the central ports, significantly increasing their chances of being caught. This is not to say that Black Sea cities ceased to be important ports of exit as the above anecdote about the three innkeepers in Trabzon indicates. Rather, travelling through them required a different set of evasive strategies, in particular the use of state-issued documents permitting travel within the empire, which migrants often used to board and then stow away on foreign steamships until they reached their home ports. Between 1904 and 1908, Istanbul received numerous reports that Armenian migrants transiting through Samsun and Trabzon were in possession of travel documents bearing fraudulent Muslim names, and using them to illegally depart the empire for North America.[43] This may have been a cheaper alternative to leaving through Mediterranean ports, but carried with it a great deal of risk, and could not accommodate the ever larger numbers of Armenians seeking to migrate abroad in contravention of Ottoman policy.

Thus, migrant smuggling networks in the Harput region continued to direct most of their clientele southward towards Mediterranean port cities.

By the first years of the twentieth century, Armenian migrants were travelling as far Latakia, Tripoli and Beirut, likely the result of state efforts to crack down on incidents of unauthorised departures in Mersin and Iskenderun.[44] The coastal geography of these eastern Mediterranean ports with long stretches of coastal plain backed by steep rises in elevation was, like their counterparts further north and west, conducive to smuggling. Nevertheless, their incorporation into the geography of migration is at first glance surprising. Harput and Beirut were separated by over eight hundred kilometres of treacherous and rugged terrain. Furthermore, unlike Mersin or Samsun, the Ottoman east and the Levant did not possess strong social and economic ties, and thus these port cities lacked networks of kinship and compatriotism that elsewhere helped to facilitate the smuggling of migrants.

The eastern Mediterranean, was no stranger to people smuggling. By the mid-1880s, an entire industry had emerged in Beirut and elsewhere along the eastern Mediterranean coast dedicated to assisting thousands of mostly Maronite Christians from Mount Lebanon to overcome Ottoman restrictions on their ability to migrate abroad.[45] The decision by the Ottoman state to lift most restrictions on Lebanese migration in December 1898, meant that Lebanese migrants no longer needed to rely on the services of smugglers and other intermediaries to the degree they had before.[46] In November 1901, the Ministry of Interior reported that smugglers in Beirut had lost a significant and stable source of revenue after the lifting of the ban on Lebanese overseas migration, but that they were developing strategies to attract new clientele.[47] Armenians from the Ottoman east clearly helped to make up for some of this lost revenue. A 1907 report from provincial officials in Beirut claimed that Armenians and military deserters made up the majority of the business of the city's smugglers.[48] Port cities on the eastern Mediterranean may have lacked the same historical connections with migrant sending regions in the Ottoman east that Samsun, Mersin and Iskenderun possessed, but two important factors likely help to explain their incorporation into the geography of clandestine migration. The smuggling operations that existed in cities along the coast of the Levant were generally larger and more organised than those that existed elsewhere in the Mediterranean and Black Seas, an outcome of years of unauthorised Lebanese migration coupled with the region's longer history of integration into networks of global trade. Smugglers in cities such as Beirut and Latakia had the means to accommodate a significant volume of migrant traffic and to employ more sophisticated strategies to evade the authorities. Meanwhile, the region's relatively advanced railway infrastructure, and in particular the completion in 1906 of a rail line that connected Aleppo, a city with longstanding economic ties to the Harput region, to Beirut, spared Armenian migrants from an additional several hundred kilometres of travel by foot over rough terrain.[49]

Russian-controlled Batumi, which until the Russo–Ottoman war of 1877–78 had been an Ottoman city, also emerged in the first years of the twentieth century as an important port of exit for Armenians seeking to migrate to North America. The benefit of embarking from a port under the control of a foreign power was obvious: once in Batumi, no Ottoman authorities stood in between the migrant and a steamship bound for Marseille or Liverpool. Nevertheless, the trek from the Anatolian interior to this eastern Black Sea port was especially perilous, requiring migrants to traverse the Lesser Caucasus Mountains that marked the frontier between the Ottoman and Russian empires. Israel Safarian, whose story introduced this Chapter, made the trip from his home village in the district of Kiğı, a region approximately one hundred kilometres north and east of Harput/Mezre. His story testifies to the fact that clandestine migration to North America was only possible through these well-organised networks of intermediaries. The Kurdish guides who led Safarian and the caravan he was a part of for the Russian border, for example, ensured that they did not fall victim to bandits and escaped detection by Ottoman authorities while en route. Despite the relative benefits of departing through Batumi, travelling there was neither easy nor cheap between paying guides and bribing Russian border guards. Its emergence as an important port of exit for the Harput region's ever expanding clandestine migration business is yet another example of the central role that geography played in this story.

By 1908, the Harput region was connected to a vast array of port cities, each of which possessed its own advantages for ensuring that Armenian migrants could depart the empire free from interference from the Ottoman state. The constant forging of new links between the interior and the coast, a process that involved vast distances and an ever-expanding array of intermediaries, is a testament to the versatility and ingenuity that sustained these migration networks throughout this period.

Port City Migration Networks

After an overland journey that at times exceeded two weeks, migrants arrived at one of the bustling ports on the Black or Mediterranean Sea coasts. There they were met by a dense network of intermediaries responsible for everything from arranging their clients' ocean passage to smuggling them aboard foreign steamers waiting just offshore. The available evidence on these port city smuggling networks reveals impressively coordinated operations that involved a broad and diverse set of actors transcending lines of ethnicity, religion, nationality and class.

Upon his arrival in Batumi, Israel Safarian and his fellow migrants were taken directly to a boarding house owned by natives of his home district of Kiğı. Decades after he had migrated to Canada, the recollection of his time in the Black Sea port remained vivid and painful. He described being forced to wait weeks in increasingly difficult conditions while his hosts made arrangements for his passage to Marseille. He accused the innkeepers of defrauding their clients by providing meagre rations while charging for three full meals a day, and bitterly recounted leaving Batumi deeply indebted to these fellow countrymen whom he referred to, perhaps ironically, as *aghas,* or feudal lords.[50] A year after arriving in Brantford, Safarian received a letter from his father complaining that an associate of the innkeepers, perhaps the migration agent in Kiğı with whom he initially contracted to assist with his journey out of the Ottoman Empire, had presented his family with a bill for charges Safarian had accrued while in Batumi.[51]

In the absence of similarly detailed accounts, it is impossible to gauge how representative Safarian's experiences were. Nevertheless, the broad outlines of his experiences while in Batumi are reflected in Ottoman source material. As the case of Hazar, Minas and Ahmed, introduced in the opening to this section of the book, suggests, innkeepers were centrally important to the success of these port city smuggling networks. They were the gateway to the underground world that assisted migrants on to foreign steamers and out of the clutches of state authorities. Because of their work, they appear with some regularity in Ottoman documents. In January 1898, for example, an Iskenderun-based innkeeper, Hagop, was accused of paying bribes to a wide range of powerful officials in the city in exchange for allowing his North America-bound clients to freely transit through the port.[52] Nearly three years later authorities in Iskenderun expelled another local innkeeper, Osep, a native of Arapgir in Mamuretülaziz province, after documents were intercepted revealing his involvement in smuggling migrants.[53] In January 1904, officials in the Black Sea port of Trabzon complained that 'Armenian innkeepers' (*Ermeni hancileri*) were encountering little difficulty procuring travel documents and steamship tickets for their clients who sought to travel abroad in violation of the migration ban.[54] Similar charges were brought up a year later against innkeepers in Samsun.[55] For their part, officials in Trabzon proposed the adoption of measures, including the levying of a steep sixty lira cash fine for those who obtained travel documents under false pretenses, in the hope of putting an end to such activities.[56]

Ties of compatriotism played a central role in the functioning of these port city smuggling networks. Like the innkeepers in Safarian's account, those identified by the Ottoman state for their involvement in the migration business were frequently natives of communities in and around the Harput region. Connections between migration agents in the interior and port city innkeepers were likely central to coordinating smuggling operations across vast distances. But innkeepers were only one node in a much larger network of intermediaries. Given the historical connections between the Harput region and port cities on the Black and Mediterranean Sea coasts, they could rely on fellow countrymen who, like them, were deeply woven into the economic and political fabric of these places. Such individuals were well situated to assist and profit from migrant smuggling operations. For example, in early 1902 officials in Adana arrested and prosecuted several local merchants and tradesmen for their involvement in smuggling migrants. Among those arrested were two bakers, two coffee merchants, a butcher and the superintendent of a local market.[57] One of the bakers, Mustafa, a Muslim and Harput native, was accused of working closely with and paying handsome bribes to a powerful police official in the city, an Armenian named Hagop, to help keep the police from interfering in their smuggling operations.[58]

Yet in the face of the state ban on Armenian migration to North America, successfully and discreetly smuggling migrants through these port cities necessitated transcending ties of compatriotism to involve other elements of port city society. Employees of foreign consulates, for example, were commonly involved in aiding migrant smuggling activities. Foreign diplomatic missions figured prominently in the economies and politics of Ottoman port cities, and they regularly employed Ottoman subjects – often local Christians – to serve as translators and guards. These individuals in turn served as an important bridge between locals and foreigners, and many enjoyed special capitulatory protections extended to them by their employers.[59] The influence and connections they possessed were invaluable to migrant smugglers, especially as they worked to get their clients on board steamships bound for foreign transit ports. This process regularly involved clandestine boardings, carried out under the cover of night, requiring extensive coordination with shipping company personnel.

Like innkeepers, references to consular employees occur frequently in the source material. As early as April 1892, officials in Adana complained that the city's Iranian consul was providing assistance to Armenians seeking to depart for North America. The Ottoman state pressured Iranian officials to remove the consul, only to have their complaints fall on deaf ears.[60] In

September 1900, officials in Mersin discovered that several employees of foreign consulates were involved in smuggling migrants through the city. Their investigation revealed that employees of the city's Russian and German consulates were shepherding groups of migrants to a waterfront villa located outside of the central city that belonged to a local doctor, a US national. From the villa's private beach, boatmen rowed the migrants to foreign steamers waiting just off shore.[61] Three years later, one of these individuals, an employee of the Russian consulate identified as Anton, in conjunction with an associate of the local British consul, was reported to be earning a handsome fee of seven liras per every migrant they smuggled from shore to ship.[62] In November 1903, the Ottomans lodged a complaint with the Russian government accusing Anton of involvement in trafficking both migrants and weapons. Yet again, the Foreign Ministry's request was met with a terse rebuff from the Russian ambassador.[63] One month later, officials in Iskenderun accused two translators and a guard affiliated with that city's American consulate of similarly aiding local boatmen with smuggling Armenian migrants onto foreign steamers anchored in the harbour.[64] The involvement of diplomatic staff in migrant smuggling did not go unnoticed, at least by American officials. In a 1901 report by Thomas Norton, the US consul in Harput, he commented that cavasses employed by foreign missions in port cities on the Black and Mediterranean Sea coasts were personally assisting Armenian migrants with boarding foreign steamships.[65]

Boatmen, however, played the most visible role in port city migrant smuggling networks. In the absence of modern docking facilities, the responsibility for shuttling goods and passengers between ship and shore fell to boatmen, whose small wooden vessels were a ubiquitous sight in every Ottoman port. They were the very lifeblood on which commerce in these cities depended. Their economic importance and, in many cases, organised political clout made it very difficult for the Ottoman state to take meaningful measures to ensure that they did not engage in or abet illegal commerce. Their involvement in smuggling North America-bound migrants onto foreign steamers was clear to state authorities early on. In July 1890, the governor of Trabzon province reported that local boatmen in Samsun were shuttling migrants to foreign steamers anchored in the harbour at night when it was all but impossible for local officials to take action to stop them. This led to his call for the creation of a modern passenger pier that would obviate the need to rely on boatmen for ship-to-shore traffic.[66] It was in the port cities of the Mediterranean, however, where boatmen assumed an especially important role in facilitating clandestine migration. As mentioned above, boatmen in both Mersin and Iskenderun readily exploited favourable coastal geography and placid waters to construct informal launch points from which migrants could be smuggled onto foreign ships. Such points were generally set up in the vicinity of small villages located up to twenty kilometres from the central port. At this distance, they were accessible from the centre of town but far enough away to avoid the reach of lighthouses monitoring the main harbour. Under the cover of darkness, migrants in groups of up to forty were rowed to ships waiting far enough off shore to also avoid detection from coastal lighthouses.[67] Testimony given by three Ottoman officials, who witnessed such an event outside of Iskenderun in June 1899, provides a detailed picture of one of these late night rendezvous. The three men, identified as two military scribes and a Jerusalem-based policeman, were passengers aboard the French steamer *Congo* as it sailed between Iskenderun and Mersin on the night of 9 June 1899. According to a statement given to the district governor of Mersin, shortly upon departing Iskenderun's central port, the ship made an unscheduled stop. Despite the pre-dawn darkness, the officials claimed to witness two white rowboats approach the backside of the large vessel where the boatmen then unloaded, one by one, twenty to twenty-five Armenian migrants. Once aboard, the migrants were quickly spirited to a place deep in the ship's hold where they were prevented from speaking and comingling with other passengers.[68]

The details provided in the testimony of these three men hint at the impressive degree of coordination that existed between local migration intermediaries, agents of foreign shipping lines, boatmen and the crews of these ships.[69] The regularity with which carefully orchestrated late-night rendezvous took place reflects the extent to which the port city migration networks relied on the close cooperation of the diverse actors, from innkeepers and local merchants to consular employees and, of course, boatmen. The relative visibility of these events in the documentary evidence, however, suggests the parties involved were not always successful in evading the authorities and arrests of boatmen involved in smuggling migrants were not infrequent.[70] Despite the risks involved, participation in the migration industry was a lucrative business for boatmen. In a report from June 1900, officials at Iskenderun estimated that some local boatmen were making up to fifty liras daily ferrying migrants to waiting foreign steamers. The report went on to raise concerns that the fine of two liras and the short jail sentence often meted out to boatmen arrested on suspicion of human smuggling was proving to be of little deterrence value.[71]

Boatmen in Mersin and Iskenderun clearly ran impressive operations, evidenced by their high degree of coordination and their ability to smuggle large numbers of migrants at a time. Further south on the eastern Mediterranean coast, boatmen in Latakia and Beirut ran operations on an even larger scale. Ottoman officials regularly complained that boatmen in these cities had the capacity to smuggle their migrant clients well off shore and out of view of the authorities, in some cases as far as the island of Cyprus, over one hundred kilometres off the Ottoman coast.[72] Because Cyprus was under de-facto British rule, migrants smuggled there could board foreign ships freely and without fear of interdiction. The trip from the eastern Mediterranean coast to Cyprus required large vessels capable of travel on the open water with the ability to carry numerous passengers at a time, a stark difference from the rickety wooden rowboats used by boatmen in Mersin and Iskenderun.[73] As mentioned above, the ability of these large, capital intensive operations to smuggle large numbers of migrants at a time may have been a major factor leading to the incorporation of cities such as Beirut and Latakia into the geography of migration.

The available evidence on the backgrounds of these boatmen testifies to the diversity of port city life in the final century of the Ottoman Empire. One notable boatman, Kiryako, who smuggled migrants from an informal port just north of Iskenderun, was a Greek Orthodox fisherman originally from the Aegean port of Çeşme, located several hundred kilometres to the west of Iskenderun.[74] Kiryako owned numerous small boats and, according to one source, his operation employed several other local boatmen.[75] Another prominent boatman/smuggler, Mustafa, based out of the eastern Mediterranean port of Tripoli, was the scion of a local Muslim family who smuggled migrants alongside his business ferrying goods between Cyprus and various port cities along the Mediterranean coast.[76] Finally, one Muhammad, who from the mid-1890s until well into the first years of the twentieth century ran an operation out of Beirut that specialised in smuggling both people and weapons, was of Algerian origin, and claimed consular protection from the French government, thus frustrating the efforts of the Ottoman state to prosecute him.[77] The diverse backgrounds of these boatmen further underscores how migration networks in port cities went beyond links of compatriotism to include actors of various social, regional, ethnic and even national backgrounds. The coordination that existed between migration agents in the interior and these impressive and heterogeneous port city networks is key to understanding why in this period so many Anatolian Armenians were able to depart for North America in the face of Ottoman efforts to force an end to this migration.

State Officials and Clandestine Migration

The Ottoman state's efforts to put an end to the unauthorised migration of Armenians to North America opened up ample opportunities for its own officials to profit from the clandestine migration business. State officials at almost every level of the imperial bureaucracy helped to lubricate the gears that kept migration networks running relatively smoothly and with minimal interference. Civil registrars (*nüfus memurları*) responsible for issuing the travel documents (*mürur tezkereleri*) that Ottoman law stipulated were to be carried by all who moved within the empire's borders, recognised early on their value to those seeking to illegally depart the empire. Possession of an internal passport, probably the most suitable term for this system of document-based mobility control,[78] was critically important for North America-bound migrants travelling between the interior and the coast, and they could ease the process by which they transited through port cities and boarded foreign steamships. As a result, cases involving civil registrars granting internal passports to Armenians seeking to migrate to North America, usually in return for substantial bribes, abound in the documentary evidence. For example, in August 1891 officials in the Black Sea port of Giresun confiscated internal passports from twenty-six Armenians from the Harput region. The documents listed Istanbul as the group's final destination, but officials in Giresun had received word that the migrants were intending to migrate abroad unlawfully. A full investigation revealed that the group had not obtained the documents from officials in their home communities as prescribed by law. Rather, they had bribed a population registrar based in the district of Karahisar-ı Şarki, located just to the south of Giresun, to illegally grant them internal passports for Istanbul. According to their statements, each member of the migrant caravan paid the registrar twenty-five kuruş for the documents, more than five times the legally stipulated cost.[79]

Twenty-five kuruş appears to have been on the very low end of the price scale for a fraudulently issued internal passport, especially as larger numbers of Armenians sought to skirt state efforts to enforce the migration ban. In 1898, officials in Samsun apprehended several migrants, each of whom was found to be in possession of an illegally obtained internal passport. The documents were traced back to a civil registrar in Malatya, a city located in Mamuretülaziz province, just over one hundred kilometres to the west of Harput/Mezre, triggering an investigation. According to a letter sent to the Ministry of Interior by an anonymous self-described 'trustworthy informant' (*muhbir-i sâdık*), the registrar managed to successfully quash the investigation and avoid losing his job by paying out cash bribes worth one hundred and fifty liras and numerous other unspecified 'gifts' (*hediyeler*). If the informant's report was anywhere close to accurate, then the registrar's willingness to pay such a significant sum suggests that selling internal passports was an impressively lucrative enterprise, and one that he was not eager to lose. For his part, the informant ended his report with an ominous warning that 'the more that the common people witness this kind of behaviour from state officials, the more it risks inflaming their hatred of them,' and by extension, the state itself.[80] The sale of travel documents continued to be a profitable business throughout this period. Several months later in 1898, a local merchant in Harput accused the province's chief civil registrar of illegally profiting from the sale of passports valid for international travel to Armenians seeking to travel unlawfully to North America.[81] In August 1907, four migrants paid a combined sum of sixty-four liras to a migration agent based in the Çemişgezek district of Mamuretülaziz province who then obtained internal passports with fraudulent Muslim names from a local civil registrar.[82] Even the US consul in Harput wrote of the important role that fraudulently issued internal passports played in facilitating clandestine migration, writing that would-be migrants could expect to pay 'five pounds, or more, to lubricate the official machinery.'[83]

In port cities, a variety of state officials played similarly important roles in the clandestine migration business. For example, in July 1892, as Istanbul ratcheted up its efforts to put a stop to the widening stream of Armenians seeking to migrate abroad, the Ministry of Interior issued a stern threat to police forces in several port cities that officers found to be turning a blind eye to or actively abetting unlawful migration would feel the full force of the law.[84] The ministry's concerns were well founded, as police officers continued to profit, sometimes quite flagrantly, off of migration. In 1900, a prominent police official in Adana identified as Hagop was implicated for his involvement in smuggling Armenian migrants onto foreign steamships in the port of Mersin. Hagop allegedly used his position to serve as an intermediary connecting migrants waiting in Adana for an opportunity to depart the empire to those in the port of Mersin working to arrange their steamship travel.[85] Two years later, he was arrested on suspicion of being involved with another migration ring, a charge for which he was later convicted and sentenced to an unusually stiff three year prison sentence, forced to return all bribe money, and slapped with a forty-five lira fine and a six-year suspension from duty.[86] Three years later, police officials in Beirut were found to be involved in an elaborate scheme to shake down Armenian migrants transiting through the port. In May 1907, officers in Beirut arrested a party of twelve migrants from the Harput area immediately after they arrived at the city's train station. According to the testimony of one police officer, the migrants were promptly released after a well-known smuggler in the city, Hussein Hariri, paid a significant bribe. The next evening, a group of twenty migrants arrived by train and were again arrested and then released under similarly dubious circumstances. The officer testified that his colleagues had a prior arrangement with the smuggler Hariri in which he allowed his clients to be arrested. The bribes he paid for their release gave the police an opportunity to profit handsomely while allowing Hariri to continue his illicit business essentially freely and in the open.[87] Indeed, it appears that the level of police involvement in clandestine migration in Beirut was so great that local smugglers expected as a matter of course that they could operate without fear of arrest, an issue addressed in greater detail in Chapter 3.[88]

Given their problems with chronic underpayment, it is perhaps not surprising that rank and file port city police officers sought to benefit from clandestine migration. Some of them, such as the aforementioned Hagop, may have been natives of migrant-sending communities and thus embedded in the same socio-economic and cultural milieus that helped to give rise to port city networks. Yet, the participation of state officials in the migration industry was not the sole domain of the rank-and-file police officer or the middling provincial bureaucrat. Case in point, in August 1907, the newly appointed governor of Mamuretülaziz province sent a long, strongly worded letter to the Ministry of Police. In the letter, he described an elaborate plot to smuggle migrants that involved a diverse and powerful cross section of provincial officialdom. In March of that year, eleven Armenians from the district of Palu, located roughly eighty kilometres to the east of Harput/Mezre, were arrested on suspicion that they had returned from the United States in contravention of Ottoman law.[89] In line with state policy concerning Armenian return migrants, officials in Palu ordered that the eleven be marched from Palu to Samsun, forced onto a steamship and deported from the empire. Having just returned from years toiling in North American factories bookended by two arduous transhemispheric journeys, the returnees were desperate to avoid this fate. Through an associate based in Palu, word of their predicament reached the powerful banker and migration agent, Artin Harputlian. A plan was subsequently devised that, if successful, would spare the eleven men from deportation. Following protocol, the eleven returnees were sent from Palu to Mezre before setting off for Samsun, where they were processed and had their photographs taken so that they would be on file in case they ever attempted to reenter the empire. Artin and his associates planned to intercede at this point of the deportation process, and switch the returnees with another group of individuals who were seeking to migrate to North America. This latter group was to assume the names and identities of the eleven Palu returnees complete with forged documents provided by the police chief of Mamuretülaziz province.

In addition to the police chief, several other prominent local officials were involved in the plan's execution including the provincial gendarmerie commander, Mirza Bey, and a number of others of lesser rank. After the group of returnees arrived in Harput from Palu, certain precautions were enacted to avoid arousing suspicion. For the next four days, police officials involved in the plot kept the eleven returnees confined and under constant watch in the local government building. The switch was scheduled to take place on Friday at prayer time when traffic at the government building would be at a minimum. Finally, rather than having the returnees' photographs taken outside the government building's prison complex, as was customary, the group was instead to be escorted to the studio of a local photographer whose services were not normally used in deportation cases. On the day of the switch, the returnees were taken from the government building to the photographer's studio while their replacements were hastily dispatched to Samsun. Shortly thereafter, the weary group of would-be deportees was released on their own recognisance and hastily returned to their homes in Palu.[90]

Despite its cunning and ingenuity, the plot unravelled after officials in Samsun arrested the group that had replaced the original returnees and had them sent back to the Harput region. The subsequent arrest of those involved in the plot shook the provincial officialdom of Mamuretülaziz to the core. The Ottoman state had known of Artin Harputlian's connections to high-ranking provincial officials since as early as 1905.[91] The investigation into the migrant switching incident, however, revealed that Artin, who was a member of the provincial council and thus himself a government official, regularly conducted business related to his migrant smuggling activities within the walls of the government building and in plain sight.[92]

The fact that the plot involved so many high-ranking provincial authorities was a jarring indication of just how deep their ties to the region's migrant smuggling business ran. Given the effort with which the central Ottoman state sought to put an end to Armenian migration to North America, however, it is difficult to imagine that these smuggling networks could have operated at high volume and for more than two decades without the cooperation of state officials at nearly every level. This is more than just a story of rampant corruption and venality, however. The actions of these officials reveal the complicated role that state power played in shaping the migration process. As will become clearer in the next Chapter, personal benefit was not the sole factor driving state officials' response – or lack thereof – to clandestine migration, as instead their actions were shaped by numerous political and social dynamics that put them at odds with the imperatives of the central state.

Conclusion

Over a century before the clandestine migration of the early twenty-first century Mediterranean dominated headlines around the world and piqued the interest of scholars of contemporary global migration, dense migrant smuggling networks traversed the Mediterranean and Black Sea coasts of the Ottoman Empire. As is the case today, the emergence of these networks was a direct outcome of state efforts to target forms of mobility deemed dangerous or otherwise problematic. Istanbul's efforts to prevent Armenians from migrating to North America in the late nineteenth and early twentieth centuries required the forging of relationships that transcended religious, ethnic and linguistic differences and spanned impressive stretches of space and time. Without this social and spatial flexibility, migration between the Harput region and North America would have been impossible.

The clandestine migration networks of the twenty-first century have rendered the Mediterranean in the words of anthropologist Maurizio Albahari 'the world's deadliest border,' a factor that has only contributed to the global interest in the current migration and refugee crisis along Europe's southern and eastern border. Armenian migrants a century before did not encounter nearly the same degree of risk as their modern day counterparts. Not once have I encountered a report either in Ottoman or in Western accounts of migrants dying as they travelled between the Harput region and the coast, while transiting through Ottoman port cities, or in the process of being smuggled from shore to ship. If clandestine migration is a natural outcome of state efforts to make mobility more difficult, then the more sophisticated the strategies and the more powerful the weapons at the state's disposal, the more dangerous the migration process becomes. Institutions such as the European Border and Coast Guard Agency, known as Frontex, have deployed cutting-edge surveillance technology along the Mediterranean to interdict boats filled beyond capacity with migrants from crossing into European Union waters. They have partnered with officials in sub-Saharan Africa and elsewhere to prevent migrants from getting anywhere close to the border.[93] The governments of Hungary and Bulgaria, meanwhile, have erected fences and stationed well-armed guards alongside their respective borders with Serbia and Turkey. Far from halting migration, strategies for evading state authorities have evolved and the geography of migration has consistently shifted, as was the case in the Ottoman Empire in the late nineteenth and early twentieth centuries. But in doing so, migration has become only more difficult and dangerous, to a degree almost unimaginable a century before.

Ottoman officials could only have dreamed of the technologies and strategies of migration enforcement available to their contemporary counterparts. Thankfully for those who sought to migrate in the face of Istanbul's ban, they did not. Even for its day, the Ottoman state was relatively weak. But this is not to say that it did not have a powerful effect on shaping the migration process, as this Chapter has shown. At the same time, migration exposed many of the tensions and contradictions that underlay Ottoman governance in the late-Hamidian era.

3

The State

In late September 1893, the governor of Adana province, Abdülhalik, sent a long communiqué to the Ministry of Interior. For the past several months, Istanbul had been receiving numerous reports from its diplomats in Liverpool and Marseille about the steady flow of Ottoman Armenians transiting through the two cities en route to North America. Concerningly for the governor, the consuls pointed the finger squarely at officials based in port cities such as Mersin for failing to put a stop to unauthorised migration. As provincial governor, Abdülhalik knew that Mersin's failures were his failures; the proverbial buck stopped with him. Eager to prove to his superiors in Istanbul that he and his subordinates were doing everything in their power to enforce the migration ban, he decided to inject a little drama into his description of these efforts. A few days before, police officials in Mersin executed a late-night raid targeting a group of clandestine migrants. Word had arrived that four Armenians attempting to depart the empire for North America were holed up in a small vessel used by foreign shipping companies to transport goods and passengers to steamships docked in the city's harbour. Officials in Mersin sent word to various foreign consulates in the city that any vessel under their jurisdiction, or belonging to a foreign or Ottoman national under their protection, was subject to search. Furthermore, the consulates would be held responsible for any ship that left the port without authorisation. No doubt the governor believed that Istanbul would be impressed with his subordinates' display of strength directed towards Western diplomats who were accustomed to operating on Ottoman soil with virtual impunity. Meanwhile, the harbourmaster was ordered to station guard boats (*muhafaza sandalları*) just off shore to ensure that no clandestine steamship boardings took place during the night. As morning broke, the four Armenians, sensing that there was no escape, left their hiding place and were arrested the moment they stepped foot on shore.

With the four men in custody, police in Mersin began a full investigation. Interrogations of the men revealed a tortuous and harrowing path that eventually led to their arrest. They had arrived in Mersin ten days earlier hoping to clandestinely board a foreign steamship. Fearing that local authorities were on to them, the four men left for Tarsus, a small inland city located between Mersin and Adana. Several days later, sporting new outfits, they returned to Mersin with the assistance of their Adana-based smuggler, Daniel Chekerjian. On the night of the raid, they were delivered to local boatmen who, in exchange for a few liras, began ferrying them to a French steamer waiting just off shore.[1] Before reaching the ship, the boatmen suddenly stopped. They searched their hapless passengers for weapons, and finding none, robbed them of more than one hundred liras worth of cash and valuables. They then transferred the four men to the foreign transport vessel, where they were forced to hide until being driven out when morning broke. Based on descriptions the unlucky migrants provided in their testimony, local police brought in a number of boatmen for a lineup. The four men identified the perpetrators who robbed them, and the boatmen were swiftly taken into custody. Orders were then given for the arrest of their smuggler, Daniel Chekerjian, who, as of the letter's writing, had yet to be apprehended.[2] Several days later, the French embassy penned an angry letter protesting the insolent demand from officials in Mersin that their ships were subject to search. 'Captain's of postal ships,' the letter stated, 'have every right to refuse such invasive and unlawful requests.'[3]

Whether the governor's dramatic recounting of the raid had the intended effect of assuaging Istanbul's concerns about the efficacy of the migration ban is unclear. While it would seem to lend credence to his assertion that officials in the province were doing everything in their policy to enforce state policy, evidence of the many obstacles frustrating these efforts lurk just below the surface. The roles of Daniel Chekerjian and the boatmen in the migrants' testimony reflect the growing sophistication, even at this relatively early date, of the clandestine migration networks that were the focus of the previous Chapter. The French embassy's angry letter, furthermore, serves as a reminder of the constraints that the international system of the late nineteenth century placed on the Ottoman state's ability to exercise sovereignty over its own realms. Finally, the governor's description of the raid describes an intricate operation involving the cooperation of a broad cross-section of officials in Mersin that only resulted in the interdiction of four would-be migrants. It is unlikely that Istanbul was entirely impressed with this result, given the degree of effort involved.

In the end, the governor's descriptions of Mersin's raid notwithstanding, the Ottoman state's efforts to prevent Armenian migration to North America were doomed to fail. Read out of context, the governor's letter could seemingly imply the existence of a powerful and well-oiled system of enforcement in Ottoman port cities. In reality, throughout the 1890s and the first decade of the twentieth century, questions remained about where responsibility for the enforcement of the migration ban should lie: either with officials based in the provinces of the Ottoman east from where most migrants came, or with officials in coastal provinces that served as their primary points of exit. Finding a resolution to this dilemma was made more difficult by a set of ancillary problems. The Ottoman state had a long history of mobility control efforts directed at managing migration within its own borders. As more Armenians departed the empire for North America in the late 1880s and 1890s, initial efforts at prevention focused on modifying this system of policing internal mobility to put a stop to unauthorised overseas migration. This strategy, however, laid bare a major tension between the state's desire to preempt forms of mobility it deemed illegitimate, while simultaneously not impinging on those it considered to be legitimate. This in turn triggered intense disagreements between officials stationed in different regions of the empire. Far from being monolithic, efforts to enforce the ban revealed an Ottoman state apparatus beset by rancourous conflict and, at times, outright hostility, as various provincial bureaucracies accused one another of failing to adequately prevent unauthorised migration. Adding fuel to these feuds was the fact that officials were often responding to specific political, social and economic forces at play in their respective provinces. These local considerations in many cases put these officials in direct conflict with the imperatives of the central state. The failure of the migration ban is not simply a cliché story about the weakness of the late-Ottoman state. Instead, these efforts fell victim to a series of insuperable tensions and contradictions inherent in the exercise of state power in the final decades of empire.

'Internal' Solutions to an 'External' Problem

In the initial weeks and months that followed the promulgation of the ban on Armenian migration to North America in 1888, the state lacked an official strategy on how to handle those caught while attempting to depart the empire. In the summer of 1888, several groups of Armenians from the Harput region were arrested in Istanbul on suspicion that they were attempting to illegally migrate abroad. These groups of migrants were then returned to their home communities in the Ottoman east with the central treasury covering the cost of the journey. In May of 1888, the expense of covering steamer travel from Istanbul to Samsun for fifty-five North America-bound migrants arrested in Istanbul forced officials with the Ministry of Interior to plead to the grand vizier for money from an emergency fund to help defray the immense cost.[4] In an October 1888 communiqué, the Ministry of Interior called for a more proactive approach to preventing unauthorised overseas migration, noting that Armenians who travelled to the United States risked having their minds polluted by seditious organisations operating in an environment of 'utter permissiveness and freedom' (*serbest ve hürriyet-i kamiliye*).[5]

By 1890, a coherent strategy had begun to emerge. Managing and policing domestic mobility had a long history in the empire and state officials chose to draw from this deep well of experience. In the late nineteenth century, the internal passport (*mürur tezkeresi*) was the beating heart of Istanbul's efforts at domestic mobility control. Document-based mobility control in the Ottoman Empire had a history dating at least as far back as the sixteenth century. The Ottoman state occasionally mandated the issuing of travel documents to control the flow of domestic migration to Istanbul with the hope of maintaining social and political stability in the empire's seat of power.[6] By the early nineteenth century, however, the social and political upheaval occasioned by the destruction of the Janissary Corps in 1826, coupled with a series of destructive wars fought against Russia and Greece, provided the impetus to create a stronger system of internal migration controls.[7] Throughout the 1820s and 1830s, the Ottoman state promulgated a number of decrees intended to strengthen mobility controls within the empire's borders. Finally in 1841, two years after the inauguration of the Tanzimat reforms, the Ottoman state issued a series of regulations known as the *Menʾ-i Mürur Nizamnamesi* (Regulations Pursuant to the Restriction of Movement) that created the legal framework for an empire-wide internal passport system. This set of regulations remained in place with some modifications until 1911, when the second constitutional government officially abolished it.[8]

The 1841 regulations stipulated that any individual seeking to travel beyond the boundaries of a township (*kaza*) needed to be in possession of an internal passport. In order to obtain one, an applicant was required to present a certificate of identity (*ilmühaber*) signed by his or her local headman (*muhtar*) or a religious official in their home district or current place of residence. This certificate was then submitted to a local civil registrar responsible for granting internal passports. The document provided information including the bearer's place of birth, occupation, the name of the locality that issued the internal passport, and the bearer's destination.

By the late nineteenth century, internal passports also contained detailed descriptions of the bearer's physical characteristics and religion. By the late nineteenth and early twentieth centuries, the internal passport assumed a standardised and easily reproducible form. The left and right sides of the document provided detailed information about the bearer's physical characteristics, serving the same purpose as a photograph in a modern day identification document. Standardised text in the middle of the document provided space to stipulate the number of dependent women and children travellers, and, not unlike modern passports, included verbiage directing any state official that the bearer encountered during travel to provide 'any and all necessary aid and assistance.' Upon arriving at his final destination, the bearer was to present his passport and register with local authorities – usually a neighbourhood headman or guild master (*kethüda*). Travelling without an internal passport, failing to register, or using fraudulent documents were all punishable by stiff penalties that included steep fines and jail time.[9]

The internal passport system as outlined by the *Menʾ-i Mürur Nizamnamesi* represented an attempt to render a diverse and rapidly changing imperial population more legible to the central state. In line with the Tanzimat-era ethos that stressed equality before the law, the internal passport requirement applied to all imperial subjects irrespective of ethnic and religious difference. The twin processes of state centralisation and modernisation embodied by the Tanzimat reforms went hand in hand with the imperial economy's increasing reliance on a mobile population engaged in trade and the sale of labour power.[10] In response to this development, the internal passport system was intended to foster the emergence of an empire-wide information grid in which an individual's movement could be traced and information shared between officials stationed at all points along the way. In so doing, the document would allow the state to fix its mobile subjects in bureaucratic space even as they moved through physical space.

In practice, however, enforcement of this elaborate system proved difficult for the cash-strapped and understaffed Ottoman bureaucracy.[11] Armenians seeking to travel to North America in the face of the migration ban early on took advantage of the many gaping holes in the internal passport system, using the documents to facilitate travel to port cities and to gain access to foreign steamships. Armenians were not the only group to engage in this practice. As Engin Akarlı shows, Lebanese migrants also used internal passports to bypass restrictions on overseas travel. Their widespread misuse of internal passports is in part what led the Ottoman state in 1898 to partially lift the ban on Lebanese migration. In that year,

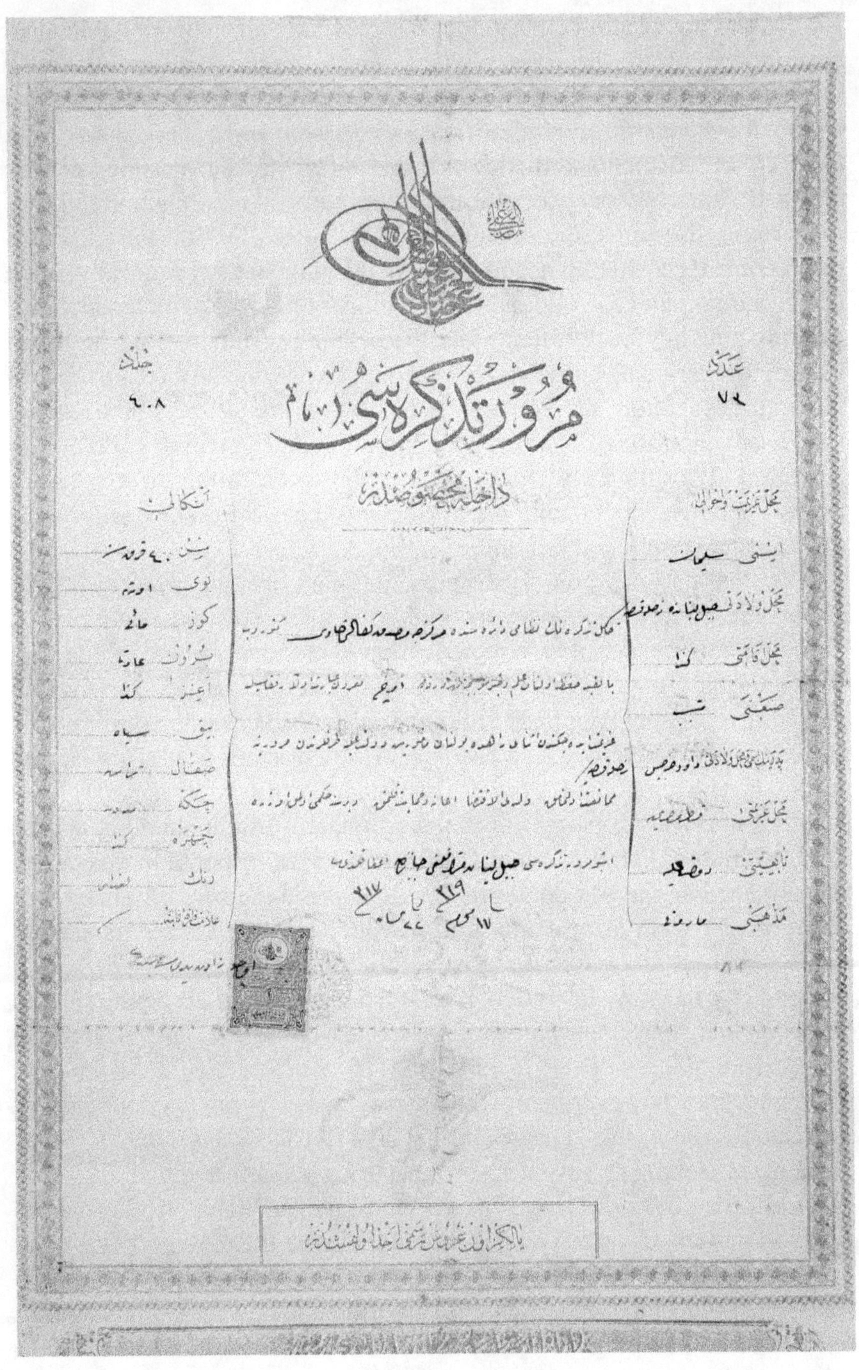

An internal passport issued in Mount Lebanon to Suleiman, May © Image courtesy of the Cumhurbaşkanlığı Devlet Arşivi

Istanbul began issuing special travel documents, essentially a modified version of the internal passport, to residents of Mount Lebanon that permitted them to migrate legally in return for promising that they would maintain their Ottoman nationality and avoid involvement in political activities deemed to be inimical to the empire and its interests. This policy was not extended to other groups in the empire, and, as Akarlı accurately notes, thereby further reinforced Mount Lebanon's special status within the broader imperial system.[12] Nevertheless, it marked a not-so-tacit admission that the state had failed to prevent unauthorised overseas migration from the region, at least in part because Lebanese migrants were so successful at exploiting weaknesses in enforcement of the internal passport system. [13]

Beginning in the early 1890s, as the number of Armenians unlawfully migrating to North America steadily increased, officials experimented with a series of modifications to the internal passport system in hopes of making it a more effective tool in enforcing the migration ban. In the end, however, these efforts laid bare several contradictions underlying Ottoman mobility control efforts. In June 1891, for example, the grand vizier reported that officials in the Ottoman east were requiring Armenians who applied for an internal passport to provide the name of a relative or close associate who could guarantee that they would not use the document to migrate abroad. By vouching for an internal passport applicant, the guarantor was agreeing to pay a significant financial penalty if the document was misused. In June 1893, the Ministry of Interior reported that Mamuretülaziz was stipulating that Armenians granted an internal passport register every three months with local authorities at their final destination. Failure to do so entitled officials in the province to collect a cash bond (*kefalet-i nakdiye*) worth twenty-five liras from the document's guarantor. It was hoped that the threat of such a fine, more than enough to inflict considerable economic hardship on the guarantor, would provide a strong enough disincentive against misuse of the document.[14]

The 1891 report from the grand vizier expressed optimism about the potential effectiveness of such measures as deterrence against unauthorised migration. At the same time, it raised concerns that provincial officials were demanding cash bonds in the absence of clear legal regulations governing their use. The *Men'-i Mürur Nizamnamesi* and subsequent amendments to the internal passport system mention nothing about the use of guarantors and cash bonds, and it appears that provincial officials enforced these requirements in an ad hoc and extra legal fashion. Not surprisingly, there was much confusion and numerous problems with coordinating the enforcement of cash bonds – especially when the various provincial bureaucracies involved were not on the same page. For example, in March 1893, the Ministry of Police complained that Armenians who arrived in Istanbul with internal passports backed by a guarantor remained undeterred and continued to depart clandestinely for North America. Officials in the imperial capital, the report continued, faced a range of logistical difficulties in tracking down guarantors of internal passports based in communities in the distant Harput region or elsewhere in the Ottoman east and ensuring that cash bonds were collected from them. Despite being an imperfect solution, the report nonetheless advocated that the policy continue and measures be implemented to improve enforcement.[15] That same year, officials in Adana complained that their counterparts in the interior were dragging their feet when it came to collecting cash bonds, rendering the practice ineffectual as a deterrent against unauthorised migration.[16] In response, officials in Mamuretülaziz complained that guarantors' 'obstinacy' (*taʾannud*) was making enforcement difficult.[17] While officials there did not bother to spell out what form this so-called 'obstinacy' took, it appears that guarantors had at least some legal recourse open to them to fight these substantial fines. Before collecting cash bonds, provincial officials first needed to obtain the approval of local courts, but given the policy's extra-legal nature this permission was frequently withheld. As a result, the Ministry of Interior granted Mamuretülaziz the power to bypass the courts and directly demand payment from guarantors.[18]

Problems persisted however, as officials in various coastal provinces continued to complain that their counterparts in the interior were either unable or unwilling to enforce their own policy. In November 1896, officials in Iskenderun complained that Armenians arriving in the city in possession of internal passports authorising travel to Beirut or Izmir were using the documents to migrate abroad instead. They requested permission to demand that Armenian travellers transiting through the city provide the name of a guarantor if it was discovered that officials in their home province failed to do so.[19] The Ministry of Interior rejected Iskenderun's request on the grounds that only an official in the province where the internal passport was granted could demand that a guarantor be provided.[20] By the first years of the twentieth century, officials in Mamuretülaziz and other interior provinces had all but ceased demanding guarantors from Armenians who requested internal passports. In a telegram to the Ministry of Interior, the governor of Mamuretülaziz claimed that instead of discouraging unauthorised migration, the practice only forced North America-bound Armenians to seek out the services of clandestine migration networks where possession of an internal passport was not essential.[21] As was discussed in the previous Chapter, in places such as Mersin,

Latakia and Beirut, migrants were increasingly smuggled on to steamships from informal piers located outside of the city, thus obviating the need to board from the central port where undocumented travel was much more difficult. Some migrants, meanwhile, bribed local population registrars who then issued fraudulent documents not backed by a guarantor. By the turn of the twentieth century, the practice was becoming increasingly ineffective as a preventative measure against unauthorised migration and Istanbul was quickly souring on its use. In April 1902, the grand vizier's office ordered that jurisdictions cease demanding guarantors from Armenians who sought an internal passport, citing malfeasance (*bir takım su-i istimalat*) involved with the collection of cash bonds as a primary justification for the move.[22]

Ottoman officials experimented with other controls on the internal mobility of Armenians in the hopes of curbing unauthorised overseas migration. In May 1893, representatives of the shipping company, P.M Kourtzi & Co., owned by a Greek Orthodox Ottoman subject, wrote to the Ministry of Interior complaining that officials in the Black Sea port of Trabzon were not permitting Armenian travellers headed for Istanbul to board the company's ships. According to the letter, Armenians attempting to travel by steamship from the port city to other destinations within the empire were being restricted to certain vessels flying the Ottoman standard in the hope that by limiting travel options in this way, those attempting to migrate to North America would be unable to access and stow away on steamships bound for European transit ports. The letter denounced what the representatives believed was the unfair targeting of their company, complaining that, 'our ships, unable to take on passengers at Trabzon, return to Istanbul entirely empty . . . We can assure that any passenger that boards at Trabzon will be disembarked at Istanbul.'[23]

Looking into the matter, the Ministry of Interior discovered that officials based in the provinces of Trabzon, Aleppo and Adana were all to varying degrees limiting Armenian steamship travel 'without official authorisation from either the grand vizier or this ministry to do so.'[24] Trabzon defended the practice stating that it was necessary to prevent 'those individuals from the Harput region (*Harput ve cıvarı ahalisinden*) from boarding foreign ships and surreptitiously migrating to North America.' That this practice, which was only applied in situations when a reasonable suspicion existed that an individual might attempt to migrate abroad unlawfully, was causing complaint among some who were inconvenienced by it was of little consequence if it succeeded in preventing illicit departures.[25] The Ministry of Police, however, disagreed with Trabzon's defense of the policy, and raised concerns that singling out Armenian travellers and preventing them from boarding certain steamships would 'undoubtedly become a source of great complaint and dissatisfaction' for those affected, and risked becoming a bigger 'political headache' (*siyasetten dahi mazarret*) for the central state.[26] In the end, the grand vizier tentatively sided with Trabzon, concluding that only 'those who aroused suspicion' (*da'i-i zann ve şüphe olan eşhas*) should have their steamship travel limited, a vague directive intended to be interpreted narrowly so as to minimise any possible disruption.[27] The policy appears not to have been in effect for very long, however, as few subsequent references to it exist in the source material. In 1900, seven years after the grand vizier conditionally approved the practice, officials in the port city of Samsun wrote to the Ministry of Interior similarly requesting permission to limit Armenian travel to steamships flying the Ottoman standard. This time, Istanbul responded by denying the request, arguing that to restrict the legitimate mobility of Armenians seeking to travel within the empire for purposes of work or trade risked 'generating much complaint' (*da'i şikayat olacağı*), assuring that 'those suspected of harbouring a desire to migrate abroad illegally simply won't be granted internal passports in the first place.'[28]

The central state's concern in 1900 about restricting the ability of Armenians to move through the empire hinted at a fundamental tension that underlay the strategy of relying on the empire's system of internal mobility controls to prevent unauthorised overseas migration. As mentioned above, the *Men'-i Mürur Nizamnamesi* of 1841 was promulgated against the backdrop of an imperial economy that was becoming steadily more reliant on a mobile labour force. By the final decades of the nineteenth century, the primarily Kurdish and Armenian-populated provinces on the empire's eastern periphery had emerged as a vital source of migrant labour. Workers from the region could be found from the Istanbul waterfront to the coal regions of the Black Sea coast and the cotton fields of the Çukurova region. Underscoring this point, a July 1894 report from the province of Adana estimated that every year between sixty and seventy thousand 'labourers of unknown circumstances' (*mechulülahval amele*) travelled to the region from adjacent provinces.[29] Thus, the Ottoman state was forced to strike a delicate balance between this increasing reliance on a mobile labour force and the desire to prevent banditry, vagrancy and other forms of mobility that it deemed dangerous or illegitimate. The internal passport system was designed in part to resolve this tension by requiring that all who moved within the empire's borders were in possession of the document, and tasking the officials who granted these documents with the further responsibility of determining the legitimacy of an applicant's request for one.

Efforts to strengthen internal mobility controls in order to prevent unauthorised overseas migration, whether by requiring guarantees for internal passports or by restricting steamship travel, risked altogether upending this delicate balance. Increasingly, officials based in provinces in the Ottoman east were loath to demand guarantees backed by cash bonds from internal passport applicants or to adopt similar measures that they feared could hinder domestic mobility.[30] After all, restricting the ability of Armenians to move within the empire's borders for purposes of trade or the sale of labour power could have profound social, political and economic consequences for sending and receiving regions alike. The response to an 1896 announcement sent from Adana to the province of Diyarbekir advertising the availability of work in the cotton-belt city nicely illustrates this point. Several residents of Diyarbekir allegedly used the call as a pretext to acquire internal passports for travel to the coastal province, only to clandestinely migrate to North America soon after their arrival.[31] The Ministry of Interior's response to the incident encapsulated the many difficulties inherent in curtailing some forms of mobility while not simultaneously impinging on others. In a communiqué sent to officials in several coastal provinces, the ministry conceded that, 'although those travelling within the empire for legitimate purposes can under no circumstances have their mobility restricted, eternal vigilance is required to ensure that prohibitions against unauthorised international departures (*diyar-ı ecnebiyeye azimet-i memnu*) are enforced.'[32] By 1896, it was becoming increasingly clear to many within the Ottoman bureaucracy that merely modifying already existing controls on internal mobility was inadequate to the task of preventing unauthorised overseas migration, in large part due to the inherent difficulty in distinguishing legitimate and illegitimate intent. Instead, the fact that the Ministry of Interior placed the onus of maintaining 'eternal vigilance' squarely on the shoulders of officials based in coastal provinces reflected a fundamental shift already well underway in the state's understanding of where responsibility for enforcing the migration ban lay.

The Spatial Politics of Enforcing the Migration Ban

As long as the internal passport system remained an important component of Ottoman state efforts to crackdown on unauthorised migration to North America, much of the burden for enforcing the migration ban rested on the shoulders of officials based in migrants' home communities. In the end, they were the ones responsible for determining whether an applicant for an internal passport had legitimate reasons for requesting one, and rejecting those they deemed suspicious. Furthermore, only these officials could enforce the system of cash bonds that emerged in the early 1890s as a strategy to dissuade Armenians from unlawfully migrating abroad. Almost immediately, however, the many challenges frustrating this approach to enforcement of the migration ban became clear.

Over the course of the 1890s, responsibility increasingly fell to officials based in provinces on the Black and Mediterranean Sea coasts. On the surface, such a shift may appear self-evident. After all, nearly every Armenian migrant en route to North America was forced to transit through these coastal regions if they hoped to board steamships bound for European transit ports. Yet as the last decade of the nineteenth century dawned, most Ottoman coastal cities were ill-equipped to carry out the functions of surveillance and mobility control that today are taken for granted as basic functions of the modern port. As mentioned in the previous Chapter, as late as 1890, the port of Samsun lacked a proper pier critical to monitoring passenger traffic, with most ship-to-shore traffic handled by local boatmen.[33] Considering that Samsun was a major urban centre on the Black Sea and by the 1860s an important steamship hub, this fact is a testament to the degree of underdevelopment that existed in many Ottoman ports. By one estimate, nearly twenty thousand labour migrants boarded steamers from the port of Samsun for travel to Istanbul in 1867 alone.[34] Port cities such as Mersin and Iskenderun were just beginning to emerge as major economic centres in the last decades of the nineteenth century, but also lacked critical commercial and surveillance infrastructure.[35] As Sibel Zandi-Sayek has shown, even in the port city of Izmir, one of the empire's most important economic centres, the Tanzimat state encountered great difficulty in its efforts to exercise greater control over the social and economic life of the city. In 1869, construction began on a modern quay that could more easily accommodate the rapidly expanding volume of steamship traffic. The project was the centrepiece of a grand initiative to engineer a more orderly waterfront befitting of a growing hub of regional and global trade. The effort required overcoming numerous obstacles that ranged from a chronic lack of funds to widespread resistance among segments of Izmir's population, against what they feared was an assault on their social and economic interests.[36] The expensive and difficult process of modernising Izmir's waterfront likely served as a cautionary tale about the risks of attempting such ambitious undertakings in the empire's secondary ports.

Nevertheless, beginning in the early 1890s the Ottoman state began taking more serious measures to strengthen the surveillance and border control mechanisms in port cities such as Samsun, Mersin and Iskenderun.

These efforts were bolstered by growing concerns over drugs, weapons and people smuggling, with the latter two especially seen by the state as twin scourges linked to armed Armenian political groups.[37] Indeed, Ottoman efforts to secure ports of entry and exit grew especially acute following the violence of the mid-1890s that gripped much of the Armenian and Kurdish regions of the empire. One such measure intended to bolster the surveillance capacity of secondary ports was the creation of pier commissions (*iskele komisyonları*). These commissions were tasked with informing the Ministry of Interior of security threats posed by smuggling and other illegal activities taking place in the central port and surrounding coastal regions. Beginning in 1896, many pier commissions began sending monthly reports to Istanbul with details regarding the traffic passing through their respective jurisdictions. The reports vary in detail and length depending on the commission. Generally, they provided information regarding the passengers who transited through the port, such as their ethnicity, nationality (if not an Ottoman subject) and date of arrival or departure. In addition, on the margins of many of these reports were detailed descriptions of noteworthy events that transpired over the course of the month. These sources provide glimpses into the evolution of Istanbul's perspective on port cities as trade entrepôts and centres of economic activity, as well as important nodes of surveillance, security and mobility control.[38] Although pier commissions cooperated closely with local gendarmes and other officials, they reported directly to the Ministry of Interior. For our purposes, the reports of various pier commissions provide significant insight into the many problems that plagued port city efforts to prevent unauthorised migration.

Not surprisingly, pier commission reports frequently pointed to the increasing sophistication of clandestine migrant smuggling operations as the primary factor frustrating efforts to curb unauthorised migration. In August 1899, for example, the pier commission in Iskenderun claimed success in preventing unlawful departures from the city's main port, but complained that the sparsely inhabited coastline stretching to the north of the city remained largely unwatched, allowing smugglers to operate with little interference.[39] Patrolling the wide-open coastline flanking cities such as Iskenderun and Mersin, required infrastructure and resources that provincial governments generally lacked. Less than a year after the Iskenderun pier commission's report, a representative of the district governor of Iskenderun recommended construction of a new police station (*karakol*) on the road linking Iskenderun to Payas, a twenty kilometre stretch known as a hotspot for migrant smuggling operations.[40] The recommendation reached the grand vizier's desk where it was readily approved.[41] Meanwhile, three years later, the pier commission in Mersin wrote of the resource limitations that were severely curtailing their efforts to implement effective coastal surveillance. The commission complained that efforts to prevent smuggling operations were limited by the fact that they had only a small police boat at their disposal for monitoring the vast coastline on either side of the city. Moreover, according to the report, the vessel, which was allotted a paltry monthly operating budget of 150 kuruş, was tasked with keeping watch on ships moored in harbour as well as investigating any suspicious activities occurring outside of the central port. The commission recommended that it be granted control of an additional larger police boat and requested authorisation to coordinate coastal surveillance operations with vessels controlled by provincial customs officials.[42]

These measures were at least partially successful as reports of arrests related to migrant smuggling in Mersin and Iskenderun increased in the first years of the twentieth century. Officials in these cities, however, were disappointed to discover that the punishments meted out to alleged migrant smugglers rarely fit the supposed severity of the crime. In June 1900, frustrated by the high rates of recidivism among local boatmen arrested for migrant smuggling, the pier commission in Iskenderun cabled Istanbul requesting permission to confiscate and auction off (*füruht etmek*) rowboats of repeat offenders. Such drastic measures were warranted, the commission argued, because the small fines and short prison sentences legally prescribed for such crimes provided woefully inadequate deterrence against engaging in what was a lucrative illicit business.[43] The Ministry of Interior refused to authorise a proposal that would effectively deprive local boatmen of their means of subsistence.[44] Boatmen guilds continued to wield significant power in Ottoman port cities, and the ministry's decision, which on the surface ran counter to the high priority Istanbul placed on preventing unauthorised migration, may have been motivated by concerns over the potential economic and political fallout of such a policy.[45] Meanwhile, two years later, officials in Mersin raised a similar complaint that efforts to prevent migrant smuggling in and around the Mediterranean port city were frustrated by these meagre punishments.[46]

As the first decade of the twentieth century dawned, Istanbul continued to maintain that prevention of unauthorised migration rested on the ability of port city officials to maintain a 'complete and earnest degree of vigilance.'[47] This expectation was further complicated, however, by the fact that many of these officials were themselves profiting handsomely off of the migrant smuggling business. Pier commissions from Samsun to Beirut regularly pointed to police corruption as a major obstacle in preventing unauthorised migration.[48] In 1907, for example, the pier commission in Beirut sent a series of reports to the Ministry of Police accusing several police officers in the city of openly colluding with local migrant smugglers. According to the commission, smugglers felt comfortable enough to operate in broad daylight and in plain sight of police stationed in the central port. On one occasion, over thirty migrants were loaded onto the French steamer *Congo* while numerous police nonchalantly looked on. When a police officer dared to reproach one of the smugglers, accosting him from a safe perch on shore, the smuggler responded brazenly, 'what are you yelling for? You know what this is about! We've paid you off, and not for cheap either!'[49] On another occasion, the same smuggler, who had apparently grown quite accustomed to local officials staying out of his business, brandished a firearm in an effort to ward off a police boat that had been dispatched to investigate his activities.[50] The Ministry of Police, for its part, dismissed the commission's report as useless handwringing, faulting the members for producing these long-winded missives rather than pro-actively tackling the twin scourges of migrant smuggling and corruption.[51] While Istanbul was often quick to criticise port city officials for the ineffectiveness of their efforts to prevent unauthorised migration, it appeared either unable or disinclined to take a more active role in bolstering these efforts by rooting out corruption, meting out tougher punishments to migrant smugglers, or enhancing coastal surveillance.

As the geography of migration expanded throughout the late nineteenth and early twentieth centuries, responsibility for preventing migrant smuggling and unauthorised departures fell to officials in a growing number of port cities. The Mediterranean coast in particular, from Mersin to Beirut, began to emerge as the epicentre of the struggle to enforce the migration ban. Rather than coordinating their efforts, however, the relationship between officials stationed in these cities was more often characterised by one-upmanship, recrimination and deflection of blame. For example, in January 1903, the district governor of Iskenderun reported that an English steamer had recently arrived in the city after two days anchored at Mersin. On board were no fewer than twenty North America-bound Armenian migrants who had allegedly been loaded onto the ship by smugglers operating from a small pier outside the city's central port. The district governor faulted local officials in Mersin for failing to put a stop to the clandestine boarding. Eager to rebut the governor's report, officials in the Mediterranean port city conducted their own investigation into the matter, claiming that only six migrants had been smuggled onboard the ship, and that their alleged smugglers were already well known to local authorities.[52] Five days later, the governor of Adana reported the arrival of another English steamer, *Sumerian Prince*, in Mersin, this time with thirty Armenian migrants aboard. The migrants, the governor claimed, were members of separate caravans smuggled onto the ship at Beirut, Latakia and Iskenderun, respectively.[53] In response, the governor of Beirut acknowledged that he was aware that Armenian migrants were aboard the ship, but he insisted they had boarded the vessel at Cyprus.[54] Officials in Iskenderun, meanwhile, claimed that a police informant sent aboard the *Sumerian Prince* upon its arrival in the city reported that the thirty Armenian migrants had boarded at Beirut and Latakia. Iskenderun ended the report by reassuring Istanbul that all available steps were being taken to ensure that no Armenians made it aboard the ship while it was docked in the city's harbour, including the deployment of a large police vessel to keep a constant watch on ship-to-shore traffic.[55]

These conflicting reports only served to further frustrate the central state's efforts to track the frequency, volume and changing geography of migrant smuggling. At the same time, however, port city officials were eager to showcase their successes at interdicting migrants. This tendency was on display, in the account discussed in the introduction of this Chapter of the successful 1893 raid on a migrant smuggling ring and its clients in Mersin. At times, these tales of success were little more than petty games of one-upmanship. In the summer of 1903, for example, officials stationed in the town of Aintab, located in the interior of the province of Aleppo, forwarded to the provincial governor a letter they had recently intercepted that was addressed to an Armenian family in the Harput region. The letter's author, a member of a large caravan of North America-bound migrants, wrote about the group's ill-fated attempt to leave the empire through the port of Iskenderun, which ended in disaster with the arrest of several of the caravan's members. The lucky few that avoided this fate decided to attempt to depart from Mersin, hoping for better fortune there.[56] In his report to the Ministry of Interior, the governor of Aleppo boasted that the letter was proof that his province's efforts to prevent unauthorised migration were bearing fruit, as North America-bound migrants were now compelled to travel to neighbouring provinces where coastal surveillance was clearly weaker.[57]

The discord and rancour between officials in coastal provinces and their counterparts in the interior was even more pronounced. In January 1892, the governor of Adana sent a communiqué to the Ministry of Interior expressing frustration over what he argued were halfhearted efforts by officials in the provinces of Mamuretülaziz and Maraş to enforce the migration ban. The governor assured the ministry that officials in Adana had done all they could to halt unlawful departures. He complained, however, that the sheer volume of Armenian migrants attempting to clandestinely transit through Mersin was hampering these efforts. He concluded his missive with a pointed accusation directed at his counterpart in Mamuretülaziz, proclaiming 'these facts suggests to us that officials in (these migrants') communities of origin are entirely uninterested in preventing them leaving for the coast.'[58] In response, the governor of Mamuretülaziz assured Istanbul that his province was employing all the measures at its disposal to prevent unauthorised migration. Yet, it was impossible to distinguish between the large numbers of labour migrants who legally travelled from the province each year to seek work in Adana from those seeking to migrate illegally to North America. Overseas travel, he continued, could only be undertaken from a port city such as Mersin, thus officials there were best situated to enforce the ban. The governor ended with a swipe at his counterparts to the south, asserting that, 'migrants seem to encounter few problems leaving out of Mersin suggesting to me that the problem lies with them and their inability to properly police that city's harbour and piers.'[59] The exchange exhibits a surprisingly hostile and recriminatory tone not often present in the staid and prosaic language of Ottoman bureaucratic correspondences. It nonetheless embodies many of the tensions that plagued the Ottoman state's efforts to prevent Armenian migration to North America. The governor of Adana's comments reflected Istanbul's anxieties about the growing sophistication of migrant smuggling networks, and underscored the difficulties that officials stationed in coastal provinces faced in their efforts to police the human traffic passing through the empire's port cities. The statement of his counterpart in Mamuretülaziz, meanwhile, echoed much of Istanbul's own reasoning for placing much of the burden for preventing unauthorised migration on the shoulders of port city officials.

Such disagreements continued as the volume of Armenian migration to North America steadily grew. Officials in migrant-sending provinces such as Mamuretülaziz and Diyarbekir continued to argue that port cities were better positioned to enforce the ban on migration to North America.[60] Meanwhile, coastal provinces became increasingly vocal in their support of measures such as requiring guarantees backed by cash bonds for internal passports granted to Armenian travellers that put more of the onus for enforcing the migration ban on their counterparts in the interior.[61] This was a battle that coastal provinces were destined to lose. Istanbul's desire to avoid impeding legitimate domestic mobility was compounded by concerns that limiting the ability of Armenians to migrate within the empire might have especially dire consequences for a region already beset by political and economic instability.

Coastal provinces nevertheless continued to bemoan the perceived intransigence of their counterparts in the interior who they felt were not taking enough effective action against unauthorised migration. For example, in September 1899, officials in Mamuretülaziz sent a telegram to Adana reporting that a caravan of twenty-three Armenians had recently left the province for Mersin. Officials in Mamuretülaziz suspected that the group was attempting to migrate abroad, and requested that authorities in Mersin interdict the caravan before they departed the empire.[62] In response, the governor of Adana cabled the Ministry of Interior to complain that officials in the interior had grown overly accustomed to sending such requests, burdening officials in the coastal province with the responsibility of locating and detaining these migrant caravans before they succeeded in absconding abroad. The governor acknowledged that the warnings sent to him from Mamuretülaziz had resulted in the arrest of over one hundred Armenians suspected of being en route to North America. He nevertheless expressed irritation that his counterparts in the interior province were not themselves acting on this information. Pursuing and apprehending caravans of migrants, he continued, interfered with the ability of officials in Adana to attend to other duties, and he ended by emphatically asserting that responsibility for preventing unauthorised migration rested with officials stationed in migrants' communities of origin and not with him.[63] The Ministry of Interior forwarded Adana's report to the governor of Mamuretülaziz, inquiring as to why officials there were not acting on information that suggested these groups were attempting to unlawfully migrate abroad.[64] The governor responded with assurances that officials there were following protocol, and once again emphasised that responsibility for implementing the migration ban lay with his counterparts on the coast. He ended, however, with a surprisingly frank admission of the scale of the challenge he, and indeed the Ottoman state's entire bureaucratic structure, faced in enforcing the migration ban, stating, 'the local population has become so accustomed to the high wages they earn in America . . . that it is virtually impossible to prevent them from leaving.'[65]

As a result of these internecine squabbles between provincial bureaucracies, Istanbul regularly received contradictory accounts about the factors hampering its efforts at enforcing the migration ban. In August 1902, the pier commission in Iskenderun sent a report accusing their counterparts in Mamuretülaziz and Diyarbekir of failing to enforce regulations governing the granting of internal passports. According to the complaint, dozens of Armenian migrants had passed through the city in recent months in possession of internal passports authorising travel to Beirut and Jerusalem. When commissioners contacted officials in these places, however, they discovered that the individuals in question never arrived, having presumably used their internal passports to access foreign steamers bound for European transit ports. Iskenderun was in no position to impede the mobility of individuals who were in possession of valid internal passports, the report continued. Rather, the responsibility of properly vetting individuals who requested internal passports to ensure they did not fall into the wrong hands lay entirely with officials in the applicant's home province. The failure of such officials to perform even the most basic duties associated with their position, the letter declared, was making it all but impossible to prevent Armenians from unlawfully migrating abroad.[66] The governor of Mamuretülaziz' response, meanwhile, cast doubt on the commission's accusations. Since the beginning of the year, he claimed, officials in his province had granted only three internal passports for travel to Beirut and none for Jerusalem.[67] Iskenderun's report did not specify the number of individuals it alleged had illegally used their internal passports to travel abroad. By 1902, this number may have been rather small given the numerous other avenues open to Armenians seeking to bypass the ban on migration to North America. It is nonetheless difficult to believe Mamuretülaziz' claim that not a single internal passport had been issued for travel to Jerusalem given that city's importance as a pilgrimage site.[68] Regardless, for the central state, the exchange was another reminder of the difficulties that existed in coordinating mobility control efforts across provincial bureaucracies that were often driven by competing interests and agendas.[69]

Meanwhile, the struggle over whether officials stationed on the coast or those in the interior were best positioned to enforce the migration ban, continued unabated. In March 1903 the governor of Aleppo wrote the Ministry of Interior to complain yet again about his counterparts in the interior and their lax enforcement of even the most basic mobility control policies. Earlier that month, officials in Aintab apprehended a group of migrants allegedly bound for North America who for two weeks had managed to travel through the Anatolian interior without once being asked to produce an internal passport, which no one in the group possessed. For the governor, the fact that the group was arrested only after they crossed into his province was proof positive of his interior counterparts' flagrant disregard for the law. Such negligence, he continued with a bit of dramatic flair, was not only the primary reason that unauthorised Armenian migration to North America continued unabated, but also contributed to 'assault and murder' (*cerh ve katil*) as migrants returning from abroad in possession of dangerous contraband felt 'free to move about without a care.' The governor concluded his breathless warning with a recommendation that

Istanbul hold accountable to the fullest extent of the law those officials in the interior whose failure to fulfil their responsibilities was abetting such behaviour.[70]

Tensions between provincial officials certainly contributed greatly to the challenge the Ottoman state faced in its efforts to put a stop to unauthorised migration to North America. Officials on the coasts and their counterparts in the interior, however, were not operating in a vacuum. Rather, whether in Harput, Mersin, or Beirut, their actions were shaped by the political and economic dynamics specific to each region. This is in part why officials in Mamuretülaziz or Diyarbekir were reticent to enforce measures that risked hindering the domestic labour mobility upon which the populations and economies of these provinces were reliant. Meanwhile, state authorities in port cities found their own efforts to prevent unauthorised migration frustrated by the actions of members of their own ranks, many of whom willingly aided and abetted local migrant smuggling efforts. Those officials who sought to enforce policies of the central state – such as the migration ban, which challenged the entrenched interests of local and regional power brokers – found that the backlash could be unrelenting and swift.

Central State Imperatives, Local Politics

On the surface, the lack of uniformity in how officials in different provinces enforced – or did not enforce – the ban on Armenian migration to North America flew in the face of the centralising logic of the Tanzimat and Hamidian eras. The creation of an imperial bureaucracy severed from local political and economic power bases had been a primary aim of the Ottoman modernisation project from its inception. Ideally, even the lowest ranking gendarmes were 'supposed to be a stranger to the region (they) policed.'[71] As Rifaat Abou-El-Haj has argued however, scholars, by projecting their own prejudices and political agendas onto their analyses of Ottoman centralisation and modernisation, have distorted our understanding of this process.[72] Rather than a linear process in which officials appointed by and loyal to the central state supplanted local power brokers, the empire continued to rely until its demise on an assortment of such intermediaries in order to meet needs ranging from revenue extraction to military conscription. Scholars have pointed to this fact as a major obstacle frustrating the Ottoman state's ability to enforce its will across the empire's vast realm, even as it grew in size and sophistication throughout the nineteenth and early twentieth centuries. As the previous Chapter demonstrated, however, involvement in the clandestine migration business was not merely limited to local intermediaries with little incentive to enforce the will of the central state. Rather, officials appointed from outside the Harput region and with ostensibly few local ties frequently became willing participants in these illicit operations, or otherwise hindered the ban's successful implementation. Indeed, the uneven enforcement of the ban on Armenian migration to North America laid bare the extent to which Istanbul's authority was shaped and limited by many different political and socio-economic dynamics at play in the Harput region, as well as by the personal agendas and interests of its own representatives on the ground. To illustrate this point, it is worthwhile returning to the case of Artin Harputlian, the provincial banker and migrant smuggler whose sophisticated operation was discussed in the previous Chapter.

In August 1907, the newly appointed governor of Mamuretülaziz province, Halid Bey, penned a strongly worded letter detailing alleged collusion between Artin Harputlian and several high-ranking local officials in the case that had led to the banker's arrest: the brazen switch of a group of recently arrived returnees facing deportation from the empire with a caravan of local Armenians eager to travel to North America. His letter was hardly the first time that high-ranking bureaucrats in Istanbul had heard of the case. In fact, the Ministry of Justice had just ordered that the charges levelled against Harputlian and his associates in the plot be lifted and for the accused parties to be released from custody. The governor was livid, and he hardly bothered to conceal his anger as he wrote the long letter. He not only desired to demonstrate the clear and incontrovertible guilt of Harputlian and his associates, but he also wanted to take the Ministry of Justice to task for dismissing the charges on what he felt were blatantly, even criminally flimsy grounds.[73] The governor's stake in the case was high. He had been appointed to the post only months before Harputlian executed his now infamous plot, which he had carried out in plain view within the walls of the provincial government building. Clearly, neither Harputlian nor his co-conspirators were particularly concerned that the newly appointed governor might intervene to put a stop to their flagrantly unlawful behaviour. By disrupting the plot and arresting those involved, including the provincial chief of police and several other prominent local officials, Halid was signalling his willingness to take on the powerful players involved in the clandestine migration business.

Halid's predecessors apparently had little stomach for such an undertaking. Since the late 1880s, the province of Mamuretülaziz had been the epicentre of a vast tangle of underground migrant smuggling networks. Nonetheless, it seems that until Harputlian's arrest, only one prominent local power broker with suspected ties to these networks had ever faced sanction for his activities. After a long-time governor of Mamuretülaziz died in early 1903, his replacement removed a prominent member of the provincial council, Ziya, in response to several accusations of corruption levelled against him. Among other things, the disgraced councilman was accused of 'opening (the council's) door to bribery and bleeding dry those Armenians seeking to go to or return from North America.'[74] The tenure of the governor responsible for Ziya's removal proved brief, however, and upon taking office, his successor, Fehmi, reinstated the councilman.[75] When Ziya was the target of further accusations of wrongdoing by an anonymous accuser, the new governor emerged as one of his fiercest defenders.[76] It is unclear what prompted the replacement of the governor responsible for Ziya's removal from the council, especially given the brevity of his tenure, or why Fehmi was so quick to reverse the actions of his predecessor. It is certainly possible that members of the province's economic and political elite, many of whom also had close ties to the migration industry, did not view the governor's action favourably, and responded by petitioning Istanbul for his removal. Certainly, taking on these entrenched migrant smuggling networks carried a significant degree of risk, and was something that a governor without strong local ties would want to avoid if he hoped to remain in the good graces of some of the province's most influential powerbrokers.

This was a lesson that Halid was learning the hard way. The governor, however, was eager to vigorously prosecute Artin Harputlian and the others involved in the migrant-switching scheme as doing so would serve as a stern warning to others in the province that open defiance of central state policy would not be tolerated under his watch. And he had many powerful allies of his own who supported his bold action. In May 1907, the United States consul in Harput reported that the governor's investigation into the matter had resulted in the arrest of 'scores of officials.' He continued by saying '(t)he progress of this matter has brought about the division of officials and leading personages in the (province) into two classes or parties, supporters and enemies of the (governor)'.[77] The fact that the consul even bothered to comment on the case hints at the extent to which Halid's actions disrupted the established order in the province. In fact, he had stirred up a veritable hornet's nest. Halid's letter to the Ministry of Police was merely part of a broader investigation he was conducting in hopes of proving that the Ministry of Justice's decision to free Harputlian and his co-conspirators was part of a web of conspiracy reaching all the way to Istanbul. The governor looked to his many local allies for support in this endeavour, asking many of them to provide testimony to help bolster his case. The transcripts of these testimonies reveal the depth of the division the consul referenced in his letter, one that transcended simple binaries of Armenian and Muslim, local and outsider and centre and periphery. Among those to provide statements was Minas Fabrikatorian, a member of a prominent family of local industrialists, and a bitter adversary of the banker-cum-smuggler. In his statement, Fabrikatorian was quick to emphasise Harputlian's guilt both in the migrant switching scheme, and in bribing the justice official. Perhaps in an effort to embellish the severity of Harputlian's alleged crimes, he claimed that the returnees involved in the switch were known revolutionaries, a charge unmentioned elsewhere in the documentation of the case.

Fabrikatorian's connection to the case is unclear, and the information he provides is largely hearsay.[78] His eagerness to provide assistance to the governor's investigation was perhaps connected to a bitter property dispute between the Fabrikatorian family and the Harputlians, a feud that pitted the region's most successful industrialists against its most powerful finance capitalists.[79] In addition to Minas Fabrikatorian, the governor collected the testimony of six other individuals all of whom attested to Artin Harputlian's guilt, and that together depicted the banker as an intensely powerful and corrupt wheeler-dealer able to wield tremendous influence over officials at every level of the Ottoman bureaucracy. For example, one minor local official, Hussein Farid, spoke of the deep ties between Harputlian and prominent individuals in the Ministry of Justice. He then dramatically lamented that, 'the infidel (Harputlian) does not fear the sultan . . . and by forcing us to engage in corruption, he is able to set Armenians free while Muslims languish in prison.'[80] The governor's investigation was hardly neutral, and many of those who gave testimony had a personal stake in undermining Harputlian's power and influence in the region's politics. Nonetheless, given the scope of his smuggling operation, the degree to which it operated in the open, and his position in the highest echelons of the provincial administration, the image these testimonies paint of Artin Harputlian as a man entirely unafraid to throw his weight around with little concern for the consequences certainly contained more than a kernel of truth.

Indeed, Harputlian's power and influence proved too great for Halid and his allies. The governor's efforts to force a reversal of the Ministry of Justice's decision ended in failure. Artin Harputlian remained a free man and a prominent figure in the political and economic life of the Harput region well into the second constitutional era, no doubt a testament to the bevy of allies he possessed at the local, regional and imperial levels.[81] As a prominent hometown banker with a hand in numerous economic and political ventures, it is perhaps not entirely surprising that he could weather the governor's challenge to his power. But this was not merely the case of powerful and recalcitrant local broker defying the authority of the central state. Rather, most of the high-ranking local officials implicated in the migrant-switching conspiracy were almost certainly not natives of the region. The most prominent among them, the police commissioner Hacı Salih, had been transferred to the post only a few months before from a similar position in the nearby province of Bitlis.[82] This fact testifies to the astounding rapidity with which state officials could insinuate themselves into these local networks.

The story of Artin Harputlian and the migrant switch, however, is not merely one in which the power of the central state was pitted against the interests of local actors. Rather, it provides a vivid demonstration of how state power was mediated through actors who, regardless of whether they derived their power locally or were appointed by the central state, operated with their own agendas that did not always match those of the centre. These officials, whether based in Mamuretülaziz, Diyarbekir Samsun, or Mersin, also operated within and were shaped by the locally specific constraints of the social and political environment. The case against Artin Harputlian and its subsequent dismissal serves as a useful parable demonstrating that regardless of the importance the Ottoman state placed on preventing migration abroad, its authority was exercised within conditions and by agents often inimical to its imperatives.

Conclusion

Many factors contributed to the Ottoman state's failure to enforce the ban on Armenian migration to North America. Attempts to bolster enforcement by modifying already existing systems of domestic migration controls only deepened the inherent tensions in Istanbul's efforts to prevent forms of mobility deemed illegitimate while not impinging on those it sought to allow or even to encourage. Meanwhile, as the onus for preventing illicit migration moved from officials based in migrants' home provinces to port cities from which they sought to embark on their overseas journeys, the Ottoman state's limited capacity to police and surveil these points of entry and exit, *de rigueur* functions of the modern port, was made painfully manifest. Furthermore, the increasingly sophisticated smuggling networks that operated in these port cities, transformed many state officials into either passive bystanders or active abettors to the steady flow of Armenian migrants to North America they had been tasked to stanch. Like any complex organisation comprised of human actors operating in numerous different socio-economic and political contexts, the Ottoman bureaucracy was hardly monolithic in its approach to enforcing the migration ban. Instead, miscommunication, disagreement and outright rancour between officials stationed throughout the geography of migration further opened the door to migrants and smugglers seeking to outwit the state. Finally, as stories such as that of Artin Harputlian make clear, local politics and the powerful actors that animated them could easily frustrate and impede the ability of the central state to exercise power on the ground.

The failure to prevent Armenian migrants from departing the empire for North America provides important insights into the limits of the Ottoman state's authority in the empire's final several decades. Nevertheless, as the past two Chapters have also demonstrated, state power was an important force in shaping the ways in which people migrated, forcing those who sought to leave to make difficult and dangerous decisions about how, where and when to do so. As efforts to enforce the migration ban evolved and improved in the face of these many difficulties, strategies to evade the state necessarily grew more sophisticated, daring and expensive. This dialectic would not only shape how migrants left the empire, but also their experience of return. The second part of this book shifts the focus to the issue of return migration. As Armenians returned from their sojourns in North America, they once again faced numerous challenges as they sought to reenter the empire and to reach their home communities in the interior of the Ottoman east. Some of these difficulties were familiar, still others brand new. As for the Ottoman state, its response to return migration would be shaped in part by lessons learned in the process of enforcing the ban on those seeking to go abroad. Meanwhile, issues such as mobility control, surveillance and policing and the relationship between subject and state would be cast in a new light. It is to this part of the story that we now turn.

PART II. FORTIFYING THE WELL-PROTECTED DOMAINS

In April 1906, Ohannes Topalian made the more than one hundred kilometre journey from his residence in the Anatolian city of Kayseri to the bustling interior city of Sivas. A naturalised American citizen, Topalian hoped to secure a passport from American consular authorities in that city so that he could return with his family to North America. Fifteen years earlier, Topalian had migrated (via Egypt) to the United States, where he remained for over ten years. After a decade abroad, he left the United States so that he could return home to marry the bride his father had arranged for him. When he arrived at Mersin and presented his American passport, he was promptly refused entry. Determined to find an alternative route home, Topalian went to Egypt. After six months there, he arrived in Izmir, and this time was permitted to reenter after he presented Ottoman travel papers he had procured in Egypt. After several days of travel through the rugged Anatolian interior, he arrived in his native Kayseri. Topalian married and started a family, but it was never his intention to remain permanently in the land of his birth, and he longed to return with his family to the United States. While at home, he lived much like any other Ottoman subject, paying taxes on his family's ancestral lands, and keeping the fact of his naturalization a guarded secret. Topalian knew that if word got out to local authorities that he had illegally travelled abroad and acquired United States citizenship, he could face arrest and deportation. Discarding his American passport while he was in Egypt had been part of his strategy to conceal his status.

When he arrived at the American consulate in Sivas, he presented the consular officials with documents he hoped would prove that he was indeed a citizen of the United States. His certificate of naturalization, which he still possessed, showed that he had been admitted as a citizen of the United States in Providence, Rhode Island, in March 1898. He also provided his military discharge papers that indicated he had served with the United States Army in Cuba during the Spanish–American War, after which he had received an honourable discharge. To remove any lingering doubt about his identity, he performed military drills for the consular staff, which, according to the consul, he did 'fairly well.'

For consular officials in Sivas, Topalian was a bit of an anomaly. Few Armenians in their district migrated to North America, and thus they were not accustomed to interacting with locals claiming to be American citizens. The neighbouring consular district of Harput, however, was home to hundreds, if not thousands, of such individuals, most of whom, like Topalian, had reentered the empire clandestinely after sojourning illegally in the United States. The consulate forwarded a report on Topalian's case to the American legation in Istanbul, and asked for advice on how to proceed.[1] After ten days, a response arrived refusing Topalian's request for a new passport. According to embassy officials in Istanbul, the circumstances surrounding Topalian's return, in particular the fact that he had concealed his status from officials of the Ottoman state amounted to a forfeiture of his United States citizenship.[2] Undeterred, Topalian made alternative plans to return to the United States and to eventually bring his family over. Nearly a full year later, in March 1907, he appeared at the American consulate in Cairo and again requested that he be issued a new passport. It seems Topalian hoped that American consular officials in the de facto British colony would be more favourably disposed to his case than were their counterparts in the Ottoman Empire. Unfortunately, such was not the case, and once again Topalian's request was rejected.[3]

Topalian's story reflects many of the challenges faced by Armenians as they sought to return to their home communities in the Anatolian interior after long sojourns abroad. Since the early 1890s, the Hamidian regime had sought to prevent Armenians returning from North America from reentering the empire. By the beginning of the first decade of the twentieth century, and especially following the assassination attempt on Sultan Abdülhamid II, these efforts took on an increasing urgency. As it became increasingly difficult to reenter the empire through conventional means, Armenian returnees were forced to find alternative, circuitous and often creative routes back in. Once back home, many returnees felt compelled to hide the fact that they had migrated abroad illegally, especially those who had been naturalised as United States citizens while abroad. By the waning years of the Hamidian regime, Armenian returnees faced the almost constant threat of being deported from the empire, and, as Ohannes Topalian learned, could expect little to no assistance from the United States government. Part I of this study investigated the ways in which

Ottoman policy shaped the migration process as Armenians endeavoured to leave the empire. The two Chapters that comprise Part II of this study focus on return migration. As the Ottoman state sought to limit and eventually to prevent Armenian return all together, it devoted increasing attention and resources to surveilling and fortifying the empire's coastal 'borders.' Meanwhile, determining the status of Armenian returnees who had naturalised as United States citizens while abroad became a test of the empire's ability to navigate the troubled waters of international law and diplomacy. The Hamidian regime's success in securing the approval of the United States government to effectively strip returnees of their status as American citizens would prove a major victory for the Ottoman state and a disaster for Armenian migrants with implications for the future even after the Armenian genocide and the demise of the Ottoman Empire.

4

Return

Ohannes Topalian's story provides us with some insight into what drove Armenian migrants to make the perilous journey home in the years preceding the 1908 revolution. Like the generations of labour migrants from the Ottoman east who went to Istanbul or elsewhere in the empire in search of work, sojourning in North America was an overwhelmingly male phenomenon. Those who left their home communities before marriage often found few prospects, choosing to either send for a bride or return. For many, returning home to marry in the land of their birth was the more attractive of the two options. Furthermore, as Topalian's experience shows, this offered them the opportunity to visit ailing or elderly parents, and to take care of other pressing family affairs that were difficult to address from the other side of the world. The sense of filial duty remained strong in spite of the great distances that separated the Harput region from the growing Armenian migrant colonies in North America. The letters that Israel Safarian received from his family while he sojourned in Canada speak to the pressure many migrants were under to make money and return. In one such letter, his father implored him to, 'come home this fall, because I am quite old. Let us see each other once more afterwards God's will be done come what may.'[1] In another, his brother-in-law cautioned him to 'live stingily so that you will be able to return home as soon as possible . . . When you return to your homeland, you should not miss America.'[2] Meanwhile, in 1901, the US consul based in Harput reported that returnees from North America were: 'here largely to revisit their families, seek wives, settle estates, and especially to look after property and family interests seriously affected by the events of 1895.'[3] Everything from divorce to illness and grievous injury also drove migrants to return.

Return migration was a relatively common phenomenon across most migrating groups in the late nineteenth and early twentieth centuries.

Armenians were certainly not alone in facing a long and arduous return trip across oceans, through grimy and crowded transit ports, and over rough terrain. They did have an added obstacle from which these other groups were mercifully spared: the Ottoman state. Istanbul's anxieties concerning the return of Armenians from North America, especially those who had naturalised as US citizens while abroad, persisted throughout the period leading up to the 1908 revolution. Nonetheless, its policies governing return were not consistent, vacillating between a partial and full ban, and including a brief period in which most Armenians were permitted to reenter the empire under certain conditions. Not willing to take their chances on returning through regular ports of entry, however, many found creative and clandestine ways to reenter the empire, a fact that only heightened the state's concerns about the phenomenon. After an uprising in the district of Sasun in 1904, followed by an attempted assassination of the sultan carried out by Armenian militants a year later, preventing Armenians from returning from North America suddenly became a major priority for the Ottoman state. Although the numbers of Armenians seeking to reenter the empire were rather small when compared, for example, to the much larger volume of Lebanese return migration, after 1905 their efforts to return through clandestine channels drove some state officials to demand nothing less than the complete fortification and militarisation of the Mediterranean coastline.[4] This was not an initiative driven primarily by the centre, but rather first-and-foremost by provincial officials stationed in the empire's coastal regions. Thus, this Chapter offers glimpses into the inner-workings of a border in the making.

Estimating the Rate of Armenian Return

Determining with any degree of accuracy the volume of Armenian return from North America to the Ottoman Empire, especially for the period preceding 1908, is a difficult task.[5] The few historians who have studied Armenian migration in the pre-World War I period acknowledge that these migrants generally did not intend to settle permanently when they set out on their long journeys from the Ottoman interior to North America. Nevertheless, the prevailing assumption is that few actually returned to the Ottoman Empire, and thus the topic is given short shrift.[6] With the intent of providing more information about the phenomenon of return migration, beginning in 1908 the United States Commissioner General of Immigration began providing detailed annual statistics on immigrant departures. These statistics, which are categorised by ethnicity and nationality, show that on average between the years of 1908 and 1914, more than seven hundred Armenian migrants left the United States annually, ranging from a low of 165 in 1908 to a high of 1,117 in 1914. The vast majority of those departing presumably intended to return to their home communities in the Ottoman Empire.[7] Robert Mirak cites these numbers as definitive proof that 'few Armenians actually repatriated' in the years preceding World War I and the Armenian genocide.[8] Indeed, the total number of departures from the United States between 1908 and 1914 amounts to just over ten per cent of the total number of Armenian arrivals in the same period, and would appear to lend credence to this assertion. While arguably not an insignificant rate of return, it is significantly less than rates of repatriation among other migrating groups such as Lebanese or Italians.[9]

Comparing the number of Armenians who returned from the United States to the Ottoman Empire with the volume of migrants arriving to the United States in the same period, however, leads to a somewhat misleading result. Given the costly and protracted voyage that separated Armenian migrants from their home communities in the Ottoman interior, the overwhelming majority who returned did so only after years and sometimes decades-long sojourns in North America. Thus, the vast majority of Armenians counted as having departed the United States between 1908 and 1914, first arrived *before* – and sometimes well before – 1908. This point is significant because Armenian migration after 1908 was quantitatively and qualitatively a different phenomenon from that which took place before. The number of Armenians migrating to the United States spiked dramatically in the years following the 1908 revolution and the lifting of the migration ban, from an annual average of approximately 1,700 between 1899 and 1908 to over 5,000 between 1908 and 1914. Thus, it is perhaps more accurate to compare numbers for Armenian departures from the United States provided for the years 1908–1910, an annual average of 439, to the median number of Armenian arrivals to the United States for the three years *preceding* 1908, a figure totaling 2,139. Doing so yields a rate of return of just over twenty per cent.

The available statistics for Armenian return migration after 1908, however, cannot serve as a useful baseline for estimating the rate of return before 1908. The constitutional government that took power following the revolution also liberalised state policies governing the return migration of Armenians from North America to the Ottoman Empire. As was the case with the volume of Armenians leaving the empire after 1908, rates of return increased dramatically in response – peaking in 1914, the year preceding Ottoman involvement in World War I and the Armenian genocide. Manoog Dzeron characterised the large numbers of Armenians who returned to the village after the revolution as having been, 'enchanted by the tumultuous hurrahs praising the Turko–Armenian national unity of 1908 . . . (formed) caravans returning from the American shores to the homeland.'[10] Before 1908, a combination of Ottoman state policies and the prevailing political and economic conditions in the Ottoman east likely dissuaded many who otherwise might have from returning. Indeed, Mirak goes as far as to state, 'the devastation of Turkish Armenia during 1894–1896 . . . compelled the vast majority to regard their move to the United States as a permanent break . . . and not simply as a temporary, money-making sojourn.'[11] The archival record, both Ottoman and otherwise, however, belies this notion that the massacres of the mid-1890s forced Armenian migrants to give up entirely on their hopes of returning home. Indeed, the available evidence suggests that rates of return increased in the years that followed the violence. While 1908 was certainly a turning point in terms of the volume of return migration, in what follows, I argue that the rate of return during the final years of the Hamidian regime was much higher than has been previously assumed.

Armenian migration to North America only began in earnest in the late 1880s. Thus, a significant volume of return would not be expected until the mid-1890s at the earliest. News of the pogroms and massacres targeting Armenian communities throughout the Ottoman east probably dissuaded many from returning, even as the aftermath of the financial panic of 1893 in the United States drove other migrant groups to return in higher numbers. Nonetheless, Armenian migrants did return to the Ottoman Empire during the mid-1890s in sufficient numbers to trigger a diplomatic row between Istanbul and Washington (and a public relations nightmare for the Ottoman Foreign Ministry) over the arrest and detention of returnees found to be in possession of US passports.[12] Spotty statistical data on return migration is available beginning in the late 1890s that hint at a rate of return not drastically lower than the years immediately following the 1908 revolution. For reasons that will become clearer below, following the massacres of the mid-1890s, and in response to a spike in the numbers of Armenians returning to the empire after sojourns in North America, the Ottoman state began allowing returnees to reenter the empire on a conditional basis through the Black Sea port of Samsun. For several months in 1898, the pier commission in that city reported the numbers of Armenians returning under this policy to the Ministry of Interior, only to abruptly discontinue the practice in October of that year for reasons that are not entirely clear.[13] From April to October of 1898 (excluding the month of August for which the data is missing), 244 Armenians returned from North America through Samsun, an average of forty per month, surpassing the yearly total of Armenian departures from the United States reported by the US government in 1908.[14]

Although the data is much spottier after October 1898, what does exist points to rates of return in subsequent years generally consistent with the volume being reported by Samsun in the middle of that year. In May and June 1899, Samsun recorded twenty-eight Armenian returnees, and thirty-eight in November and December.[15] After the Ottoman state ended the policy allowing for conditional return through Samsun, these occasional reports on Armenians reentering the empire cease altogether. Other sources, however, continue to point to a healthy rate of return. In 1901, the US consul in Harput reported that at least 'three hundred naturalized (United States) citizens of native (Ottoman) birth' resided in his consular district alone, a rough estimate that did not include those returnees who were not naturalised citizens.[16] In 1905, meanwhile, authorities in Mamuretülaziz estimated that between four and five hundred Armenians had returned to that province from North America in the four years since the end of the policy permitting conditional reentry at Samsun.[17] Taken as a whole, the available data suggests that an average return of two hundred Armenians from North America a year is both a plausible and perhaps even a conservative estimate. Considering that the annual average rate of outmigration from the Ottoman Empire to North America between 1890 and 1907 was less than two thousand, this points to an absolute minimum return rate of just over ten per cent. Given the many specific challenges that Armenian migrants faced in their efforts to reenter the empire in the years before the constitutional revolution, this rate of return is noteworthy.

From a Partial Ban to a Blanket Prohibition, 1888–1897

When the Ottoman state issued the ban on Armenian migration to North America in 1888, the perceived threats posed by return migration were key in shaping the new policy. For Istanbul, migration and return were two sides of the same coin – all part of a broader effort by Armenian revolutionary organisations to 'position minds' and foment sedition, both within and outside of the empire's borders.[18] The spectre of Armenians returning to the empire after having naturalised as United States citizens and benefiting from the extraterritorial privileges granted to nationals of that country made prevention of both migration and return all the more imperative.[19] Yet the decree inaugurating the policy did not officially ban Armenian return from North America. Instead, the initial logic impelling the policy was that the best way to mitigate the threat posed by return migration would be to prevent Armenians from leaving in the first place.

Furthermore, especially in these early years, a significant proportion of Ottoman Armenians who travelled to North America did so for 'legitimate purposes' such as trade or education.[20] The Ottoman state did not want to impede the travel of those whose globetrotting provided a clear economic and political benefit. For example, one such individual, Hagop Bogigian, a native of the Harput region and a prominent Oriental rug dealer in Boston, maintained significant business interests in the Ottoman Empire. In his memoirs written in the early 1920s, Bogigan reckoned that he returned to the land of his birth to conduct business and restock wares at least forty times in the final decades of the nineteenth century. His economic and political ties to the empire were so strong that beginning in the early 1890s, he volunteered to assist the efforts of Ottoman diplomats in the United States to monitor the activities of Armenian political activists and organisations operating in the country.[21] An overly restrictive policy on Armenian return to the empire risked ensnaring individuals like Bogigian whose ability to come and go as he pleased was a political and economic boon. More importantly, a draconian ban on return risked incurring unwanted attention from the United States government, especially if those kept from reentering were naturalised US citizens.

Additionally, Ottoman law was somewhat ambiguous when it came to the reentry of Ottoman subjects returning from international travel. The 1867 Ottoman Passport Law (*Pasaport Nizamnamesi*) required that all Ottoman and foreign nationals be in possession of a passport when entering or exiting the empire's borders.[22] The bulk of its seventeen articles, however, dealt with the treatment of foreign nationals found to be in violation of the law. Ottoman subjects who reentered the empire without proper documentation, meanwhile, appear to have fallen under the jurisdiction of the regulations governing internal mobility, and faced small fines or short jail sentences before being returned to their communities of origin.[23] In July 1893, however, the Ottoman state issued its first policy explicitly addressing the return of Armenians from unauthorised sojourns in North America. Over the course of that year, Istanbul's anxieties about the supposed link between overseas migration and Armenian revolutionary politics reached a fevered pitch. In July, rumours began circulating among various government ministries that armed Armenian revolutionaries were seeking to infiltrate the empire in order to provoke an insurrection in the Harput region.[24] A report from the Ottoman consul in New York City implicated Gaspar Nahigian, the head of a prominent clandestine migration network discussed in the second Chapter of this book, in an alleged effort to smuggle weapons and money in preparation for this revolt.[25]

Motivated by such reports, in August of 1893, the palace issued a decree declaring: 'those Armenians who have adopted United States citizenship and then proceed to return to the Ottoman Empire, even if they have issued passports by the United States government for that purpose, will not be allowed to reenter the imperial realm.'[26] The text of the decree made clear that this new policy was motivated by the belief that Armenians were 'absconding' (*firar*) to the United States with the goal of 'changing nationality' (*tebdil-i tabiiyet*) and then returning to the empire to 'engage in seditious activities intended to undermine public order (*ihlal-i asayiş*).'[27] The architects of this policy were well aware that targeting returnees who possessed valid travel documents issued by the United States government carried with it a great deal of diplomatic risk. Indeed, its implementation required unilaterally abrogating an informal agreement between the Ottoman Empire and United States that governed matters related to nationality and naturalization. In justifying the new policy to their American counterparts, Ottoman officials emphasised that it was aimed at preventing Armenians who had naturalised as US citizens from abusing their status in order to foment sedition, a practice that was no different than American efforts to restrict the entry of certain foreigners into its own borders.[28] The effect of this policy on the US–Ottoman relationship is a central focus of the next Chapter. Meanwhile, the text of the decree explicitly targeted only those returnees who had adopted American citizenship (*Amerika tabiiyetine girmiş olan*). Determining who had done so, however, was not as straightforward as it might seem. For the Ottoman state, possession of a US passport was considered unambiguous proof of having unlawfully obtained American citizenship. State policy was less clear about how to handle those who arrived without a passport, and did not otherwise give cause for suspicion.

As a result, Ottoman officials responsible for enforcing the ban appear to have erred on the side of a capacious reading of the decree's mandate and refused to grant entry to most returnees. For example, in December 1894, the Armenian Patriarchate in Istanbul petitioned the palace on behalf of several Armenians who had recently arrived from the United States only to be barred from the empire by officials in several port cities. According to the patriarchate, the group of returnees, who at the time of the petition's drafting were stranded on the island of Cyprus, had travelled to North America looking for work only to fail in their efforts to find anything sufficiently remunerative to warrant remaining overseas. Stressing that the migrants' motivations for travelling abroad were strictly economic in nature and thus entirely unworthy of suspicion, the petition emphasised the financial hardship their de facto exile was causing their families.[29] Taking the petition's characterisation of the migrants' plight at face value, they were not among the class of returnees that the previous year's decree had officially banned from reentry. Regardless, they found themselves in a precarious limbo as they struggled to reunite with their families in their home communities. In a similar case from that same month, a returnee was arrested upon arrival in the Black Sea port of Giresun and subsequently 'placed in chains generally reserved for (the transportation of) murderers and thugs' as officials there prepared his expulsion from the empire.[30] This shabby treatment earned Giresun a strong rebuke from the grand vizier who reminded them that the state's policy on Armenian return only extended to those who had adopted US citizenship while abroad. Further investigation, meanwhile, revealed that the returnee, identified as Kevork, had in fact secured permission to return to the empire from Ottoman officials in Egypt while on a stopover there.[31] In response to continued confusion regarding the policy, in September 1895, the Foreign Ministry's Office of Legal Counsel issued a clarification. The statement declared that Armenians who had migrated to North America for the purposes of work or trade (*kesb ve ticaret*), even if they had done so unlawfully, were not to be denied entry if there was no evidence suggesting that they had naturalised as US citizens or engaged in seditious activities while abroad.[32]

Nevertheless, migrants who desired to avoid becoming victims of confusion over Istanbul's policy on return, simply found ways to reenter the empire through the backdoor. One common strategy involved obtaining internal passports in Egypt and using these documents to reenter the empire, in a way taking advantage of the Ottoman state's dogged defense of its embattled imperial pride. By the early nineteenth century, Egypt had emerged as a de facto independent entity under the control of Mehmed Ali Pasha, whom Istanbul had appointed as governor shortly after Napoleon's failed invasion and occupation of the province (1798–1801). After falling under the British occupation in 1882, Egypt was defined by a confusing pastiche of overlapping sovereignties that included the descendants of Mehmet Ali Pasha, the khedives, who maintained extensive powers over the everyday lives of Egyptian subjects; the British, who controlled the commanding heights over the country's economy, military and foreign affairs; and the Ottomans, who remained nominal suzerains. Istanbul retained little real power in Egypt, but nevertheless worked strenuously to cultivate the illusion that the distant province remained an integral part of the empire, in part by governing mobility between the two as if this were indeed still the case. As a result, travellers could enter the Ottoman Empire and move within its borders with internal passports granted by the khedival regime, and by all accounts, most encountered little difficulty in obtaining the documents. Indeed, this appears to have been a common method for bypassing Ottoman border restrictions. For example, in 1898, Ottoman consuls stationed in several North American and European cities refused to grant visas for travel to Palestine to a group of American Jews en route to the 'holy land.' Undeterred, the group stopped in Alexandria where they had little trouble obtaining internal passports allowing them passage to Jerusalem.[33] Throughout the mid-1890s, reports of Armenian returnees reentering the empire with travel documents issued in Egypt abounded.[34] The problem was acute enough that in November 1897, the Ottoman High Commissioner in Egypt (*Mısır Fevkalade Komiseri*) requested that khedival authorities more thoroughly vet individuals seeking Ottoman travel documents in an effort to reduce the volume of 'suspicious persons' (*eşhas-ı muzzira*) entering the empire via Egypt.[35]

Other returnees, meanwhile, reentered clandestinely with the assistance of smugglers in Beirut and other cities whom they paid to row them to shore out of view of the main port.[36] In 1897, with reports piling up of returnees reentering the empire through these surreptitious means, and confusion regarding state policy governing the return of Armenians from North America, Istanbul extended the ban to include all who had migrated unlawfully, regardless of their citizenship status or suspected involvement in revolutionary politics.[37] Returnees nevertheless continued to find ways to skirt the ban. In late 1897, a group of twelve Armenians were rounded up for questioning by officials in Mamuretülaziz province after they were found to have returned from unlawful sojourns in North America. In their statements, they revealed a wide range of strategies for reentering the empire. Half had returned through Samsun where, despite official policy, they were granted entry and issued travel documents permitting them to continue on to their home communities in the Harput region. The remaining six, however, had followed much less direct paths home. Four obtained internal passports from khedival authorities in Egypt, one after having been in that country for more than a year, and reentered the empire from there. One was admitted at the Mediterranean port of Jaffa. Proceeding from there to Jerusalem, he secured travel documents from the Armenian Patriarchate before setting out for Harput. The final returnee mentioned in the report arrived at the port of Batumi, travelling from there to Russian-occupied Kars. While in Kars, he secured an internal passport from Ottoman authorities stationed in the city, probably by convincing them he was returning from a sojourn in the southern Caucasus. Documents secured, he trekked home through the inhospitable and rough terrain of northeastern Anatolia.[38]

In a report to the Ministry of Interior that accompanied the profiles of the twelve returnees, the governor of Mamuretülaziz, echoing a familiar theme, attributed their ability to reenter the empire to the failure of port city officials to enforce state policy.[39] At the same time, however, his counterparts on the Black Sea coast were dealing with a dramatic increase in Armenian migrants returning from North America and seeking to reenter the empire. Over the course of several months in late 1897 and early 1898, the governor of Trabzon province sent several communiqués to Istanbul complaining of the numerous challenges preventing his office from implementing the full ban on return. Notable among these was the unwillingness of foreign shipping companies to accept those who had been denied entry back on their ships without compensation, stranding dozens of Armenian returnees in Samsun.[40] In response, officials in the port resorted to detaining returnees in the city's jails, further taxing already overcrowded facilities.[41] With the anti-Armenian violence of the mid-1890s quickly receding into the past, migrants who had been anxiously following the grim news coming out of the Ottoman east from the relative comfort of North America were eager to return home, if only for a visit. Samsun feared the volume of return would only grow, with little at their disposal to put a stop to it. Once again, Istanbul was forced to change course.

From Blanket Prohibition to a Policy of Conditional Reentry, 1898–1901

In early January 1898, facing growing numbers of Armenian returnees attempting to reenter the empire through Samsun, the Council of Ministers (*Meclis-i Vükela*) effectively reversed the full ban on return issued only months earlier. In its stead, the Ottoman state would, on a conditional basis, begin allowing Armenians to return to the empire through the port of Samsun.[42] Those suspected to have adopted US citizenship while abroad or to be members of outlawed political organisations would remain banned. Admitted returnees were to have their identities verified by local officials, after which they would be dispatched under armed guard to their home communities in the interior. A year after the policy was introduced, the United States consul in Sivas described the process in stark terms, stating, '(the migrants) are treated as semi-criminals. They are escorted in groups by mounted police who are said to ill use them, and they are kept in jail in the towns en route.'[43] Upon arrival in their home communities, returnees were transferred to the custody of local officials, investigated for criminal or otherwise suspicious behaviour, and released upon providing a guarantor who, backed by a cash bond (*kefalet-i nakdiye*), could vouch that they not be involved in illegal activity.[44]

This policy was an acknowledgement of weakness and it was rooted in pragmatism, as the Council of Ministers themselves made clear, stating, 'These returnees are brought to our shores by foreign steamships and just dumped here (*ecnebi vapurlarıyla getirilüp bırakılmalarından dolayı*). Given these circumstances, it is simply impossible for us to implement a policy based on debarment and deportation (*kendilerinin geldikleri mahallara iadeleri gayr-i kabil*).'[45] The Ottoman state was in no position to dragoon foreign steamship lines into assisting with enforcement of its migration policies, as the United States government would do beginning in the first decade of the twentieth century.[46] The emergence of an international passport system backed by reciprocal agreements between nation states that would inscribe into international law the sovereign right to determine who was allowed to enter and who was not was still several decades away. Istanbul, at least for the time being, could expect little help from representatives of European shipping companies or foreign diplomats in its efforts to enforce the ban on return. Furthermore, it was loath to further deplete its treasury on steamship passage for those officially banned from reentering the empire but deemed by port city officials to be otherwise of low risk. Instead, the Ottoman state turned to this policy of conditional return, applying tried-and-true strategies to ensure that any possible threat posed by those readmitted to the empire was mitigated. In lieu of a systematic method of surveilling and policing returnees once they were back in their home communities, the onus for monitoring their behaviour fell instead to guarantors who were on the hook for large cash fines if the individuals they vouched for acted against the interests of the state. Unlike when this practice was unsuccessfully employed to dissuade Armenians from migrating to North America, at least now returnees and guarantors would be together in the same place, making it much easier for local officials to enforce cash bonds.

A certain cruel irony underlay the policy of conditional entry. Those who had been granted permission by the state to migrate in exchange for renouncing their Ottoman nationality and vowing never to return, generally the wives and dependent children of Armenians already in the United States, were ineligible. This was a policy that benefitted only those who left unlawfully and returned without documents. Yet such returnees were not so easily kept out. In July 1899, thirty-four returnees arrived in Samsun in hopes of being allowed to reenter the empire. Among them were nine, including women and children, who had been given authorisation to migrate to North America on the condition they agreed not to return. The twenty-five returnees who had migrated unlawfully were admitted, but the nine legal migrants were denied entry. The captain of the steamship that brought them, however, refused to board them, and officials in Samsun were forced to dispatch the entire group under armed guard to Harput.[47] Meanwhile, the year before, Samsun was faced with a difficult dilemma about how to handle a recently arrived returnee, identified as Mariam, who had legally migrated along with her husband, only to return to the empire months later after the marriage fell apart.[48] After months waiting in a dingy jail cell in the Black Sea port while officials in her home province of Mamuretülaziz wrangled with the Ministry of Interior for a decision on her case, she was permitted to return home.[49]

Complaints about prolonged detention like that endured by Mariam, and other forms of abuse against recently arrived returnees were common. In July 1898, the Ministry of Interior sent a communiqué to officials in Samsun warning them against mistreating returnees or subjecting them to long stints in the city's jails. Of particular concern were claims that returnees were being escorted in shackles through major population centres in the interior, in plain sight of consular officials, missionaries and other foreigners who were liable to give Istanbul grief about such treatment.[50] Reports of abuse nevertheless continued. In October 1898, seventeen recently arrived returnees, all natives of the Harput region, petitioned the patriarchate claiming to have been unlawfully detained in Samsun for the past month, despite the fact that officials in the port city had determined the group was not suspicious. They begged the patriarchate for assistance in obtaining their freedom before the harsh Anatolian winter left them stranded in the port city.[51] Two years later, in May 1901, Kevork Tashjian petitioned the patriarchate to intercede on behalf of his son who he claimed was being held by officials in Samsun and being threatened with deportation on grounds that he had naturalised as a US citizen. Tashjian insisted that his son had not 'forsaken the nationality of his ancestors (*aba 'an cedd teba'a-i saltanat-ı seniyyeden . . . terk-i tabiiyet etmediği*).' Furthermore, he stressed that his son had gone to North America strictly to find work, hoping to put to rest any suspicion that he might have been involved in seditious activity.[52] Unfortunately it is not clear how either case was resolved. Files kept by the US consul based in Harput on numerous returnees living in his consular district, meanwhile, also contain stories of prolonged detention at Samsun, or of large bribes paid to officials there in return for permission to travel into the interior.[53]

For most Armenian returnees, reentering the empire at Samsun under this policy was preferable to doing so clandestinely given the risks and expense involved in obtaining the necessary travel documents or paying smugglers. Perhaps in response to stories of returnees suffering indefinite detention and other forms of abuse at the hands of Ottoman officials, however, many continued to turn to such avenues of reentry. In late 1899 and early 1900, several reports arrived to the Ministry of Interior suggesting that some Armenians returning from North America were continuing to travel through Egypt to obtain internal passports, while others were entering the empire clandestinely and then procuring travel documents for passage to the Harput region with the assistance of church officials in Jerusalem.[54] Some, meanwhile, were arriving at port cities on the Mediterranean where conditional reentry was not permitted, hoping still that local officials might admit them. This in turn generated confusion about how to handle such cases. In October 1898, seven Armenians arrived at the port of Iskenderun after sojourns in North America. Authorities refused them entry and ordered them back on to the steamship on which they had arrived. The group refused to heed the order, claiming to be loyal Ottoman subjects and demanding to be admitted to the empire. Upon contacting the Ministry of Police, the city's pier commission ordered the migrants to be deported.[55] Rather than passively accepting this fate, the pier commission's report on the incident claimed that the group then sailed from Iskenderun to Mersin where they were granted entry and permitted to continue their journey back to the Harput region.[56] Officials in Iskenderun pressed the Ministry of Interior to clarify protocol for such situations. It is not clear how the ministry responded, but in January 1900 officials in the city admitted ten returnees and allowed them to travel to their homes in Bitlis province.[57] The next month, the Ministry of Interior gave permission to officials in Adana to admit Armenian returnees with the same conditions governing reentry through Samsun.[58] This expansion, would be short lived, as the next year the Ottoman state's policy on return would once again undergo a profound shift.

1901–1908 Banning Return, Securing the Coasts

In May 1901, the Council of Ministers announced a quite sudden reversal of the policy of conditional reentry. Several factors likely contributed to this decision.[59] In March of that year, the United States government informed Istanbul that its diplomats in the empire would no longer guarantee protection to Armenian returnees residing in the empire who claimed US citizenship. The message came with assurances that Washington respected the Ottoman state's right to debar Armenian returnees, and expressed a willingness to surrender certain individuals who sought to claim consular protections to the custody of local authorities when requested.[60] The latter assurance was a notable departure from earlier American policy. This decision removed a critical diplomatic obstacle to the enforcement of a more hardline ban on Armenian return. Furthermore, allowing conditional reentry through Samsun, a practice later expanded to include other Ottoman ports such as Mersin, had resulted over the past several years in a considerable increase in the volume of Armenians returning to the empire from sojourns in North America. As has been discussed above, this policy amounted to a major concession on Istanbul's part that too many impediments stood in the way of a stricter approach to return migration. Certain measures such as requiring admitted returnees to provide guarantors backed by cash bonds were intended to minimise the risks the state associated with large-scale return. Nevertheless, the belief that Armenian returnees posed a major and intrinsic threat to the empire's political stability persisted. The US government's increasingly accommodating attitude towards Istanbul's treatment of returnees coincided with reports that Armenian revolutionaries were attempting to infiltrate the empire.[61] While several obstacles had frustrated enforcement of the ban on return migration, it was no longer tenable for the Council of Ministers to support a policy that had, in their eyes, encouraged Armenians to return to the empire.

After the policy change, Armenians longing to return to families and communities in the Anatolian interior could no longer enjoy the relative convenience and safety of reentering the empire at Samsun. Once again, they were confronted with the spectre of having to enter through the back door. How this affected the volume of return migration is not entirely clear. As mentioned above, however, in 1905, the governor of Mamuretülaziz estimated that at least four to five hundred Armenians had returned to his province alone since the full ban was reimposed. Sustaining this volume of return in the face of the ban necessitated more creative and organised methods of clandestine reentry. In June 1904, officials in Ankara complained that Armenians returning from North America were travelling into the Anatolian interior with internal passports they had obtained in the Aegean port city of Izmir. The documents were made to appear as if the bearer had been working in the coastal metropolis when in fact he had been overseas.[62] Although officials in Izmir denied Ankara's claim, a September 1904 report from the Ministry of Police regarding a migrant who had recently returned to his home in the province of Mamuretülaziz seemed to lend further credence to the practice. The returnee, identified as Aran Khacharian, had spent nine years in the United States. After obtaining an internal passport from the khedival authorities in Egypt, he reentered the empire at Izmir where he worked as a butcher (*kasaplık*) for six months before obtaining travel documents that finally allowed him to return home.[63] Meanwhile, Boghos Jafarian, writing many decades after his experiences as a migrant, told a similar story about the circuitous route he and his brother-in-law were forced to take in order to bypass the ban on return:

> After working in the United States for seven years, I was anxious to return . . . I decided to return with (my brother-in-law). This was in 1904 . . . At that time, no Armenian was allowed to enter Turkey. We landed at a seaport named Finiko (Finike), on the Mediterranean Sea. We hired two horses and went to Almleg (perhaps Antalya). At Almleg, there was an Armenian called Zewer Beg, who was a high officer in the Turkish government. We explained to him our intentions to return to Kharpert (Harput). He ordered the Armenian church authorities to take out a passport for us so that we could go to Ankara . . . There we received a visa for Kharpert. We travelled through Akah, Aphion-Karahisar, Kayseri, Sivaz (sic), and Malatia, a distance of about five hundred and fifty miles. In Malatia we hired a carriage which was prohibited from transporting more than one Armenian passenger at a time. We entreated the driver not to report us to the police. We reached the outskirts of Mezireh (Mezre), we took our bags and walked home.[64]

Jafarian and his brother-in-law clearly benefitted from a wide-range of actors, including a high-ranking Ottoman official and the Armenian Church, in their efforts to return home. The report on Khacharian's return through Izmir suggests that he also had help from well-connected people while there. Meanwhile, three years later, the Ministry of Interior faulted church officials in Izmir for helping returnees who arrived in the city secure internal passports so they could travel into the interior. The ministry's report also alleged that local officials in the Aegean port were issuing the documents without bothering to properly vet the applicants requesting them.[65] While these accounts do not point to anything nearly as sophisticated and coordinated as the clandestine networks that helped Armenian migrants to leave the Ottoman Empire, they nonetheless suggest that a more organised system of facilitating return migration was beginning to emerge.

Indeed, by 1904, reports were beginning to trickle in suggesting that some who profited off of smuggling migrants out of the empire were also making money from those hoping to find a way back in. In June 1904, four Armenians from the provinces of Mamuretülaziz and Diyarbekir admitted to having reentered the empire from Cyprus. The captain of the boat that ferried them across the one hundred kilometre stretch of the Mediterranean that separated the island from the mainland unloaded the four returnees at a quiet, unpatrolled piece of shoreline just outside of the port of Mersin.

After a few days spent in nearby Adana, the four were led back to their home communities with the assistance of a muleteer guide.[66] Two years later in September 1906, three Armenian returnees were arrested just outside of the port city of Iskenderun. They claimed that a smuggler based out of Alexandria, Mahmud, whom they identified as a native of Malatya, had helped them to travel from Egypt to the eastern Mediterranean port of Latakia.[67] In June 1907, meanwhile, four Armenians returning from North America arrived at the port of Beirut aboard a Russian steamer. That evening, two 'smugglers' (*kaçakçı*) approached the ship in a rowboat and were permitted to board the larger vessel. While aboard, they secured a payment of three liras, a rather significant sum, from three of the four returnees in exchange for safe passage to shore. Upon entering the rowboat, the smugglers forced the three returnees to lie face-down, taking evasive manoeuvres as they approached landfall so as to avoid detection by the police boats prowling the harbour. After arriving on shore, their twelve liras safely in hand, the two smugglers decided to augment their earnings by turning their erstwhile clients in to the police in return for a handsome monetary reward.[68]

Beginning in 1905, reports became increasingly frequent of large numbers of Armenian returnees on the island of Cyprus awaiting an opportunity to be smuggled into the empire. According to such reports, smugglers operating from various locations along the northern and eastern coasts of the island would transport returnees to landing spots outside major port cities along the eastern and northern Mediterranean littoral.[69] This development paralleled the growing importance of Cyprus as a site of operations for clandestine migration networks helping North America-bound Armenians to depart the empire. In this way, by 1907 many Armenian returnees were reentering the empire in much the same way that others were leaving it, suggesting that by this late date, these networks were fully operational in both directions. This development mirrored increasingly intensive efforts by the Ottoman state to enforce the ban on return.

In the years immediately following the reimposition of the ban, return migration appears not to have been an issue of high priority for the Ottoman state. With few exceptions, between 1901 and 1904, the source material is largely silent on the matter, a stark contrast to the attention that Istanbul gave to preventing Armenians from departing the empire for North America in these same years. Nevertheless, stark warnings continued to trickle in about the danger to the empire's internal security posed by the return of Armenians 'whose minds had been poisoned' while abroad.[70] Then, beginning in 1905, the topic of return migration once again came to the fore. In late July of that year, the governor of Mamuretülaziz informed the Ministry of Interior that two smugglers in Beirut, working closely with 'Greek Cypriot' (*Kıbrıslı Rumlar*) boatmen, were ferrying Armenian returnees from the island to 'open stretches of beach outside of Beirut, Izmir, Iskenderun and Mersin, far from places where local police conduct regular surveillance.' Based on this information, which he claimed to have gleaned from several returnees who had successfully made it home, the governor recommended that 'officials on the coast strengthen their surveillance efforts, and ensure that known smuggling hotspots are firmly secured (*kaçak mahallarının taht-ı muhafazaya aldırılması*).'[71] Fehmi was already developing a reputation as a migration hardliner. Since his arrival in the province several months earlier, the governor had reversed his predecessors' practice of allowing returnees to remain in the province as long as they stayed out of trouble. In its place, he began to implement a draconian policy of deporting Armenian returnees who had arrived in the province since the reinstatement of the ban on return in May 1901.

Fehmi's hardline approach to return migration would quickly take hold empire-wide. It coincided with a period of growing political violence and instability in the Ottoman Empire that featured Armenian political groups at the front and centre. In February 1904, Armenians in the highland district of Sasun in Bitlis province, backed by armed fighters associated with the Hunchakian Revolutionary Party and the Armenian Revolutionary Federation (ARF), staged an insurrection. The uprising and Istanbul's violent response were redolent of the bloody years of the mid-1890s. It also brought the Ottoman state's deep-seated anxieties about the threat posed by Armenian revolutionary politics back to the fore. Then, on a balmy Friday in July 1905, a bomb exploded just outside of the mosque on the grounds of Yıldız Palace as Sultan Abdülhamid II was preparing to leave a prayer service. Years earlier, the otherwise reclusive sovereign had turned his Friday prayer ritual into a public relations effort aimed at bolstering popular support for his autocratic regime. As a result, the area outside the mosque was crowded with on-lookers hoping for a glimpse of the sultan as he entered and departed in the company of his large retinue of bodyguards. The sultan was spared from injury, but dozens of individuals outside of the building were killed in the blast. After the initial investigation revealed that militants associated with the ARF had planted the bomb, Istanbul was plunged into turmoil.[72] For the next three years, Ottoman society would be buffeted by winds of revolutionary change coming from within and outside the empire's borders. Waves of anti-government protests and strikes erupted in cities throughout the empire. Meanwhile, by the end of 1905, organised political movements in both Iran and Russia had succeeded in forcing the governments there to accede to political reform. The sultan and his government felt under siege, a sense that only grew as the 1908 revolution drew closer.

The assassination attempt on Abdülhamid took place only days before the governor of Mamuretülaziz warned the Ministry of Interior about the Armenian returnees being smuggled into the empire. As Toygun Altıntaş notes, in the aftermath of the bombing, 'orders were . . . sent out to provinces with large Armenian populations . . . to remain vigilant about similar revolutionary plots,' and to 'conduct secret investigations' into allegations of seditious activity.[73] Within this climate of escalating political tension, it is not surprising that Armenian returnees found themselves cast as prime targets of suspicion, and high-ranking officials in provinces such as Mamuretülaziz increasingly demanded that more be done to prevent them from reaching home. In October 1906, Fehmi's successor, Nuri, sent a communiqué to the Ministry of Interior that once again demanded that that coastal provinces revamp their efforts to prevent Armenian returnees from being smuggled in.[74] Both Fehmi and Nuri were placing the bulk of the onus for enforcing the ban on return migration on the shoulders of their counterparts on the coast, echoing a familiar theme from Chapter three. In response, however, there was little the officials could do but acknowledge that they were on the frontlines of this effort.

Policing vast stretches of open coastline, however, was a daunting task for woefully under-resourced local and provincial governments. This was made harder by the fact that returning migrants were increasingly reentering the empire far away from central ports, and in areas even more remote than those preferred by smugglers assisting outbound Armenian migrants. In late December 1906, the governor of İçil, a sub-district of Adana province that encompassed much of the Mediterranean coastline surrounding the port city of Mersin, sent a communiqué to the Ministry of Interior. Several days earlier, two villagers in the county of Gülnar, about 150 kilometres to the west of Mersin, reported to local authorities that they had witnessed several individuals being unloaded from a small vessel onto a deserted beach. After apprehending the group, gendarmes discovered that it was comprised of several Armenians from various provinces in the Anatolian interior returning from unauthorised sojourns in North America. They had paid a Cypriot boatman to row them to the desolate, undeveloped and un-policed stretch of coastline. The area's proximity to the northern coast of Cyprus made for a relatively safe and short trip between the island and the Ottoman mainland, and the absence of coastal surveillance meant that smugglers and their clients generally had little reason to fear interference form the authorities. It was pure serendipity, at least as far as the district governor was concerned, that the two villagers who initially reported the incident had been on the usually empty beachfront that day.[75]

Summarising the governor's report for the grand vizier, the Ministry of Interior made sure to emphasise that the complete lack of surveillance along this empty stretch of coast made this region west of Mersin especially attractive for these kinds of smuggling activities. The ministry also recommended that the two villagers be awarded medals for their decision to report the incident to local authorities. Meanwhile, squabbling between officials in different coastal provinces continued to hamstring enforcement efforts. In June 1907, the Ministry of Police upbraided officials in Mersin for failing to interdict a group of returnees who had entered the empire at a stretch of beach near the border separating Adana and Aleppo provinces. The ministry was especially irked by a message from Mersin shifting the blame for the incident onto the shoulders of officials in neighbouring Iskenderun, which Istanbul took as evidence of 'total complacency and lack of concern about fulfilling responsibilities that are of gravest importance.'[76]

For their part, officials in coastal provinces viewed enforcement of the ban on return migration as first and foremost a question of resources. This echoed similar complaints levelled by port city officials about their increasingly central role in preventing unauthorised outmigration, something for which many felt they had less than Istanbul's full support. With anxiety over Armenian return reaching a fever pitch in the years preceding the 1908 revolution, however, these demands for greater resources became much greater in scope. As the governor of İçil's report showed, the empire's Mediterranean coast featured vast stretches of empty and unwatched coastline ideal for smugglers seeking to avoid interference from the authorities. Adequately policing and surveilling such areas would require major increases in available manpower and materiel. To this end, in January 1907, after fifteen Armenian returnees had been apprehended by authorities in Mersin, and with reports coming in of many more soon to be arriving from Cyprus, the governor of Adana complained about the challenges his office faced in policing the province's 'vast and sinuous coastline.' He claimed that the province was equipped with 'nothing more than a patrol vessel (*karakol vapuru*) and a steamboat for coastal defense (*muhafaza istimbot*)' to assist in these efforts. To enhance surveillance, he requested that watchtowers be constructed at regular intervals along the shoreline, and that a massive increase in personnel be provided to both man the towers and keep a mobile watch. In response, Istanbul agreed to fund the construction of the watchtowers. To bolster the province's available manpower, an additional battalion of police along with sixty-four mounts would be provided. Such measures, the governor responded, were essential to improving coastal security, but successful enforcement of the ban on return migration would require continued assistance from the central state.[77] Several months later, the governor of Jerusalem recommended that several ships be dispatched to the eastern Mediterranean in order to maintain a constant watch along the five hundred-kilometre-long stretch of coastline between Iskenderun and Gaza.[78] In February of 1908, meanwhile, the Naval Ministry sent two gunboats to Beirut in response to a similar request from officials in that city.[79] Two months later, the governor of Adana sent a communiqué to the Ministry of Interior complaining that several gunboats promised to his office to assist in patrolling his province's coastline had yet to arrive.[80] In its note forwarding Adana's complaint to the grand vizier, the ministry stated that it had become bogged down with requests from officials up and down the Mediterranean coast for more resources to strengthen coastal surveillance.[81]

As the fateful year of 1908 dawned, an outgoing Ottoman telegraph clerk stationed in the Cypriot town Tuzla sent a letter to his superiors in the Ministry of Post and Telegraph. The document nicely captures the sense of urgency, even paranoia, that the issue of Armenian return was beginning to generate in the minds of many officials stationed on or near the Ottoman coasts. The clerk's missive was long and rambling, touching on a wide range of perceived threats to the besieged imperial government. For instance, a bizarre story about the depraved sexual escapades of a fellow telegraph clerk, an Ottoman Jew based out of the island's capital, Nicosia, was meant to serve as a parable for the dangers of entrusting to non-Muslims positions that were vital to imperial security. He also wrote of the anti-Ottoman propaganda circulating freely on the island, still a nominal possession of the empire and located only a few dozen miles off the coast of its Anatolian heartland. But it was smuggling and other illicit commerce between Cyprus and the Ottoman mainland that really exercised the clerk's bilious rage. From his point of view, clamping down on smuggling networks that operated from the island, which he argued were facilitating the infiltration of the empire by dangerous Armenian revolutionaries from North America, was a matter of life and death for the imperial government and for Islam. In addition to advocating for improved security along the Ottoman coastline, the clerk called for the immediate repair of the telegraph line that connected Cyprus to Latakia on the eastern Mediterranean coast and had been out of service since at least 1898.[82] Reactivating the dormant line, he continued, would allow Ottoman telegraph clerks on Cyprus to immediately alert officials on the Mediterranean coast when smugglers departed the island, giving them a chance to interdict these vessels and their passengers before they reached the mainland.[83] For the clerk, no less than the empire's very survival rested on the ability of state officials to communicate instantaneously throughout the entire eastern Mediterranean. Although his nearly ten-page letter at times seems little more than a fulminating and chauvinistic screed written by a soon-to-be retired middling bureaucrat, his superiors in Istanbul nonetheless took it seriously. The clerk's recommendations were forwarded to various branches of the imperial bureaucracy, while warnings were sent out to officials in several coastal provinces to be on heightened alert for Armenian returnees seeking to reenter the empire clandestinely from Cyprus.[84]

With the sense of an empire under siege increasingly pervasive at all levels of the Ottoman bureaucracy, officials from the telegraph clerk in Tuzla to the governors of Adana, Beirut and Jerusalem were advocating what amounted to a full militarisation of the Mediterranean coastline as the only effective method to enforce the ban on Armenian return. In the years before 1905, preventing Armenians from leaving the empire had received the bulk of Istanbul's attention. In the final three years of the Hamidian regime, however, the focus swung dramatically towards keeping returning migrants from reentering. The view that migration and revolutionary politics were inextricably interlinked phenomena, and that Armenian returnees posed an immediate and existential threat to the empire's security had come to dominate the state's approach to the issue in a way that it had not before. Nevertheless, the pressure Istanbul was under to redirect so much of the insolvent empire's precious resources to fortifying the coasts was bound to generate concern within the upper echelons of the state bureaucracy.

In addition to the cost involved in such an effort, however, other factors likely also tempered Istanbul's gusto to transform its Mediterranean coastline into what amounted to a hard border. Throughout the nineteenth century, the Ottoman state was forced to accept borders that cut ever deeper into territories that had once been under its dominion. By 1900, its once vast holdings in the Balkans had been reduced to a strip of territory wedged between often hostile states that had, over the course of the past one hundred years, won their independence from Istanbul. In the east, the empire's archrival Russia had long ago ended Ottoman dominance over the Black Sea; expelled it from the Caucasus; and, since the Russo–Ottoman war of 1877–78, controlled Kars and Batumi, cities that not so long ago sat far from the frontier. The Mediterranean coast was not a political boundary like the ones that separated the empire from Russia or from Greece, and it looked out on to what was still, at least nominally, an entirely Ottoman domain. While both British protectorates, Egypt and Cyprus remained de jure Ottoman.[85] As Aimee Genell has argued, the Ottoman state was willing to accept such arrangements because, 'autonomy and even foreign military occupation were preferable to losing a province to annexation or independence . . . autonomy was as much an Ottoman as a British strategy for dealing with European intervention in Ottoman domestic affairs.'[86] By 1905, Armenian migrants seeking to skirt the ban on return had become quite skilled at using the ambiguous status of Egypt and Cyprus to their advantage. Istanbul was nonetheless reluctant to respond with measures such as refusing to recognise travel documents issued by the khedival regime. After all, doing so would mark another concession to the reality that Egypt was no longer in practice an Ottoman territory. In the same vein, treating its Mediterranean coast as a hard border to be policed for the sake of preserving its internal security, and in doing so essentially walling the empire off from Cyprus and Egypt, was yet another acknowledgement of its diminished stature. Indeed, this sentiment is infused throughout the Tuzla telegraph clerk's long message. For him, the political menace and moral degeneracy that he argued had taken hold on Cyprus were, in his mind, directly connected to the loss of Ottoman governmental and Islamic moral authority over the island.[87] That such measures were being debated and undertaken in response to the actions of the empire's own subjects only further reveals the depth of the political turmoil embroiling the regime of Sultan Abdülhamid II in the years immediately preceding the 1908 revolution.

This effort to strengthen coastal security was driven by another noteworthy dynamic. Over the past two decades, borderlands and frontiers have received significant attention from historians of the Ottoman Empire and modern Middle East. The actual process by which borders were made, enforced, and secured has, with some exceptions, generally escaped rigorous study.[88] Regardless of the temporal or regional context, policing and fortification of borders is generally thought to be a phenomenon shaped and driven by the authority of the central state. Historians of immigration restriction have, however, begun to paint a different picture. Beth Lew-Williams, for example, argues that the actions of local officials in the northwestern United States tasked in the early 1880s with enforcing Chinese restriction were primarily responsible for transforming the permeable boundary separating the US and Canada 'from a legal border into a social reality.'[89] In this way, border control was not a deliberate initiative driven from the centre, but a haphazard process shaped by a bevy of intermediaries on the ground.[90] Likewise, the effort to fortify the Ottoman empire's coastal 'borders' in response to Armenian return migration was spearheaded by officials in the affected provinces in reaction to the increasing pressure put on them to enforce the ban. Thus we are once again reminded that state power in the late Ottoman Empire was exercised through multiple and often competing layers of official and unofficial actors who both shaped and frustrated Istanbul's ability to enforce its will on the ground. The degree to which these efforts at securing the coast succeeded in preventing return migration is not entirely clear. Many, state officials or otherwise, continued to seek ways to profit off of assisting Armenian returnees with skirting the ban.[91] Nevertheless, the increasingly circuitous routes that many returnees were forced to take in order to reenter the empire coupled with reports that larger numbers found themselves marooned on Cyprus awaiting an opportunity to be smuggled to the mainland, does suggest these efforts at least succeeded in making the return process that much more difficult.[92]

Conclusion

In March 1908, as yet another report arrived in Istanbul of Armenians on Cyprus awaiting an opportunity to return home, sensational rumours once again began circulating throughout the Ottoman bureaucracy of a concerted effort by these returnees to infiltrate the empire and stage an uprising at Harput. In response, the palace authorised officials on the coasts to use armed force (*kuva-yi meslaha*) if necessary to prevent their reentry.[93] Of course, the autocratic rule of Sultan Abdülhamid II would end not because of a revolution staged by globetrotting Armenian migrants, but in a palace coup staged by mid-ranking officers of the Ottoman army, mostly Muslims from the empire's remaining Balkan provinces. In the aftermath of the 1904 uprising in the district of Sasun and the attempted assassination of the sultan a year later, the effort to prevent Armenian return, increasingly deemed a major threat to the empire's internal security, preoccupied large swaths of the Ottoman bureaucracy. This concerted effort to prevent their return stood in stark contrast to the Ottoman state's handling of the same phenomenon in the years before 1905, when a generally more lenient attitude reigned.

Throughout the period in question, however, Istanbul's shifting policies on return were consistently frustrated by the creativity of Armenian migrants, many of whom were willing to go to great lengths to return to their families and their homes deep in the Anatolian interior. As this Chapter has demonstrated, a surprisingly large number of Armenians returned to the empire after sojourns in North America despite the many and often serious challenges they faced along the way. Indeed they continued to return even as the Ottoman government's hostility towards them deepened, and as the political instability that would eventually culminate in the revolution of 1908 accelerated. Those who eventually made it home, however, would soon find that their troubles were only beginning. The Ottoman Empire was not the only state adopting a harsher stance towards migrants in this period. Rather, it was part of a global phenomenon in the first decades of the twentieth century that saw governments throughout the world adopting increasingly hardline positions and policies on migration. Politics in the United States, where efforts at restricting Chinese migration beginning in the 1880s were fast becoming a template for societies throughout the world interested in cracking down on immigration, was growing increasingly hostile to the migrants arriving in increasingly larger numbers from Eastern Europe and the Middle East. As the following Chapter demonstrates, the anti-immigrant political discourse in the United States and the increasingly hardline attitude of the Ottoman state towards Armenian return would have profound consequences for returnees, plunging them into a strange and unenviable diplomatic and legal limbo.

5

Dubious Citizens

It is impossible to estimate with any degree of accuracy the number of Armenians who, like Ohannes Topalian, naturalised as US citizens while abroad. The decentralised nature of the naturalisation process in the late nineteenth and early twentieth centuries, handled through state courts with naturalization records generally kept by county governments, makes recovering such data difficult. Most Armenian migrants remained in the United States longer than the minimum of five years required to begin the naturalization process, one that was otherwise not particularly onerous. According to one estimate, by the end of the first decade of the twentieth century, however, fewer than half of all immigrants who had been in the United States for less than fifteen years had naturalised.[1] As Irene Bloemraad argues, immigrant groups in the early twentieth century, arriving mostly from eastern and southern Europe and the Middle East, were on the whole less likely to naturalize than their western and central European counterparts who arrived in the mid and late nineteenth century. She attributes this growing disinclination to adopt US citizenship in part to an environment that was becoming much less welcoming to new arrivals, as political hostility towards immigration in the country grew.[2] More specific to the Ottoman context, Kemal Karpat notes that contemporary observers believed that Armenian migrants were much more likely to acquire US citizenship than their Lebanese fellow countrymen.[3] The source material consulted for this book suggests that of those Armenian migrants who returned to the Ottoman Empire between 1890 and 1908, a majority (and perhaps an overwhelming majority) did so as naturalised citizens of the United States. Drawing sweeping conclusions from the available evidence, however, is somewhat problematic as such returnees were much more likely to come into contact with state authorities (Ottoman and American) than those who had not acquired US citizenship while abroad.

Nevertheless, assuming that Lebanese and Armenians – two migrant groups with many more similarities between them than differences – did naturalize at significantly different rates, the reasons for this may be found both in Ottoman migration policies and in the specific gender dynamics of citizenship and nationality in this era. As was discussed in Chapter one, after 1896, the Ottoman state exempted Lebanese citizens from its strict policies on international travel, permitting them to migrate abroad as long as they promised to retain their Ottoman nationality and to refrain from engaging in subversive politics. Akram Khater's pioneering work has demonstrated that for many Lebanese, permanently returning to their homes on Mount Lebanon after sojourns abroad was of paramount importance.[4] This may explain their reluctance to naturalize, if doing so could imperil their ability to return home. Armenians, meanwhile, enjoyed no such luxury. Aside from a brief period between 1898 and 1901, after 1897 they were strictly forbidden from returning to the empire regardless of their citizenship status. Meanwhile, a different set of state policies likely served as an incentive for Armenian men to acquire US citizenship. In 1896, Istanbul began permitting Armenians to immigrate permanently to the United States if they agreed to forsake their Ottoman nationality and never again return. As noted earlier, this became the primary method by which the spouses and dependent children of Armenians already residing in the United States left the Ottoman Empire. Until the passage of the Cable Act in 1922, citizenship law in the United States mandated that a wife's citizenship match that of her husband. Thus, by naturalising as a US citizen, an Armenian migrant could extend his newly acquired status to his spouse and dependent children still residing in the Ottoman Empire. He could also seek out the assistance of American diplomats stationed in the empire in securing official permission for their families to migrate, as evidenced by the frequency of such cases in the records of the US consulate in Harput.

This was of little help to the many Armenian migrants such as Ohannes Topalian who left their home communities as single men. The desire to marry and have children often necessitated a return to the Anatolian interior. Furthermore, Topalian was hardly alone in thinking that his status as a US citizen – and decorated war veteran to boot! – would prove helpful when the time came to once again leave the Ottoman Empire for North America, this time with a family in tow. Regardless of what drove Armenians to adopt US citizenship, those who returned to the Ottoman Empire after doing so were putting themselves in the middle of a political firestorm, whether knowingly or unknowingly. In the final decade of the nineteenth century, concerns over the Ottoman state's treatment of such individuals when they returned to the empire threatened to trigger a prolonged diplomatic row between Washington and Istanbul. Against the backdrop of the anti-Armenian and anti-missionary violence of the mid-1890s, the controversy also created a public relations disaster for the empire. At the same time, negotiations revealed a great deal of overlap between the United States and the Ottoman Empire's respective positions on questions of immigration, sovereignty and the right of governments to exclude. As tensions faded toward the dawn of the twentieth century, the two governments' policies concerning the status of returnees who had naturalised as US citizens came increasingly into alignment. By 1901, the same year that the assassination of President William McKinley would further enflame anti-immigrant sentiment in the United States, American diplomats informed Ottoman officials that they would no longer extend the protections of citizenship to most Armenian returnees residing in the empire. After the Ottoman sultan survived an assassination attempt on his own life, the state began vigorously deporting Armenian returnees in the empire unlawfully. As this Chapter argues, this policy would not have been possible without assurances from Washington that it would not intervene on behalf of those individuals who claimed to be US citizens. While the Ottoman Empire may have been consigned to the lower levels of 'the global legal regime' throughout much of its final century, especially when it came to questions related to the treatment of foreign nationals in its territory, this marked an important and noteworthy exception.[5] For their part, Armenian migrants found themselves at the receiving end of the policies of not one but two powerful states who increasingly viewed them as troublemakers, criminals and pariahs. In many ways, their experiences foreshadowed what would become a common experience of migrant groups in the twentieth and twenty-first centuries, whose fate would become increasingly intertwined with the vagaries of international diplomacy and national politics.

Defining Ottoman Nationality in an Interconnected World

In 1869, the Ottoman state introduced a detailed framework that would serve as the basis for Ottoman nationality law for the remainder of the empire's existence. The Ottoman Nationality Law (*Tabiiyet-i Osmaniye Kanunnamesi*) officially ended the Ottoman legal practice of distinguishing between Muslims and protected non-Muslims (*dhimmi*), instead favouring an Ottoman legal identity that applied equally to all subjects of the empire regardless of their religion. The Muslim/non-Muslim binary that had governed the Ottoman state's relationship with the populations living and travelling within its domains was replaced with one that divided the world principally between Ottoman nationals (*tabiiyet-i Osmaniye*) and foreign nationals (*tabiiyet-i ecnebiye*).[6] In this way, the Nationality Law emerged out of the broader Tanzimat-era effort to create an empire-wide Ottoman identity that transcended the multitudinous religious, ethnic and regional identities held by the empire's diverse populations.

As Will Hanley notes, however, the promulgation of the Nationality Law was motivated by a more pressing and immediate concern.[7] The law outlined the ways in which Ottoman nationality could be acquired: patrilineal descent, birth and over five years of continuous residence in the empire. Just as important, were the provisions that laid out the process by which an Ottoman subject could legally forsake his or her nationality for that of a foreign power. The Ottoman state reserved the right to 'refuse permission for Ottomans to quit Ottoman nationality and (conversely) . . . strip those who acquire(d) foreign nationality of their Ottoman nationality and bar them from Ottoman territory.'[8] The intent was to make it as difficult as possible for Ottoman subjects to adopt the nationality of a foreign power. In doing so, the drafters of the Nationality Law hoped to minimise what many nineteenth century Ottoman statesmen saw as one of the greatest threats facing the empire: the Capitulations. Beginning in the sixteenth century, the Ottoman state began granting certain extraterritorial privileges to the subjects of foreign realms resident in the Ottoman Empire. These capitulatory agreements were initially intended to provide legal protections to non-Muslim subjects of certain foreign powers as a way to promote commerce and preserve peaceful relations with the empire's Christian neighbors.[9] By the nineteenth century, however, the number of states whose nationals enjoyed the extraterritorial protections afforded by the Capitulations had swelled. An 1830 treaty between the Ottoman and United States governments extended these privileges to US citizens. Furthermore, whereas the Capitulations had originally applied only to certain individuals, usually merchants, by the middle of the nineteenth century, they had been extended to include all nationals of capitulatory powers. When the Treaty of Berlin admitted the Ottoman Empire to the Concert of Europe in 1856, the Capitulations were enshrined in international law, leaving the Ottoman Empire little power to challenge them.[10]

In the decades that followed, the enhanced global trade and mobility ushered in by the steamship era coupled with the growing economic and diplomatic influence of Western powers in the empire opened numerous avenues for Ottoman subjects to claim foreign nationality or secure other forms of diplomatic protection. For example, as Lale Can states, 'to encourage mercantile relationships and expand their spheres of influence, European consuls . . . grant(ed) letters of extraterritorial protection (*berat*) to thousands of Ottoman Christian protégés and, increasingly, to Muslim clients.'[11] In 1863, the Ottoman state issued a regulation aimed at significantly restricting the ability of its subjects to claim such protections.[12] In a similar vein, the 1869 Nationality Law sought to curb another way by which Ottoman subjects could claim extraterritorial privileges: namely through adopting the nationality of a capitulatory power. Importantly for the Ottoman state, the Great Powers grudgingly accepted that the Nationality Law did not 'infringe on the rights and privileges granted under the capitulations and established by custom.'[13] In subsequent years, Istanbul negotiated separate bilateral agreements regarding citizenship and naturalization with several governments, including Britain and France, both of which agreed not to extend extraterritorial protections to erstwhile subjects of the sultan who had naturalised without first obtaining the assent of the Ottoman state.[14]

In 1874, the Ottoman Empire reached a similar agreement with the United States. Modeled after a treaty signed between the United States and Germany, the document permitted the Ottoman state to deem any naturalised citizen of the United States who returned to and resided in the empire for a period of more than two years as having reverted to their Ottoman nationality.[15] While the agreement required Istanbul to recognise the status of all former subjects who naturalised as US citizens upon their return to the empire, its provisions were sufficiently satisfactory to win the Ottoman state's approval. The United States Senate, however, refused to provide consent to a binding treaty. As a result, for the remainder of the 1870s and 1880s, the document operated as an informal agreement between the two governments.[16] Nevertheless, from the perspective of the United States government, the agreement was similar to those it had reached with other foreign states on matters concerning citizenship and naturalization.[17] For its part, despite not being legally obligated to do so, the Ottoman state continued to honour the agreement. This was likely because until the late 1880s, relatively few Ottomans migrated to the United States, and only a fraction of these migrants acquired US citizenship while abroad. As the last decade of the nineteenth century dawned, however, growing numbers of Ottoman subjects leaving the empire for North America led Istanbul to reconsider its position.

In May 1891, the governor of Mamuretülaziz wrote to the Ministry of Interior complaining of the growing number of people in his province unlawfully migrating to North America.[18] His letter reached the desk of the grand vizier and from there to the Council of Ministers, the imperial government's most powerful policy-making body. Responding to the information enclosed in the letter, the council declared that the return of individuals claiming to be US citizens was the greatest of the threats that unlawful overseas migration posed to the empire's security. In response, it recommended an alteration to the agreement with the United States that would firmly cap at two years the amount of time a returnee to the Ottoman Empire could maintain his US citizenship before reverting to Ottoman nationality. The aim was to close a loophole that allowed naturalised American citizens of Ottoman origin who resided in the empire to maintain their status beyond the two-year residency limit by renewing their passports at an American embassy in a neighbouring country.[19] As the volume of Armenian migration steadily increased in the early 1890s, the spectre of suspected Armenian revolutionaries securing US citizenship and then returning to the empire to engage in seditious activities under protection of the Capitulations led to calls for more urgent action. In October 1893, the Council of Ministers approved a Foreign Ministry proposal to unilaterally abrogate the naturalisation agreement with the United States government. This action voided the two-year residency provision, and allowed Ottoman officials, in line with the 1869 law, to expel returnees who claimed US citizenship upon arrival.[20] While the council's decision did not explicitly target Armenians, it was clearly issued in line with the Ottoman state's decision in July of that year to no longer permit Armenians in possession of passports, or other evidence that they had unlawfully naturalised as US citizens, to reenter the empire.[21]

From Istanbul's perspective, this unilateral action was justified given the perceived scale of the threat posed by Armenian return and the non-binding nature of the agreement with the United States. Although the United States was not the only destination for Ottoman migrants, Armenians or otherwise, the Ottoman state viewed the US's approach to questions of citizenship and naturalization with particular concern. The 1802 Naturalization Law, which until 1906 served as the primary legal framework governing the naturalization process, mandated the swearing of an oath of intention and a minimum five-year residency in the United States as prerequisites for citizenship.[22] The swearing of oaths and residency requirements were hardly unusual facets of naturalization policies in Europe and elsewhere in the nineteenth century. Indeed, the 1869 Ottoman Nationality Law also stipulated a five-year residency period for those seeking to naturalize. In the Ottoman Empire, the naturalization process was firmly controlled by the central state. In contrast, until the 1906 Naturalization Act, state level courts in the United States handled naturalization cases with little to no oversight from the federal government.[23] Aristide Zolberg argues that the

American naturalization process grew out of an approach to citizenship as a voluntary association, which: 'challenged head on the common law doctrine of "perpetual allegiance," which held that a subject was indissolubly linked to the sovereign and which constituted the foundation stone of the entire European state system.'[24] By the late-nineteenth century, this liberal and decentralised approach to naturalization had for some become 'a tool for political machines to increase the number of loyal voters on the eve of local, state, and federal elections.'[25] Meanwhile, according to Dorothee Schneider, some immigrants purchased forged naturalization papers not primarily for voting purposes, but rather 'to gain access to public jobs or to ease admission at the border.'[26]

For Ottoman officials, the United States government's seemingly lackadaisical approach to naturalization was both befuddling and deeply concerning, especially given its status as a capitulatory power. In a December 1893 report the Ottoman foreign minister, Said Pasha, explained to the grand vizier that American policy on naturalization was an outgrowth both of its republican political system and its freewheeling approach to political expression, stating:

> Of all the foreign states with whom we have relations, the only other republic is France and even their naturalization law emerged out of that country's imperial past and institutions. The United States, meanwhile, has long had a republican government, and it affords just about anyone and everyone freedom of opinion. In this way, it should not be afforded the same treatment as other states.[27]

The minister's comments, animated it seems by a dyspepsia-inducing vision of revolutionaries operating in an environment of absolute permissiveness and switching nationalities as easily as others changed outfits, echoed concerns that had been driving Ottoman policy on overseas migration since the late 1880s. But the reality of US citizenship was more complicated and less threatening – at least as far as the Ottoman state was concerned – than what Said and many other officials feared. The late nineteenth century witnessed a steady increase in the numbers of Americans travelling abroad, including many naturalised citizens returning to their countries of origin, often permanently or for long stretches of time. As Craig Robertson shows, this growth in international travel made determining who was and was not entitled to the protections of American citizenship while abroad a matter of pressing importance. Doing so was made difficult, however, by the fact that federal law did not provide a standard method of proving citizenship. The passport for example, which was not a requirement for international travel in this period, was not always accepted as *prima facie* evidence of the bearer's citizenship status.

As will be discussed in further detail below, confusion over who could and could not claim the status of citizenship meant that consular officials stationed overseas were often left to make such determinations on a case-by-case basis. This created a paradoxical situation whereby citizenship was granted locally and with little oversight by the federal government, and yet outside of the United States, consular officials, federal employees who often had little or no grounding in citizenship law, possessed extensive discretionary power to determine whether an individual could claim diplomatic protection as a US citizen.[28] This fact, along with the State Department's extensive power to set policies concerning the status of naturalised citizens living outside of the United States, would eventually come to benefit the Ottoman state as it took an increasingly hard line against Armenian returnees residing in the empire.

After the Ottoman state introduced its policy barring Armenians found to be in possession of US passports from entering the empire, followed by its unilateral abrogation of the naturalization agreement with the United States, the Foreign Ministry was left to work feverishly to limit any diplomatic fallout. In August 1893, the Ottoman ambassador in Washington, DC, Alexandros Mavroyeni, wrote to Secretary of State Walter Gresham to communicate Istanbul's concerns about Armenian return migration and what he argued was the threat these returnees posed to the empire's internal security and sovereignty. The ambassador equated the newly introduced Ottoman policy banning Armenian holders of US passports from the empire to the Monroe Doctrine, which he held up as a supreme example of the United States asserting its sovereign right to protect itself from the meddling of foreign powers.[29] In response, Gresham corrected the ambassador's misreading of the doctrine's intent, pointing out that it concerned the involvement of European powers in the affairs of 'those states located south of the American Republic.' He also assured Mavroyeni that the United States government would not countenance its citizens, naturalised or otherwise, fomenting political instability in any foreign state.[30] Unconvinced, Mavroyeni stressed Istanbul's belief that the vast majority of Armenians migrating to the United States were doing so with the goal of naturalising as US citizens so they could return to the empire under Washington's protection and engage in sedition. Once again acknowledging the ambassador's concerns, Gresham nonetheless criticised the Ottoman government for excluding an entire class of American citizens primarily because of 'their race (*leur race*).' If the United States government were to reject certain Ottoman nationals on similar grounds, the secretary continued, he would vigorously oppose such an unjust policy.[31]

Gresham's response likely raised more than a few eyebrows at the

Ottoman embassy. After all, the United States was now more than a decade into the era of Chinese exclusion (1882–1943), a period marked by a series of legislative acts that barred most Chinese (later extended to include most East and South Asians) from entering the country. Mavroyeni's interpretation of the Monroe Doctrine may have been off mark, but he was certainly familiar with the politics that surrounded Chinese exclusion. Indeed, his invoking of the doctrine in his correspondence with the secretary of state was likely intended to draw a parallel between the Ottoman approach to Armenian return migration and the United States government's own justification for its policies towards Chinese migrants. For much of the nineteenth century, a prevailing sentiment took hold in the West that equated the freedom of both mobility and commerce with civilisation, and decried the undue restriction of either as being 'vexatious and oppressive'.[32] As Beth Lew-Williams shows, in the late 1880s when growing violence against Chinese migrants in the western United States led the administration of President Grover Cleveland to explore an expansion of Chinese exclusion, it first sought to do so through negotiations with the Chinese government. This approach was in line with the prevailing view that comity and free intercourse between states were benchmarks of an enlightened world order. Washington hoped that it could reach an agreement with the Qing government whereby the embattled dynasty would give consent to the United States government to exclude Chinese immigrants while continuing to maintain an open door to American commercial interests.[33] When in September 1888 the Qing Dynasty rejected the treaty that emerged out of these negotiations, the Cleveland Administration quickly changed its tune. Just a little over two weeks after receiving word of the Chinese government's decision, the Senate passed and the president signed a new exclusion bill marking a unilateral and drastic expansion of restrictionist policies aimed at Chinese immigrants. According to Lew-Williams, '(d)espite America's long history of negotiating immigration policy with foreign nations, Cleveland now asserted that immigration control was America's sovereign right.'[34] In a message to Congress that year, the president argued that 'excluding from its border all elements of foreign population which for any reason retard its prosperity (was) the admitted and paramount right and duty of every Government.'[35]

From Mavroyeni's perspective, by debarring Armenians found to be in possession of US passports, the Ottoman state was invoking the same sovereign right that animated American efforts to restrict Chinese immigration. What's more, the fact that citizens of the United States could claim extraterritorial privileges while on Ottoman soil only magnified the threat such individuals posed to the empire's security and prosperity.

The secretary of state's chiding comments about the unfair targeting of Armenians notwithstanding, Mavroyeni's diplomatic efforts were paying off. In December of 1893, Grover Cleveland, in the first year of his second non-consecutive term as president, touched on the Ottoman Empire's policy towards Armenian returnees in his annual address to congress, stating:

> Turkey complains that her subjects obtain citizenship in this country not to identify themselves in good faith with our people, but with the intention of returning to the land of their birth and there engaging in sedition . . . The Ottoman government has announced its intentions to expel from its dominions Armenians who have obtained naturalization in the United States since 1868. The right to exclude any or all classes of aliens is an attribute of sovereignty. It is a right asserted and, to a limited extent, enforced by the United States.[36]

Cleveland's address borrowed liberally from the arguments he had put forward in defense of the 1888 Scott Act passed during his first term in office that expanded Chinese exclusion. For Mavroyeni, reading these words must have come as a relief. The president was unequivocally acknowledging that the right of states to exclude individuals who were 'detrimental to the moral and physical health of its people'[37] was a principle that applied to the Ottoman Empire, even when those excluded were US citizens.

At the same time, Cleveland's address also included a stern warning directed at Istanbul, cautioning Ottoman officials not to engage in 'unnecessary harshness of treatment' against US citizens.[38] The president's comments were in response to reports that some Armenian returnees discovered to be in possession of American passports were being detained or otherwise mistreated upon their return to the empire. As 1894 dawned, the issue of the Ottoman state's treatment of returning Armenians risked exploding into a full-blown diplomatic and public relations crisis for the empire. In February, the *New York Times*, in an article titled 'Outrages on American Citizens,' reported on statements made by a former consul general in Constantinople, William Hess, accusing Ottoman officials of detaining and abusing naturalised US citizens of Ottoman birth in contravention of international law.[39] That same month, another article, 'Outrages on American Citizens,' claimed that A. W. Terrell, the American minister plenipotentiary to the empire, had been forced to dispel a rumour published in a French daily that Washington had dispatched a warship to Ottoman waters in an effort to secure the release of two American citizens of Ottoman–Armenian origin reportedly being held by provincial officials in Aleppo.[40] Meanwhile, in October, Terrell wrote a pointed letter to the Ottoman Foreign Ministry stating: '. . . I feel confident that the conduct of some Turkish officers who in times of past have imprisoned naturalized American citizens who have committed no offense except having changed their nationality will not be repeated, for . . . such acts could only . . . disturb (our) cordial relations.'[41]

For Mavroyeni, this controversy could not have come at a worse time. To the American public, reports of capricious 'Turks' mistreating US citizens of Armenian origin for the 'crime' of carrying an American passport only magnified the outrage being generated by the barrage of articles appearing in the country's major dailies on the anti-Armenian and anti-missionary violence in the empire's eastern provinces. Nevertheless, image management was central to Mavroyeni's job description, and he was deeply in tune with the political sentiments and sensitivities of the American public and its economic and political elites in particular.[42] He fully understood that news of fellow Americans being arrested and imprisoned in a foreign country on account of citizenship status was not going to be received warmly. At the same time, he was working to craft a counter-narrative that would play into the growing anxiety among many in the United States about the perceived nexus between immigration and radical politics. He had some formidable allies to help him in this task. In June 1894, the Ottoman consul in Chicago, Charles Henrotin, a prominent man-about-town who had also served as first president of the Chicago Stock Exchange and as a director of the 1893 Chicago World's Fair, granted an extended interview to the *Chicago Herald*. Owned by his friend and fellow Chicago socialite, James W. Scott, Henrotin could be sure the paper's coverage would be sympathetic to his defense of his Ottoman employers. In the interview, the consul argued that the empire's policy of debarring Armenians returnees who were United States citizens was justified on the grounds that they were 'engag(ed) in a revolutionary movement against the established order of the (Ottoman Empire).' He then mused, 'What would the United States government do if some of its former citizens were to return . . . under the protection of foreign passports, attempt to revolt a body of its people . . . (and) plot(ting) the overthrow . . . of the federal authority?'[43] Mavroyeni was no doubt pleased by the subsequent article, convinced that the good citizens of the United States' second-largest city would find it difficult to ignore someone of Henrotin's stature.

Meanwhile, in 1895, two pamphlets were published and widely distributed to defend the Ottoman government against charges that it was directing the massacre of Armenians in the empire's eastern provinces. In addition, the pamphlets also addressed at length the controversy surrounding the treatment of Armenian returnees to the empire who claimed US citizenship. Both pamphlets were published anonymously and distributed with the support of the Ottoman Foreign Ministry, but were later attributed to Alexander Russell Webb. Webb, a journalist by trade, had served as US consul to the Philippines beginning in 1887. While there, he converted to Islam; he would devote much of the rest of his life to educating the American public about his adopted faith, its history and the cultural practices of Muslims.[44] By the mid-1890s, his work had brought him into close contact with Ottoman state, which supported his efforts to raise awareness about Islam. In return, he proved to be a willing mouthpiece for the world's largest and most powerful Muslim state on issues of both a spiritual and, at least in the case of the 'Armenian Question,' political nature.[45] Both pamphlets contain numerous excerpts of newspaper articles along with the statements of prominent Americans supportive of the Ottoman position interspersed at various intervals with Webb's own commentary. They also include an English translation of the 1869 Ottoman Nationality Law in order to demonstrate to readers that Armenians who returned to the empire after naturalising as US citizens without the permission of the Ottoman state did so in violation of imperial law. Webb then echoes Istanbul's assertion that Armenians who adopted American citizenship did so solely for the purpose of securing capitulatory protections. To bolster this argument, he includes an excerpt of an 1893 report from the United States' chief diplomat in the Ottoman Empire, A. W. Terrell, in which the diplomat declared: 'The European emigrant in the United States generally naturalizes in good faith: The Asiatic very rarely does. I am in a position to know that it is the rule, rather than the exception, that the Armenian returns soon after he is naturalized, and goes back with the intention of remaining.'[46] Mavroyeni had used these same comments from Terrell in his correspondences with the secretary of state, hinting at the close cooperation between the ambassador and Webb in the production of the pamphlets.[47] By echoing this characterisation of Armenians as untrustworthy 'Asiatics,' both Webb and Mavroyeni were eager to tap into the deep well of racism that existed in the late-nineteenth century United States. There was a certain irony to this, however, as the ambassador had worked tirelessly during his time in Washington to depict the empire and its populations as civilised and European to an otherwise skeptical American audience.

As educated and relatively prominent native-born citizens, both Charles Henrotin and Alexander Russell Webb were ideally suited to advance Ottoman efforts to present Armenian returnees in an unsympathetic light. Both men endeavoured to link the Armenian return issue to broader concerns that were driving the growth of anti-immigrant sentiment in the United States at the end of the nineteenth century. People arriving from locations outside of western and central Europe were increasingly seen as bearers of both pathological and political contagion. The image both Henrotin and Webb evoke of alien miscreants seeking to adopt American citizenship as a flag of convenience in order to sow discord in their homeland grafted well onto the political discourse being mobilised in support of tightening the United States' immigration and naturalisation laws. The ground was indeed quite fertile for such arguments to take root. In December 1894, the *Washington Post*, among the most prominent dailies in the United States, published a blistering editorial warning readers that, 'Armenians are a very noisy and troublesome people who pretend to flee to America as to a haven of refuge (only to return) to the scene of their alleged suffering.' The piece then called the citizenship of such returnees into question, stating: 'It is difficult to believe, that (Armenians) would go back if Turkish rule were the barbarous and dreadful thing they would have us think it is. We . . . believe that they go back because they imagine that their naturalization in this country will protect them in acts of wanton offense and contempt at the expense of Turkey.'[48] Whether the *Post* was directly swayed by Mavroyeni's efforts is unclear. The ambassador was nevertheless pleased enough by it to forward the article to the Ottoman foreign minister in Istanbul.[49]

By 1896 a clear tension existed between the sympathy many Americans felt for the victims of anti-Armenian violence in the Ottoman east, and their increasing ambivalence about Armenians as an immigrant group, especially in the context of the controversy surrounding those who returned to the empire. This tension was on clear display in Grover Cleveland's final address to Congress that year. In it, the president lamented the loss of Armenian life in the Ottoman Empire to what he attributed as 'the rage of mad bigotry and cruel fanaticism.' Similar statements of ire directed against the empire had become a quotidian refrain in American politics over the course of the mid-1890s. Cleveland then turned his attention to the security and safety of US citizens in the Ottoman Empire. He assured Congress that all was being done to ensure that 'our missionaries in Ottoman territory, who constitute nearly all the individuals residing there who have a right to claim our protection on the score of American citizenship.' Cleveland's formulation, however, implied that there existed a class of citizen in the Ottoman Empire that the United States government did not have an obligation to protect: namely those Armenians who had naturalised as citizens and subsequently returned to their homeland.[50] In his address to Congress three years earlier, the president had defended the Ottoman state's sovereign right to debar such returnees, but warned Istanbul against detaining and mistreating them given their status as US citizens. Now in 1896, his words seemed to foreshadow a shift in Washington's policy concerning the citizenship status of naturalised Armenians who returned to the Ottoman Empire, one that would become more evident as American outrage over the Armenian massacres faded in subsequent years.

Despite Mavroyeni's efforts to turn American public opinion in favour of the Ottoman Empire, however, as the treatment of Armenian returnees generated a firestorm in the United States, Washington used its sizeable diplomatic leverage to intervene on their behalf. In December 1895, the late Walter Gresham's successor as secretary of state, Richard Olney, submitted a report in response to a Senate resolution that demanded a full investigation of allegations of violence against American citizens and property in the Ottoman Empire. The report, titled 'Armenian Outrages,' provides extensive information about the deliberate attacks on missionary property that had taken place over the past two years. It also references several instances of alleged violence against native-born US citizens travelling in the Ottoman Empire. Although none of these incidents were connected to the massacres underway in the Ottoman east, Olney nevertheless points to them as evidence of Istanbul's weak and ineffectual response to the deteriorating political situation in the empire.[51]

Against this backdrop, he describes three cases in which Ottoman authorities, in violation of the Capitulations, had detained or otherwise mistreated Armenian returnees who claimed US citizenship. The report acknowledged the Ottoman Empire's right as 'a sovereign state to exclude or deport for adequate cause . . . aliens whose resort to its territories may be pernicious to the safety of the State.'[52] Nevertheless, Olney stridently defends the United States' rights under the Capitulations to extend extraterritorial protections to its citizens without exceptions, declaring: '[the] Government (of the United States) is unable to forego its right in (the Ottoman Empire) and can not (sic) relinquish jurisdiction over any citizen, even though after naturalization he return (sic) to his native land and identify himself with its political conspirations.'[53] Olney's discussion of the individual cases, however, far from revealing a picture of Ottoman intransigence worthy of such a full-throated defense of American capitulatory rights, instead reflects the distinct imbalance of power that existed between the United States and Ottoman governments. The first two cases involved naturalised citizens who had been detained on suspicion that they were members of seditious political organisations. In the first, Ottoman officials released John Arakelian after the US consul in Sivas 'made energetic representation to the Porte against the detention of a citizen of the United States on criminal charge.'[54] After his release, Arakelian left the empire at the request of the

Ottoman state.[55] In the second case, another returnee, Mardiros Mooradian, was arrested after he was found to be in possession of documents that connected him to the outlawed Hunchakian Revolutionary Party. Upon the request of the American consul in Istanbul, Ottoman authorities promptly handed over the documents. Convinced that Mooradian had committed no criminal act under US law, the consul demanded that he be released to the custody of consular officials.[56] Once again, Ottoman officials quickly bowed to diplomatic pressure, recognising the right of the United States to extend extraterritorial protections to Mooradian.

The third case, however, is especially revealing of the diplomatic power the United States could bring to bear over the Ottoman Empire, and the extent to which the controversy as it was reported in the American press did not match the reality on the ground. In August 1895, seven men were arrested in the province of Aleppo on suspicion that they were Armenian revolutionaries. One of the men, Melcoun Guedjian, had until recently been residing in the United States, naturalising as an American citizen in December 1894. He had entered the Ottoman Empire at the port of Iskenderun where he was smuggled in with the help of local boatmen, after which he prepared to set out for the long overland journey to his home community in the Harput region. Before leaving the port city, he was mugged and robbed. In a report he filed on the incident with the local constabulary, Guedjian claimed to be a British national. With the help of the British vice-consul in the city, however, local officials were eventually able to determine that his nationality claim was false, a fact that helped to lead to his arrest. When apprehended, Guedjian was found to be in possession of several documents of a political nature and more than eight hundred pounds in cash. He then promptly confessed to being a member of the Hunchakian Revolutionary Party. After a court in nearby Aleppo found him guilty of fomenting sedition, Guedjian was sentenced to a lengthy prison sentence. At first, American diplomatic officials refused Guedjian's requests to intervene on his behalf, convinced that Ottoman authorities had provided sufficient evidence that he had engaged in 'armed resistance to Turkish authority.' Not wanting his case to become a precedent for trying US citizens under Ottoman law, however, the State Department ordered AW Terrell to pressure the Ottoman government to remand Guedjian to the custody of his office on grounds that the trial and subsequent conviction were in violation of the Capitulations. Terrell's intervention succeeded, and the grand vizier ordered that Guedjian be sent to Istanbul. After initially refusing to heed the order, the governor of Aleppo was eventually forced to comply, and by December 1895, Guedjian was in American custody.[57]

In many ways, Melcoun Guedjian embodied the Ottoman state's worst fears about Armenian return migration. If Olney's report is to be believed, he was an admitted member of an outlawed Armenian political organisation, and claimed to be a national of not one but two capitulatory powers. Nevertheless, the speed with which the grand vizier vacated Guedjian's lengthy prison sentence and remanded him to American custody suggests that in contrast to some of the sensational reports circulating in the United States, in face of diplomatic pressure, Istanbul was quite constrained in its treatment of returnees, even those it considered to pose a major threat to the empire's internal security. In a strikingly similar case less than one year later in July 1896, the Ottoman state came under pressure from Washington to release nine Armenian returnees, all of whom claimed American citizenship, after they were arrested on suspicion of being revolutionaries. Officials in Aleppo, where the group was being detained, argued that the United States government had no right by its own law to extend protection to the returnees given their alleged involvement in efforts to overthrow the Ottoman government.[58] The American Legation, meanwhile, pointing to the Guedjian case as a precedent, demanded that the group be remanded to its custody.[59] After a couple of months of pressure, the Ottoman government agreed to release the group.[60] As long as the United States government continued to demand that returnees who had naturalised as American citizens were to be afforded extraterritorial protection under the Capitulations, the Ottoman state was restricted in its treatment of such individuals. While Washington recognised Istanbul's right to debar returnees who were citizens, a policy that aligned with its own approach to Chinese immigrants, it steadfastly opposed efforts to treat them as Ottoman subjects once in the empire. As 1896 came to a close and an uneasy peace once again began to descend over the Ottoman east, both popular and governmental interest in the United States in the fate of the empire's Armenian populations began to wane. With William McKinley prepared to take the oath of office as the next president of the United States, the controversy over the Ottoman state's treatment of naturalised American citizens also began to fade. The same was not true of the rising anti-immigrant sentiment taking hold in American political discourse. With this shift in popular opinion also came a profound transformation in how the State Department and American diplomats in the Ottoman Empire viewed the status of Armenians who sought to return home.

From Crisis to Compromise, 1897–1901

In January 1898, the Council of Ministers issued the policy allowing Armenians returning from North America conditional reentry at Samsun. As was discussed in the previous Chapter, this decision was in response to return migration and helped to further accelerate the volume of such migration in the aftermath of the massacres of the mid-1890s. Returnees found to be in possession of US passports or other evidence that they had changed citizenship while abroad remained banned from the empire, as did those who had been given authorisation to migrate in exchange for forfeiting their Ottoman nationality. Thus, for those returnees who had naturalised as US citizens while sojourning in North America, it was imperative that they conceal this fact from Ottoman authorities when they reentered at Samsun and for as long as they remained in the empire. Indeed, in June 1901, the American consul in Harput, Thomas Norton, reported that of the three hundred naturalised American citizens he estimated resided in his consular district none 'felt free to allow the fact of their citizenship to become known to the Turkish Authorities.'[61] For most Armenians, returning home constituted a *de facto* reversion to Ottoman nationality. While concealing their US citizenship was a necessary price to pay to return home, it would nonetheless have profound consequences for their status moving forward.

Meanwhile, by the late 1890s, the treatment of Armenians who claimed US citizenship upon their arrival in the empire was no longer a source of major diplomatic friction between the Ottoman and United States governments. If anything, a more cooperative relationship began to emerge that would foreshadow an increasing convergence in the two states' policies on the status of Armenian returnees. The story of one such individual, Ohannes, from the province of Erzurum, is emblematic of this dynamic. In September of 1898, he arrived in Samsun after having resided in the United States for several years. Ottoman authorities in the Black Sea port had been expecting him because of a warning that the Ottoman consulate in New York had sent to the Foreign Ministry stating that Ohannes, who was alleged to have been spreading 'pernicious ideas' (*efkar-ı muzzira*) while abroad, was seeking to reenter the empire. Immediately upon his arrival, Ohannes declared that he was a US citizen and demanded to be taken to the American consulate. Ottoman authorities notified the consulate, which promptly dispatched a representative to assist with the situation. With the representative present, Ottoman authorities searched the returnee's bags, finding an Ottoman identity card (*nüfus tezkeresi*), an American passport and several pamphlets and books. Following the search, Ohannes was remanded to the custody of the consulate along with his belongings. The next day, the consul requested that Ohannes be granted permission to return to his hometown in the Anatolian interior so that he could convalesce from a bad bout of tuberculosis. The request was quickly denied on grounds that he had naturalised as a US citizen in contravention of imperial law and was thus permanently barred from the empire. The consul demonstrated no inclination to protest the decision, agreeing to help arrange Ohannes' removal from Ottoman territory. In return, officials in Samsun acceded to the diplomat's request that the ailing returnee be given safe passage to Batumi, just across the Russian frontier, to continue his convalescence there.[62] Thus, in contrast to similar episodes earlier in previous years, the incident was resolved amicably, with Ottoman and American officials careful to respect one another's jurisdictional claims.

Regardless, both governments viewed the absence of a legally binding treaty between them governing naturalization as less than ideal. An 1899 report by the Ottoman foreign minister cited the lack of such an agreement as the greatest source of friction between the Ottoman Empire and the United States, especially given the continued ability of naturalised American citizens of Ottoman origin to claim extraterritorial protection under the Capitulations. He blamed the United States Senate's refusal to consent to the 1874 naturalization treaty for the situation, and ended his report citing statements from the American Minister Plenipotentiary, Oscar Strauss, that future ratification was unlikely given the continued deep divisions in that legislative body.[63] Several months later, in August 1899, the consul general in Istanbul, Charles Dickinson, approached Ottoman officials with a guarantee that his government would comply with the text of the 1874 treaty if the Ottoman state agreed to do the same, effectively returning to the pre-1893 status quo. According to one official's report on the meeting, the consul general argued that such a move would alleviate Istanbul's concerns about the perceived threat to the empire's sovereignty posed by naturalised US citizens residing in the empire. The official seemed to take it as a hopeful sign that Washington was taking Ottoman concerns seriously.[64] Nevertheless, nothing appears to have come of the meeting, and for the next year and a half, little progress was made in forging a permanent agreement between the two states on the status of naturalised US citizens in the empire.

Meanwhile, the United States government was increasingly hesitant to continue extending diplomatic protections to returnees, especially those who concealed their naturalization status from Ottoman authorities. In January 1901, the State Department issued a circular entitled 'A Notice to American Citizens Formerly Subjects of Turkey who Contemplate a Return to that Country.' The document warned such individuals that they 'may expect arrest and imprisonment or expulsion' if discovered by Ottoman authorities to have naturalised without permission. Only those willing to ' regard (themselves) as a Turkish subject' were given permission by the Ottoman state to return, the document continued.[65] The information provided in the circular reflected what had been the reality on the ground for the past several years. The document's significance, however, lay not in what it said, so much as what it omitted. Nowhere did it state that naturalised citizens arrested or imprisoned by Ottoman authorities would receive the protection of American diplomats under the Capitulations. While during the tumult of the mid-1890s, Washington asserted that its citizens, native born and naturalised, were equally entitled to the rights of extraterritoriality, the document seemed to imply that this would no longer be the case.

Certainly, this is the way the American consul general, Charles Dickinson, interpreted his government's policy in the aftermath of the circular's publication. In March 1901, he once again met with Ottoman officials, including the minister of police, to discuss the status of Armenians residing in the empire after having naturalised as US citizens. An Ottoman report on the meeting claimed that the consul acknowledged that many 'American Armenians' (*Amerikalı Ermeniler*) returned from the United States 'with minds set on revolution' (*ihtilal fikri hissetmekte olduğu*). Although required to extend the protections of citizenship to such individuals, Dickinson promised to divest his office of this responsibility (*mesuliyetten azade*) when Istanbul vigorously opposed a returnee's presence in the empire, agreeing in such cases to provide Ottoman authorities 'any and all assistance' (*her türlü muavenette bulunacağı*). The consul general's statement reflected a significant departure from US policy in the mid-1890s, when American diplomats insisted that no US citizen under any circumstance was to be tried under Ottoman law. Indeed, according to the report on the meeting, Dickinson personally informed the minister of police about the change in policy, excusing his Armenian translator from the task evidently out of fear that the assistant could not be trusted to convey this sensitive and personally troubling information.[66] Two months later, Dickinson wrote to his consul in Harput, Thomas Norton, responding to information Norton had provided about the many Armenians in his consular district who were not 'allow(ing) the fact of their citizenship to become known to the Turkish Authorities.' In the letter, Dickinson stated:

> It is my duty to inform you that . . . those alleged Naturalized citizens who claim for any purpose to be Ottoman subjects, have forfeited their American

> citizenship and are not entitled to American protection. The obligation assumed by our Government and the foreign subject when he becomes naturalized, is a reciprocal one and the latter cannot return to the country of his origin, *shirk his obligation to his adopted country* (emphasis mine), masquerade as an Ottoman subject and yet claim American protection if an emergency arise (sic). If American citizenship is as valuable as we know it to be, it is worth maintaining at all times and under all hazards.[67]

Dickinson ended the letter with assurances that 'the foregoing opinion conforms to his understanding of the ruling of the (State) Department.'[68] The policy as stated by Dickinson effectively denaturalised the vast majority of Armenian returnees residing in the Harput consular district, who could ostensibly claim US citizenship. Ottoman policy since 1893 had made it clear that evidence that a returnee had naturalised as a US citizen was grounds for immediate debarment. The overwhelming majority of Armenian returnees in the Harput region had little choice but to hide their citizenship status if they hoped to remain resident in the empire. In response to Dickinson's letter, Norton wrote the State Department claiming that one of his first acts as the inaugural consul in the newly created district had been to inform 'the large class of citizens in question (that) they could no longer expect consular protection.'[69] His comment suggests that this policy had been introduced well before Dickinson drafted his letter, perhaps in conjunction with the January 1901 publication of the circular discussed above. Regardless, it was far more sweeping than the guarantees Dickinson had given to the minister of police during his March meeting with him in Istanbul.

Armenians who returned to the Ottoman Empire after naturalising as US citizens could be forgiven for believing that their new status was permanent and inalienable. By leaving US territory and returning to their homeland, however, returnees had unknowingly made themselves vulnerable to denaturalization effectively by fiat. In 1906, as Patrick Weil demonstrates, the State Department succeeded in including a provision in that year's Naturalization Act that declared 'foreign residence by a naturalised citizen was "sufficient . . . to authorize the cancellation of his certificate of citizenship as fraudulent."' But this had been *de facto* State Department policy well before 1906. According to Craig Robertson, the lack of clear guidelines for proving citizenship while abroad, a situation exacerbated by the legally ambiguous status of documents such as passports as evidence of citizenship, gave rise in the early twentieth century to an entire class of 'dubious citizens.'[70] Responsibility generally fell to individual consular agents, who possessed vast discretion in such matters to determine on a case-by-case basis whether such individuals had valid claims to citizenship. If, for example, a naturalised citizen had been living in his homeland for a prolonged period of time, especially if he could not 'claim an ongoing economic relationship with the United States,' it was within a consular official's power to conclude that the individual had voluntarily expatriated himself.[71] The 1874 agreement reached between the Ottoman Empire and United States, which Istanbul unilaterally abrogated in 1893, had set at two years the length of time a naturalized US citizen could remain in the empire before being deemed to have expatriated. In its absence, the State Department and the American Legation in Istanbul had vast authority to set policy and to determine protocol regarding the status of naturalised citizens in the empire. Dickinson's letter to Norton made clear that as a result of the State Department's new policy, in choosing to return home, the vast majority of Armenian returnees residing in the Harput region had rendered their naturalization null and void.

Much had changed in the United States since the political and diplomatic outcry over the treatment of naturalised citizens in the Ottoman Empire. In the mid-1890s, Washington was willing to leverage its diplomatic might to protect Armenian returnees whose rights as US citizens it believed were being denied. Against the backdrop of anti-Armenian and anti-missionary violence in the Ottoman east, this was a broadly popular position. Already by the early 1890s, however, hostility towards migrants who returned home, especially those who did so after naturalising as US citizens, was increasingly a component of the broader anti-immigrant fervour taking hold in American politics.[72] This development was driven by the widespread belief that such individuals were fraudulently adopting US citizenship so that they could avoid military service or paying taxes when back in their home countries. Additionally, in the aftermath of the 1886 Haymarket Affair, when a demonstration of mostly German immigrant socialists and anarchists in support of the eight-hour workday turned violent, immigrants from countries outside of western Europe were increasingly viewed as a dangerous threat to the political and social order.[73] Reflecting these developments, in August 1896, well before the popular outrage generated by news of anti-Armenian violence in the Ottoman Empire had fully subsided, the *New York Herald* published an editorial that dripped with hostility against Armenian returnees. The piece, published the day after militants with the Armenian Revolutionary Federation (ARF), some of whom were believed to be naturalised US citizens, raided the Ottoman Bank in Istanbul, proclaimed:

> The American public long ago tired of the revolutionary attempts of the Armenians who, led by men who had come to this country and gained,

> oftentimes by fraud, their status as American citizens, went back and brought the name and character of Americans and of Christianity into disrepute and disgrace. These men, these so-called Christian Armenians, have been working under false pretenses long enough, and we trust that in future greater care will be extended in granting the privileges of American citizenship to men who are unworthy of the shelter of the Stars and Stripes. Turkey has suffered much from these bogus citizens of ours . . . We do not build splendid war ships for the purpose of sending them out for the protection of misguided persons who believe that American citizenship will cover idiotic attempts to produce revolution in the name of Christianity.[74]

The editorial's language excoriating 'our bogus citizens' closely matches Dickinson's letter written five years later that justified the new State Department policy by decrying returnees who 'shirked' their responsibilities as citizens and only claimed consular protection when 'emergencies ar(o)se'. By 1901, sympathy for the plight of Ottoman Armenians had largely faded from mainstream consciousness in the United States. Meanwhile, as larger numbers of Armenians returned home in the late 1890s and the first years of the 1900s, the anti-immigrant clamour in the United States was only growing louder. The assassination of President William McKinley by Leon Czołgosz, a Michigan-born anarchist with a 'foreign' surname only added fuel to the anti-radical and nativist fire. In response, the first decade of the twentieth century would see the introduction of a raft of legislation aimed at barring suspected anarchists from the country, restricting the immigration of those believed to be unskilled or illiterate and bringing the naturalization process under federal control.[75] Against this political backdrop, from the perspective of the State Department and the American public alike, Armenian returnees in the Ottoman Empire were no longer a group deserving of either sympathy or the protections of citizenship.

For his part the US consul in Harput, Thomas Norton, did not share the hostility of his superiors towards the returnees residing in his district. In May 1901, he wrote:

> They are here largely to revisit their families, sick wives, settle estates, and especially to look after property or family interests seriously affected by the events of 1895. They are thoroughly loyal and would vastly prefer to have their status as American citizens freely known. As it is, however, impossible to enter the country with American passports, they are forced to let their citizenship lie dormant or else to forego the performance of their duties as husbands, brothers, or sons.[76]

Norton's sympathetic description of returnees as unfortunate victims of circumstance who were forced to choose between their adoptive land

and their familial responsibilities contrasted mightily with the image put forward by Mavroyeni and his allies in their mid-1890s propaganda effort, or later by the *New York Herald* and Charles Dickinson. Regardless, by the end of 1901, he was sending regular reports about Armenian returnees who sought the aid of his office only to be turned away for having not presented as a US citizen during their residence in the empire.[77] This would remain the established policy of the United States government until the end of World War I. Meanwhile, with the United States government all but stripping Armenian returnees of any hope of receiving diplomatic protection, the Ottoman state was in a position to drastically harden its policies on return migration.

Strangers in a Familiar Land – Towards a Policy of Deportation

In May 1901, the Ottoman Council of Ministers ended the policy of allowing returnees to reenter the empire at Samsun.[78] The full ban on Armenian return migration from North America first introduced in 1897 was reinstated. This decision was almost certainly influenced by the simultaneous changes in US policy towards naturalised citizens residing in the empire, which gave Istanbul tremendous leeway in how it could treat such individuals without incurring Washington's diplomatic wrath. The 1897 policy banning Armenian return from North America stipulated that all returnees were to be either debarred upon entry or deported (*def' ve iade*) if they were later found to be in the empire unlawfully.[79] Thus, someone who entered the empire clandestinely and then successfully reached his home community in the Harput region could still be removed from the empire if the fact of his return was uncovered by local authorities. After less than a year, the full ban on return was replaced by the policy allowing conditional return through Samsun. As a result, no evidence exists of returnees being deported in large numbers between 1898 and 1901. With the reinstatement of the 1897 policy, however, Armenian returnees from North America once again faced possible deportation.

As was discussed in the previous Chapter, however, between 1901 and 1904, little appears to have changed in how the Ottoman state treated returnees. Armenians could no longer reenter the empire by normal means after the Samsun policy was brought to an end, thus forcing them to rely on clandestine means of entry. Nevertheless, in these years, large numbers of returnees from North America eventually made it back to their home communities in the Anatolian interior. For those who reached home, provincial authorities in the Harput region were hesitant to pursue a hardline approach. While they complained about the inability of their counterparts on the coasts to enforce the ban on return, once returnees arrived in the interior, they claimed that little could be done to force them to leave.[80] The available evidence suggests that those who were illegally in the empire but were determined to be 'of good character' were generally permitted to remain.[81] Meanwhile, those who did face deportation found ways to contest their fate. For example, in March 1903, Dikran and Kevork, both of whom had recently returned from long sojourns in the United States, sent a petition to the grand vizier. The two had attempted to reenter the empire at Beirut only to be denied admission by authorities there. They then travelled to Istanbul and on to the Black Sea port of Giresun, where they managed to enter the empire. They were subsequently taken into custody and transported by armed guard from the nearby district of Karahisar to their home community of Çemişgezek, sixty kilometres to the north of Harput/Mezre. Almost immediately upon their arrival home, they received the news that they were to be deported, leading them to petition the grand vizier to seek a stay. In it, they argued that the order of deportation against them was unjust, claiming that they had travelled abroad for legitimate economic reasons. They then lamented the terrible financial and emotional toll that their expulsion would wreak on the families they were being forced to leave behind, comparing the prevailing sentiment in their households to that of a funeral. Several weeks later, they sent another petition, this one signed by three other returnees who were also facing deportation, in which they once again requested a stay, emphasising their good reputations and outstanding moral characters.[82] For his part, the provincial governor seemed inclined to support their case, decrying the logistical difficulties involved in deporting returnees from the interior and faulting officials in Giresun for allowing them to reenter the empire in the first place.[83] Several months later, the grand vizier's office indicated a willingness to side with the returnees as long as Mamuretülaziz could guarantee that they were indeed the upstanding property owners and family men they had claimed to be in their petitions.[84]

Their petitions indicated that Dikran and Kevork were familiar with the anxieties that animated the state's fear of both overseas migration and return, and knew what to emphasise in order to assuage them. Those returnees discovered to have returned to the empire after having naturalised as US citizens, however, quickly learned that there was little they could do to avoid debarment or deportation. Meanwhile, Istanbul was finding that US consular officials were amenable partners in enforcing its policies on return migration. Ottoman authorities regularly transferred returnees who claimed or were otherwise found to possess American citizenship to the custody of the nearest consulate, which then took on the responsibility of ensuring that the individual in question was transported out of the empire.[85] Returnees who were US citizens remained compelled to conceal the fact of their naturalization from Ottoman authorities, thus risking expatriation if they sought out consular assistance on the grounds that they were 'masquerading' as subjects of the empire.

Those who made their status known to American consular officials upon returning to the empire may have come to regret the decision. For example, in February 1904, Hayrabed Varjabedian, a native of Palu, arrived in Istanbul after sixteen years in the United States, where he had naturalised as a citizen. He had come to the imperial capital after a brief stay in Batumi, clandestinely disembarking from the steamship on which he arrived so as not to draw the attention of Ottoman authorities. He made his way to the American consulate where he declared himself to be a US citizen and requested the consulate's assistance in securing permission for his family in Palu to return with him to his adoptive homeland. Consular officials subsequently took him into custody and arranged to have him removed from the empire. Undeterred by this unfortunate turn of events, Varjabedian departed the ship on which he had been placed at the Mediterranean port of Iskenderun hoping to travel from there to Palu. The hapless returnee's hopes were once again dashed, however, when he was arrested and detained by officials while transiting through the province of Adana. In a different case from May 1903, two naturalised US citizens, a husband and wife, arrived in Mersin with their infant child. They were denied entry by Ottoman officials and forced to return to the ship on which they had arrived. Shortly thereafter, employees of the city's US consulate, where the family sought protection as citizens, rowed them to shore. When local officials demanded that the consul expel them from the empire, he refused. The officials responded to the consul's intransigence by reminding him that he was in violation of Ottoman law, and that failure to deport the couple risked triggering a 'diplomatic incident' (*mesele-i siyasiye*).[86] While it is unfortunately not clear how the case was resolved, it nonetheless demonstrates Istanbul's growing assertiveness in such matters. Clearly, the Ottoman officials involved felt they had every reason to believe that the US consul would accede to their demand to expel the family. Certainly the guarantees that Charles Dickinson had given to the minister of police in 1901 would further justify their assumption.

The year 1905 marked a major shift in the Ottoman state's approach to return migration, one that would have profound implications for the fate of the hundreds of Armenian returnees, naturalised US citizens and otherwise. As was discussed in the preceding Chapter, this hardening of policy was influenced by the worsening political situation in the empire beginning with the February 1904 uprising in Sasun and accelerated by the assassination attempt on Sultan Abdülhamid II in July 1905. It was in this context that Fehmi was appointed governor of Mamuretülaziz province in the spring of that year. Almost immediately upon his arrival in the province, he signalled a much more hardline approach to Armenian returnees than that of his predecessors. As evidence of this, in June 1905, Fehmi ordered the deportation of Aron Minassian who had recently arrived after a ten-year sojourn in the United States.[87] Throughout the summer, with the assistance of local church representatives, several other returnees petitioned Istanbul in hopes of having deportation orders against them lifted.[88] In September 1905, Fehmi recommended to the grand vizier that deportations be allowed to proceed despite such petitions seeking a reprieve on account of a returnee's supposed loyalty (*sadık*) and good moral character. 'We must adhere to the policy stipulating that those who unlawfully return be deported (*geldikleri mahale iadeleri*),' the governor wrote, 'at the very least, doing so can serve as a disincentive against illegal migration . . . and the political threats (to the empire) associated with it.'[89] One month later, Fehmi sent a report to the Ministry of Interior complaining that between four hundred and five hundred Armenians had returned to Mamuretülaziz from the United States since the full ban on return was reimposed more than four years earlier. For reasons unclear to him, he continued, these returnees had been allowed to remain in the province. Because the provincial government did not have the resources to deport these returnees en masse (*toptan*), his office had been forced to deport individuals deemed by local authorities to be suspicious (*da'i-i şüphe*) on a case-by-case basis.[90] After a long series of correspondences, the Ministry of Interior agreed that any attempt at large-scale deportation of returnees residing in the province would be fraught with logistical challenges and risked 'giving rise to complaints.' It permitted the governor, however, to continue deporting any returnee deemed 'suspicious,' even if that person had been residing in the empire for a long time, and to deport without exception all who subsequently returned to the province.[91]

I use the term 'deportation' to characterise the process referred to in the Ottoman source material as 'returning (them) to whence they came' (*mevrudlarına iade/geldikleri mahale iade*). The term 'deportation' has a particularly fraught and tragic meaning when used in the context of early twentieth century Ottoman Armenian history. For many, the term evokes the Deportation Law (*Tehcir Kanunu*) of 1915 that served as the legal framework for the murderous World War I-era evacuation of Armenian civilians, women, children and men to the Syrian Desert, and was a key component of a broader genocidal process. At the same time, as Torrie Hester argues, in the first decades of the twentieth century, deportation was emerging as a 'internationally recognised form of (immigrant) removal, which was unique in law, scope, motivation and significance.'[92] Deportation differs from other forms of removal such as expulsion because, again, according to Hester, '(it) makes the question about the destination of *where* to send a person central.' Because deportation requires the consent of the country to which the deportee is being sent, it is an inherently international phenomenon. In contrast, expulsion is less concerned with the final destination of the subject being expelled and thus can be carried out unilaterally.[93]

Ottoman policy towards Armenian returnees, particularly in the three years between 1905 and the 1908 revolution, fits somewhere between deportation and expulsion as Hester defines the two. Armed guards escorted returnees subject to deportation from the Harput region to the Black Sea port of Samsun where they were forcefully boarded at the Ottoman state's expense onto a foreign steamer. Before their expulsion, deportees' photographs were taken and copies left with various government offices to ensure positive identification if the subject were to attempt to reenter Ottoman territory. Because this process predated the international system of mobility control that emerged after World War I, one that through passport and visa requirements necessitated that international travellers secure the permission of their own government and that of their country of destination, it was not incumbent upon the Ottoman state to secure the prior consent of the United States or any other country to which a deportee might travel. Indeed, I have been unable to find any evidence as to the fate of deportees after they were forced out of the empire. While many likely returned to the United States, a large number probably also attempted to clandestinely reenter the empire through one of the many channels discussed in Chapter four. Nevertheless, this policy was hardly unilateral in its implementation. Istanbul's handling of Armenians who returned to the Ottoman Empire was heavily influenced by Washington's position on the status of naturalised US citizens residing in the empire. With the State Department's decision in 1901 to effectively strip naturalised returnees of diplomatic protection, Ottoman officials clearly believed they had a free hand to treat such individuals in any manner they saw fit. The extent to which the Ottoman policy was influenced by the diplomatic stance of the United States government was on full display in an August 1905 document from the cabinet (*Meclis-i Mahsus-u Vükela*) boasting that the American Legation in Istanbul had given its full consent to the practice of deporting Armenian returnees.[94] It is this incipient internationalism, central to Hester's own definition of the term, that leads me to characterise Ottoman policy as deportation.

The policy of deporting returnees from the Harput region long outlasted Fehmi's brief period in office. In June 1907, the United States consul in Harput, Evan Young, reported that the newly appointed governor, Halid, was vigorously deporting newly arrived returnees causing 'great consternation . . . among the (province's) Armenian residents . . .'[95] Two months later, the consul reported that Halid had told him he was 'heartily in favour of permitting all Armenians who had returned to this country some years ago . . . to continue their residence here . . . (but) . . . it would be impossible . . . in the light of his instructions in the matter, to attempt to retain or keep here any Armenians who might hereafter return to this country.'[96] Meanwhile, the Ottoman archival record is full of records attesting to the deportation of Armenian returnees. In 1907 and 1908 in particular, as the July revolution drew near, Istanbul received nearly weekly reports of deportations numbering upwards of a dozen or more at a time.[97] Generally speaking, these reports provide deportees' names and ages, sometimes accompanied by more detailed information such as the year they migrated to the United States and when and how they reentered the empire.[98] These documents together contain the names of approximately one hundred and sixty (160) Armenian returnees who were deported between July 1905 and July 1908, although the actual volume of deportation was likely higher. Most of those deported were recent arrivals, although those who had returned sometimes many years prior were not altogether spared. As will become clearer below, by 1908, returnees found it increasingly difficult to evade deportation, despite the numerous strategies they employed in hopes of doing so.

The Ottoman state's increasingly hardline approach to return migration in the first years of the twentieth century reveals an important evolution in its dealing with questions of ethnic and religious difference. Istanbul's approach to Armenian overseas migration was essentially the inverse of its policies towards Lebanese migration, and corresponded to the respective level of threat Istanbul believed they posed. In addition to Armenians, however, by the beginning of the twentieth century, increasing numbers of Muslims and Assyrian Christians were also migrating between the Ottoman east and North America. Throughout this period, the Ottoman state was concerned primarily with preventing the unauthorised migration of Armenians. Nevertheless, with the exception of the special treatment afforded to Lebanese migrants, it remained outlawed for any Ottoman subject to travel abroad without first obtaining the permission of the Ottoman state. Thus, Muslims and Assyrians attempting to unlawfully depart the empire could, like their Armenian counterparts, expect to be returned to their home communities if caught by the Ottoman authorities. Because Istanbul believed the return of Armenians from North America posed a unique threat, however, its increasingly harsh policies towards Armenian returnees did not apply to Muslims and Assyrians. This difference in approach to returning migrants who often hailed from the same communities in the Ottoman east generated confusion among officials tasked with enforcing state policies on return, and even opened up opportunities for Armenians to avoid debarment and deportation. It also required the Ottoman state to redefine its own ethnic and religious categories in ways that went against centuries of established imperial practice.

Exemplifying this dynamic, in August 1905, three men identified as Muslim natives of Mamuretülaziz province arrived in Samsun after sojourning unlawfully in the United States. The men were in possession of Ottoman passports obtained from the Ottoman consulate in New York. Authorities in the port city wrote to the Ministry of Interior to inquire whether Muslim returnees 'of the labouring classes' were subject to debarment.[99] The ministry responded that the group was to be admitted to the empire and, in line with Ottoman mobility law, subjected to a cash penalty for unauthorised migration. At the same time, it recommended that such returnees be closely vetted to ensure that Armenians were not attempting to reenter the empire with falsified travel documents acquired under assumed Muslim names.[100] In a similar case from June 1906, the Ministry of Police sent a communiqué to the Ministry of Interior asking whether it should deport an individual in their custody, an Assyrian Catholic (Chaldean) from Aleppo province named Wadih. Wadih had just reentered the empire at Beirut with an internal passport acquired in Alexandria after a long sojourn in the United States and Europe.[101] The ministry replied that as an Assyrian, he was not subject to deportation, but like Muslim returnees, *was* subject to the punishment for unauthorised migration stipulated by law.

Meanwhile, in July 1906, the newly appointed governor of Mamuretülaziz province, Halid, sent a brief telegram to the Ministry of Interior asking whether Assyrian returnees in his province were to be subject to deportation. In response, the ministry informed the governor that Assyrians were to be allowed to remain in the empire as long as they provided a signed surety guaranteeing that they would not engage in illegal activity. The reply ended with a warning to provincial officials in Mamuretülaziz to beware of any Armenian returnees who might claim Assyrian identity in order to avoid deportation.[102] In a follow-up telegram, Halid sought further clarification of state policy. Specifically, he inquired as to whether Armenians Protestants and Roman Catholics were to be subject to deportation or if they were to be treated in the same way as Muslims and Assyrians.[103] The governor's question was significant, and cut to the heart of how the Ottoman state defined 'Armenianness' in the context of its policies on migration and return migration. By the late nineteenth century, both Roman Catholics and Protestants were recognised by the Ottoman state as separate and distinct religious communities under the millet system. For much of the empire's history, the term Armenian (*Ermeni*) referred primarily to the Armenian millet, which was comprised of members of the Armenian Apostolic Church. Armenian Catholics and Protestants, although ethnically Armenian, were not members of the Armenian millet, but rather the separate Catholic and Protestant millets. The governor could be forgiven for believing that such individuals might be exempt from a policy that applied only to 'Armenians.'

In response to Halid's inquiry, the Ministry of Interior stated in no uncertain terms that Armenian returnees regardless of sectarian identity were to be subject to deportation.[104] In other words, as far as Ottoman policy on return migration was concerned, Armenian was to be interpreted as an ethnic rather than a sectarian category. The ministry's reply included another important clarification. While Assyrians were exempt from deportation, this only applied to 'natural born' (*'an asıl*) Assyrians who possessed 'no connection to Armenianness' (*Ermenilikle bir münasebeti olmayup*).[105] Armenians who converted to Assyrian Christianity, and thus under Ottoman law became members of the Assyrian millet, were still subject to deportation. The ministry may have been responding to reports that some Armenian returnees were attempting to convert to other sects of Christianity in hopes of avoiding deportation.[106] In applying an ethnicised definition of Armenianness to its policies governing the treatment of return migrants, Istanbul was ironically in alignment with the same Armenian political parties whose alleged power and influence it was seeking to curb by banning both migration and return. For organisations such as the Hunchakian Revolutionary Party and the ARF, creating a shared sense of Armenianness among Apostolic Armenians, Catholics and Protestants was a central goal. This indeed may explain why Istanbul was eager to ensure that the deportation policy was applied to all Armenians regardless of their sectarian identity, given its belief that migration and Armenian political activism were mutually reinforcing phenomena. It was certainly contrary to the empire's long history of favouring sectarian and religious identities in its efforts to classify populations, a practice that would continue until its demise.[107] Nevertheless, the anxiety that migration and return migration generated among the highest echelons of the imperial bureaucracy meant the Ottoman state was constantly willing to employ extraordinary measures to put a stop to them. Istanbul's response to Armenian return, when compared to that of other groups such as the Assyrians and Maronites, also serves as a caution not to assume that treatment of non-Muslims was uniform in this period. Instead, despite Tanzimat-era guarantees of equality under the law for all imperial subjects, wide variations continued to exist across sectarian, ethnic and geographic divides.

As the autocratic rule of Abdülhamid II entered its final years, hundreds of Armenian returnees residing throughout the Harput region and the Ottoman east anxiously wondered whether they would be forced to leave their families and home communities. Most who had naturalised as US citizens were by now well aware that, if faced with deportation, they could expect no assistance from the local American consulate. Those who were not would soon find out that their adopted citizenship no longer counted for much. For many, staying home necessitated devising strategies to evade the authorities, much as they had done while leaving the empire and once again when they returned. In May 1906, for example, a Catholic Church official based in Mamuretülaziz sent a petition to the Ministry of Interior. In it, he requested that a parishioner recently returned after a twelve-year sojourn in the United States be spared deportation. The returnee, the petition stated, was an upstanding individual and was certainly no troublemaker. Moreover, his deportation would have a devastating effect on his family members who risked losing their primary breadwinner.[108] After a brief investigation, the governor of Mamuretülaziz reported that the returnee, identified by the church official as Krikor Misakoğlu, had returned to the region three years earlier and had recently converted to Catholicism in hopes of avoiding deportation. The governor confirmed that Krikor was a family man and a property owner, details that in years past would have been grounds for allowing him to remain in the empire.[109] Regardless, the Ministry of Interior ordered his immediate deportation while reminding Mamuretülaziz that conversions could not be used as a strategy to avoid or delay deportation.[110]

Any lenience the Ottoman state had shown returnees in the past had disappeared by 1905, evidenced by another case in which a returnee with severe injuries to his legs and arms had his request to stay his deportation denied.[111] Even those with ostensibly significant political and economic clout found themselves unable to avoid this fate. In February 1908, M. N. Demirjian, the owner of a large handkerchief factory in the city of Aintab, applied to the US consulate in Iskenderun for protection as a naturalised citizen after Ottoman authorities ordered his deportation. The consul forwarded the request to the consulate general in Istanbul along with a recommendation that an exemption to the policy of denying such individuals diplomatic protection be made as Demirjian's deportation would badly impact the operation of his factory.[112] The Minister Plenipotentiary ignored the consul's recommendation, and refused to extend diplomatic protection to the unfortunate industrialist.[113] For most returnees, the best strategy to avoid deportation was to lay low and avoid contact with state officials as much as possible. In October 1906, the newly appointed governor of Mamuretülaziz, Nuri, complained to the Ministry of Interior that despite all efforts to enforce deportations, families of migrants and village headmen (*muhtarlar*) had taken to actively hiding returnees who had recently arrived in the province from the authorities.[114]

This strategy, however, was not without risk. Given the constant threat of deportation, returnees were vulnerable to everything from denouncement to extortion. For example, in August 1907, the American consul in Harput reported that fourteen returnees residing in a nearby village had been denounced as political subversives by fellow villagers following a dispute between them. The group was arrested by local officials and orders of deportation were brought against them. In response, the consul claimed success in intervening on behalf of the returnees, winning a stay of deportation after he convinced the provincial governor that the accusations levelled against them were false.[115] Meanwhile, as was discussed in Chapter three, in April 1906 an unnamed informant accused a member of the Mamuretülaziz provincial council, Ziya, of accepting bribes from returnees in return for protection from deportation.[116] The governor, Fehmi, was quick to defend Ziya against the allegations, accusing the informant of peddling in scurrilous lies. Nevertheless, given the longstanding practice of provincial officials benefitting handsomely off of abetting clandestine migration, it would be surprising if many were not also using their influence to profit off of desperate returnees seeking to avoid deportation. The now notorious case of the banker Artin Harputlian, who, like Ziya, was a member of the provincial council, certainly points to this having been the case. The eleven returnees at the centre of Harputlian's scheme, all of whom were facing deportation, paid the banker a combined one hundred liras to switch them with another group of Armenians seeking to migrate to the United States.[117] Harputlian's plan could not have been executed without the extensive involvement of wide swaths of the provincial bureaucracy, a fact that contributed to the governor's vigorous pursuit of the case against the banker and his allies.

By the beginning of 1908, the threat of deportation had cast a pall over many communities in the Harput region. In some places, anxiety was beginning to spill over into outright resistance. In May 1908, the governor of Erzurum sent a telegram to the Ministry of Interior. In it, he claimed that an Armenian church official in Kiğı was encouraging Armenians in the district to protest deportations by congregating outside of the local government building and collectively confessing to having returned from unlawful sojourns abroad while calling for an end to the practice.[118] The governor concluded his message by warning that further problems could ensue if the troublemaking official was allowed to remain in the district. The governor's accusations, which the Armenian Patriarchate in Istanbul vigorously denied, suggest that three years after Ottoman officials began deporting returnees in earnest, a sense of both desperation and anger was beginning to take hold in communities in the Harput region.[119] As political turmoil gripped the empire, building to a revolutionary crescendo in July of 1908, the threat of collective resistance to the deportation policy was no doubt concerning to both the governor of Erzurum and to Istanbul. In the Harput region that summer, news of revolution marking an end to over three decades of autocratic rule was followed less than a month later by an official order issued by the newly installed constitutional government bringing an end to the practice of deporting returnees. The sense of relief in the region must have been palpable. A new, more optimistic era appeared to be just on the horizon.[120]

Conclusion

To the leaders of the July 1908 revolution that stripped Sultan Abdülhamid II of his autocratic powers, his regime's policies towards migration and return migration were symptomatic of the deep-seated backwardness and despotism they saw as hallmarks of his rule. By lifting the *ancien regime's* policies governing both migration and return soon after taking power, the newly formed constitutional government assumed that they were bringing the empire more in line with principles of free mobility and commerce they believed to be essential markers of civilised and modern statecraft. Stripped of its broader global context, the Hamidian regime's handling of Armenian mobility in particular may indeed seem like nothing more than outgrowths of the sultan's notorious paranoia and heavy-handedness. But to dismiss it as such would risk missing how these policies paralleled a broader shift towards the emergence of an international 'melancholy order' of immigrant restriction, militarisation of borders and deportation in the twentieth and twenty-first century. As migration historians have noted, the United States was very much a forerunner in this regard. By the early twentieth century, its policies increasingly served as a model for other countries in their efforts at restriction. Istanbul was deeply familiar with these developments, and viewed its efforts to prevent Armenians from returning to their homes in the Anatolian interior as fundamentally similar to those driving immigration restriction in the United States. It is this sense that motivated the Ottoman Ambassador Mavroyeni's diplomatic and public relations efforts during the controversy over the treatment of US citizen returnees in the mid-1890s. Clearly, the Ottoman state was not entirely wrong in its thinking. By the first years of the twentieth century, Washington had largely forsaken its naturalised citizens who had returned to the empire, largely because like the Ottomans they increasingly viewed these returnees as troublemakers, subversives and fraudulent citizens. This alignment in policy between the two governments eventually allowed the Ottoman state to enforce a hardline deportation policy directed against these returnees, particularly in the aftermath of the assassination attempt on Abdülhamid II. Hardly a reflection of its fundamental backwardness, then, the Ottoman response to Armenian return migration in this era was in many ways ahead of its time. Meanwhile, the Hamidian regime's constitutionalist successors would quickly discover that it was their own liberal approach to mobility whose days were increasingly numbered.

PART III. REVOLUTION, GENOCIDE AND THE LEGACIES OF MIGRATION

The news that Sultan Abdülhamid II had reinstated the long dormant Ottoman constitution hit like a bombshell. The air was thick with optimism and the joy was palpable. Armenians marched through the streets of Istanbul with giant banners adorned with revolutionary slogans written in Ottoman Turkish and Armenian. Similar scenes played out in Salonica, Beirut and Izmir as Muslims and non-Muslims, Arabs and Jews, Greeks and Assyrians all felt a reason to celebrate. As news trickled into the Harput region about the heady events that had taken place in the imperial capital, a sense of cautious excitement began to take hold. The last several years had taken their toll on the region's Armenian communities. In village after village, stories circulated about people who had returned from long sojourns in North America, only to be deported upon being discovered by local authorities. Some barely had enough time to embrace their loved ones whom they hadn't seen in years before having to pack their bags once again, this time against their will. Meanwhile, young migrants seeking to make their way to North America for the first time were travelling as far as Beirut in hopes they could be smuggled aboard a foreign steamer waiting off shore. The cost of migrating had skyrocketed as the Hamidian regime ratcheted up their enforcement of the ban on Armenian migration to North America. Might the restoration of the constitution relieve the weary Armenian communities of the Harput region from this increasingly intolerable situation? The question lingered in the minds of many.

For Yankob,[1] Kirkor and Giragos, news of the revolution seemed almost too good to be true. The three men, all from the same village just outside of Harput/Mezre, had returned to the region two years earlier from sojourns in the United States. Like so many of their fellow villagers, the benefits of spending a few years away from home toiling in the factories of a strange land outweighed the many risks. But the pull of home was strong, and after a few years abroad, the three friends agreed that it was time to go home. The trip back proved much more difficult than the journey that had taken them to North America. The weeks-long wait on Cyprus for a boatman willing to drop them on an empty and unpatrolled stretch of beach had seemed like an eternity. The overland trip from the rocky stretch of coastline outside of Silifke through Adana and back home to the Harput region was especially harrowing. They were unprepared, however, for the nightmare that awaited them upon their return. It was hardly a secret in town that the three, like so many others in the village, had been in the United States illegally. The local gendarmes threatened to inform the provincial government of their return, which meant almost certain deportation. While each of the three men had saved a not insignificant amount of money while abroad, they found themselves spending much of it bribing local officials to keep their mouths shut. Over the course of the two years they had been back, no fewer than five of their fellow villagers had been arrested and deported from the empire. While two had managed to sneak back in, this was a fate the three friends wanted to avoid at all costs. Thus, news of the events in Istanbul gave them a sense of optimism of a sort they had not felt in a long time. When the new government talked about the restoration of constitutional rights, a return to the rule of law, and a general amnesty for those who had been jailed for political reasons under the old regime, it seemed as if they might finally have the chance to live freely and in the open without fear of deportation.

At the end of July 1908, the three friends travelled to the government telegraph office in Mezre and sent a telegram directly to the office of the grand vizier. In it, they admitted to having travelled to the United States 'for purposes of trade,' and to having returned to the empire two years earlier. They then proceeded to inquire, using none of the indirect language and rhetorical flourishes that usually graced such communications with the central Ottoman state, whether the 'extra legal' threat of 'deportation by force' had been lifted with the general amnesty for political crimes the new government had recently issued.[2] When a response arrived three weeks later, the three breathed a sigh of relief: they and all like them were included in the amnesty. A new day had truly dawned; the fear and anxiety that they had lived with for the past two years had quite suddenly been lifted.[3]

The revolutionary government strove to break firmly with the practices of their autocratic predecessors. The liberalisation of policies governing migration and mobility was a key way to do so. As the story above suggests, the effects of these new policies was felt almost immediately in the Harput region, demonstrating the power that even a weak state such as the

Ottoman Empire had in shaping the migration process. As both migration and return became much easier, the number of people circulating around the region (and the empire more broadly) increased significantly. This invited a new set of challenges, especially as the commitment to freedom of migration bumped up against the many threats and crises facing the constitutional regime. The promise of July 1908 would by the early 1910s give way to a new grim reality of perpetual war, territorial loss and political unrest. The Armenians who returned in record numbers to their home communities in the Anatolian interior in the years between 1908 and 1914 would find themselves the target of a much more vicious and violent policy of deportation than that seen during the Hamidian period, this one now directed at the region's entire Armenian population. The infant Turkish Republic's introduction of new bans on Armenian migration and return in the post-war period, meanwhile, while faintly echoing those of the Hamidian regime, would serve an entirely different purpose.

6

Revolution

True to its promise, the constitutional revolution of July 1908 marked a radical break from the past. Mere days after Sultan Abdülhamid II restored the Ottoman Constitution, which had been suspended since 1876, most of the strict restrictions on domestic and international mobility that had been key facets of his autocratic rule were lifted. The ban on Armenian migration to North America, in place since 1888, would not be enforced. Between 1908 and 1914, no longer forced to leave the empire clandestinely, Armenians flocked to North America in unprecedented numbers. Ottomans from Salonica to Jerusalem also took advantage of their newfound freedom to travel, joining what by the start of the second decade of the twentieth century was becoming an increasingly dramatic exodus. At the same time, the number of Ottoman subjects returning to the empire also spiked. This was especially true for Armenian migrants who no longer faced debarment or deportation if they returned. Furthermore, evidence suggests that following the 1908 revolution, Armenian returnees felt more emboldened to purchase lands, expand homes and open businesses with the money they earned while sojourning abroad, thus contributing to the rapid transformation of the economic landscape of the Harput region.

Although no longer engaged in a concerted effort to prevent its own subjects from migrating overseas, state power continued to shape the migration process in numerous, if often more subtle ways. Perhaps most notably, the clandestine migration networks that had been key to facilitating Armenian migration in the face of the Hamidian-era ban were quickly rendered unnecessary. This does not mean the many intermediaries that comprised these networks disappeared altogether. Instead, the migration business became much more visible as travel agents and steamship ticket sellers opened offices throughout the empire. The spatial dynamics of migration also underwent a profound change now that migrants could transit freely through Ottoman ports. Regions that hitherto had seen relatively low migration rates increasingly took advantage of the new government's liberal policies. Almost immediately, however, Istanbul's commitment to the principle of freedom of travel (*serbest-i seyr-ü seyahat*) came under challenge from numerous directions. Provincial officials, accustomed to the draconian policies of the Hamidian era, struggled to accommodate themselves to a radically different mobility control regime. Meanwhile, just as Istanbul began relaxing its policies on migration, new laws were going into effect in the United States aimed at tightening its immigration restrictions and border control efforts. As a result, the constitutional government quickly found itself dealing with an epidemic of Ottoman migrants stranded in European transit ports, unable to secure passage across the Atlantic. Finally, as the 1910s dawned, a decade in which the empire would find itself engaged in nearly perpetual warfare, the Ottoman state was faced with the acute dilemma of balancing its commitment to upholding the freedom to travel with its rapidly increasing need for military manpower. Thus, just as was the case in the Hamidian era, the constitutional government found its policies on mobility and migration frustrated by numerous, often insuperable challenges and contradictions.

The first half of this Chapter expands beyond the focus on Armenian migration that anchors the rest of this book to focus on migration throughout the empire following the 1908 revolution. The reason for this shift is simple: in stark contrast to the Hamidian regime, the constitutional government, in which several members of once outlawed Armenian political organisations had been elected to parliament, did not view Armenian migration as posing a distinct and special threat to the empire. Instead, after 1908, Istanbul's concerns about the rapidly increasing rate of Ottoman subjects travelling abroad applied regardless of the ethnic and religious identities of individual migrants. The focus returns to the Harput region in the second half of the Chapter. A mere seven years after the 1908 revolution inspired many in the empire with the promise of a liberal and tolerant constitutional order, in the midst of the First World War, a government headed by authoritarian-minded members of the Committee of Union and Progress (CUP), the organisation that spearheaded the revolution, oversaw the genocidal destruction of much of the empire's Armenian population. This unspeakable tragedy brought an abrupt end to the transhemispheric sojourns that had reshaped the Harput region's society, economy and politics. Nevertheless, Armenians left a significant legacy behind in the form of land and other property, much of it acquired through money earned in North America. As the second part of this Chapter argues, the government of the Turkish Republic, founded after the demise of the Ottoman Empire in 1922, feared that Armenians might return to seek compensation for or the restoration of lost property. To prevent this, they turned to many of the same strategies employed by their Hamidian counterparts to keep them out. These efforts largely succeeded, ensuring that these ill-gotten spoils of war and genocide could be put to use in the project to engineer a new order out of the embers of the imperial past.

Defining Freedom of Movement

On 1 August 1908, the Ministry of Interior circulated a telegram throughout the empire announcing the new government's intent to nullify all *ancien régime* migration policies that did not strictly adhere to Tanzimat-era laws governing mobility and the issuing of travel documents.[1] While these laws remained in effect throughout the Hamidian era, Istanbul's widely variable approach to the overseas migration (and return migration) of its Lebanese and Armenian subjects was in clear violation of the Tanzimat principle of legal equality. By once again aligning state policies with established law, the constitutional government was signalling very early on its intent to uphold the rule of law, something they believed had lapsed under Abdülhamid II's autocratic rule. Tanzimat-era Ottoman law did not outlaw mobility *per se*, and thus in its strictest interpretation it did not contradict the constitutional regime's commitment to freedom of travel.[2] The decision to leave the 1860s law in place was likely a temporary legal stopgap until parliamentary elections were held and new permanent legislation could be drafted. Regardless, the decision, issued less than ten days after Adbülhamid II had restored the constitution, marked an end to the discriminatory policies that had shaped both Armenian migration and return migration since the late 1880s.

For state officials who had long been at the centre of the Ottoman state's mobility control efforts, the telegram and the new government's policies towards mobility more broadly, left many questions unanswered. What would become of Hamidian-era efforts to militarise and fortify the empire's land and sea borders? What did the new government's policy of freedom of mobility mean for the *ancien regime's* sophisticated system of document-based mobility control? How would the constitutional regime handle issues such as return migration and citizenship? A few days after the circulation of the telegram outlining the new policy, the Ministry of War sought clarification of the new government's approach to ensuring the security of the empire's coasts. The ministry's request was motivated, in part, by a recent decision from Istanbul disbanding the pier commissions that the Hamidian regime had created in several port cities on both the Black and Mediterranean Sea coasts. This move had evidently generated a great deal of uncertainty among officials stationed in many of the empire's major ports about where responsibility fell for manning the coastal surveillance towers and police boats that, before the revolution, had been central to state efforts to combat smuggling and other illegal activities.[3] In a series of responses sent to the governors of various coastal provinces, the Ministry of Interior's response indicated that such questions would no longer be a central concern for Istanbul. Instead, it stated that responsibility for such efforts was to be left entirely to the discretion of provincial governments. It appeared that the resource-intensive efforts of the Hamidian regime to fortify the coasts did not align with the new government's more liberal approach to both mobility and commerce.[4]

Also symptomatic of the constitutional government's radical break was its position on the use of travel documents such as the internal passport (*mürur tezkeresi*) and the passport (*pasaport*). These documents had been the backbone of both Tanzimat and Hamidian-era efforts to police internal and international mobility. Despite its limitations, for Abdülhamid's autocratic regime in particular, the internal passport system was an important surveillance mechanism and an essential tool in maintaining social and political order. To the newly installed constitutional government, however, travel documents embodied the oppressiveness and illiberalism of the *ancien régime*. Although mandated by the still-in-effect Mobility and Passport Law, the passport – and especially the internal passport – were quickly falling into disfavour as instruments of mobility control.

For some state officials long accustomed to the draconian policies of the Hamidian era, the pace of change was bewildering. In October 1908, officials in Beirut sent a telegram to the Ministry of Interior inquiring whether a group of non-Muslims (*gayr-i müslim ahali*) should be granted internal passports for travel to Alexandria. Local officials, the telegram stated, had reason to suspect that the group was not actually seeking to travel to the Egyptian port city, but rather intended to migrate clandestinely to the United States (*Amerika'ya savuşacakları*). The short message ended with a warning that the group probably included military deserters (*asker firarileri*) trying to flee the empire.[5] The ministry responded with a reminder that it was no longer against the law for Ottoman nationals to migrate to the United States, and ordered Beirut to issue passports to the group that were valid for international travel. Meanwhile, the ministry's reply continued, because non-Muslims were not yet required to serve in the Ottoman military, it was only necessary to confirm the service status of Muslims seeking permission to travel abroad. A law mandating military service for all, regardless of religious affiliation, would not pass the Ottoman Parliament until October 1909.[6] Thus, in an ironic shift from the policies of the Hamidian era, the ministry's response implied that only Muslims were to face possible restrictions on overseas travel, at least until conscription was extended to include all imperial subjects twelve months later. Fears about military desertion would soon bedevil the constitutional regime's liberal approach to migration. For the time being, however, the exchange of telegrams revealed that issues that had been a central concern of the Hamidian-era state, such as the fraudulent use of internal passports, no longer had much relevance to a government that viewed these documents as fundamentally illegitimate. Indeed, the Ottoman Parliament would officially abolish the internal passport in early 1910, marking an official end to documentary controls on domestic mobility.[7]

Less clear was the role the (international) passport would now play in Ottoman migration policy moving forward. For some in the new government, requiring those who desired to travel abroad to be in possession of a passport upon departure was an intolerable infringement on individual liberty. Nonetheless, Istanbul continued to demand them from those who sought to enter the empire, whether Ottoman national or foreigner. In November 1908, the Ministry of Interior ordered that imperial subjects who arrived at a port of entry without a (Ottoman) passport be admitted only upon positive confirmation of their identity and the payment of a fine.[8] Two years later, the passport would become a central issue of debate in the Ottoman Parliament as it worked to draft a new passport law. At the heart of the debate was whether the law should require (*mecburî*) Ottoman nationals to obtain passports for international travel or whether the documents should be made voluntary (*ihtiyarî*). For many members of the newly created legislative body, the debate struck at the heart of the meaning and contours of the constitutional guarantee of individual liberty. Rıza Tevfik, an MP from Edirne and a firm supporter of making passports optional, boldly proclaimed: 'It is not the business of a (constitutional) government to know where I am going and what I am doing. The government will extend protections to me only if I wish it to and if I call on it to do so.'[9] In contrast, Mehmet Talat, the MP from Ankara arguing in favour of mandatory passports declared: 'I understand where Rıza Tevfik is coming from; he is one of those liberal extremists (*müfrit hürriyetperverandandır*). We have already abolished the internal passport. It's getting to the point that (*o raddeye getirelim*) we will end up getting rid of the police and gendarmerie along with the passport . . . we might as well be setting all the criminals (*erbab-i ceraim*) free.'[10] Artas Yorgaki of Salonica, meanwhile, argued in favour of a passport requirement as a necessary response to the increasingly harsh restrictionist policies being adopted by the United

States and other countries. Doing so, he hoped, would help Istanbul to manage a growing crisis involving Ottoman migrants who were stranded in European transit ports after being denied passage to the Americas.[11]

As the debate continued into the early months of 1911, those in support of the passport requirement would include everything from the added revenue from passport fees that would accrue to the state's distressed coffers to fears of terrorism to their list of arguments.[12] At the heart of the disagreement over passports were questions about the meaning of constitutional government: was constitutionalism first and foremost about protecting the liberty of the individual, or was it primarily concerned with guaranteeing the security and prosperity of society as a whole? The law that eventually passed parliament in 1911 made obtaining the documents optional for Ottoman subjects who desired to travel abroad. At the same time, included in the text of the legislation was the Ministry of Interior's 1908 order subjecting those who returned to the empire without a passport to a fine.[13] The decision to include this wording reflected an emerging consensus among Ottoman parliamentarians that passports possessed value as identification documents and as mechanisms for raising much needed revenue. In this way, the passport survived the revolution and its aftermath, albeit in much diminished form, with little value as an instrument for enforcing migration policy, its primary function before 1908.

In the years immediately following 1908, as Ottomans increasingly took advantage of the constitutional government's laissez faire approach to both domestic and international mobility, state officials worked to adjust themselves to a radically different migration control regime than the one that had existed in the Hamidian era. As Istanbul would soon discover, however, its embrace of liberal mobility policies came at a global historical moment that would put its philosophical commitment to guaranteeing freedom of travel under increasing strain.

Ottoman Liberalism, American Restrictionism

The constitutional government's embrace of a liberal approach to international migration was an object lesson in bad timing. In many ways, Hamidan-era efforts to curtail mobility through the use of documents, followed by its attempts to create a robust border security infrastructure, foreshadowed developments that would come to define the twentieth century international system of mobility and border control. As the century dawned, however, the principles of nineteenth century liberalism in which freedom of mobility was seen as a basic liberty and as a benchmark of enlightened government continued to shape the politics of migration in both Europe and the Americas.[14] Even when these freedoms were denied to entire groups of people, this discourse was mobilised to justify such practices. In the 1880s, for example, the United States government justified the policies of Chinese exclusion on the grounds that Chinese migrants were inherently unfree. In denying them the right to enter its sovereign territory, so the argument went, the US government was defending liberal values against those who by dint of their race and backward civilisation were incapable of being truly free.[15] At the same time, in the late nineteenth century, 'liberal' powers such as the United States and Great Britain viewed with contempt the restrictions on domestic and international mobility employed by the Russian, Ottoman and Qing empires, pointing to them as further evidence of the inherent backwardness and despotism that prevailed in these countries.[16] The constitutional government's embrace of freedom of mobility after the revolution was intended not only as a radical break with the *ancien régime*, but also signalled an intention to bring the Ottoman policy in line with that of nineteenth century liberal modernity.

Yet the 1908 revolution took place against the backdrop of a rapid shift in the United States and other immigrant receiving societies towards increasingly harsh and expansive restrictions on immigration. In the United States, the Immigration Act of 1903 followed by another immigration act four years later, targeted suspected anarchists, beggars, pimps, epileptics and carriers of infections diseases for restriction. After 1912, the US government began requiring that those seeking admission pass a literacy test. These laws clearly targeted immigrant groups from Southern and Eastern Europe and the Middle East who were believed to be less educated and more susceptible to political radicalisation and to infectious disease than their counterparts originating from countries further to the west and north.[17] The laws also targeted the steamship companies, increasingly the recipients of American ire for their alleged role in profiting off of and even encouraging large-scale overseas migration from Europe. The 1903 Immigration Act allowed US officials to fine these companies one-hundred dollars for each 'diseased immigrant' they brought to American shores if that individual's illness 'could have been detected at the port of departure.' The 1907 Immigration Act expanded these categories of excludable immigrants to include 'idiots, imbeciles, epileptics, and tuberculous aliens.'[18] By 1910, steamship companies were compelled to conduct rigorous health examinations before allowing immigrant passengers aboard in order to avoid such fines and penalties.

The effects of the 1903 and 1907 Immigration Acts were just making themselves felt as the new Ottoman government was lifting nearly all *ancien régime* restrictions on overseas migration. In November 1908, the Foreign Ministry forwarded a report from the Ottoman consulate in Liverpool to the Ministry of Interior that discussed the growing number of Ottoman migrants bound for the United States who had become stranded in the port city, unable to secure passage for the final leg of their trip. According to the consul, steamship companies were refusing to sell tickets to these migrants, fearing that they might be infected with trachoma or would be declared likely to become a 'public charge,' both of which were grounds for debarment from the United States under the Immigration Act of 1907. The report ended with translations of portions of the 1907 act that dealt with classes of immigrants who were likely 'to be excluded from admission into the United States.' It was hoped that that if individuals contemplating migrating to the United States understood American law, they might be more reluctant to do so.[19] Acting on the recommendations of both the Liverpool consulate and the Foreign Ministry, the Ministry of Interior forwarded translated copies of the law to all provincial governments. It then recommended that the governors take steps to warn the populations of their respective provinces about the challenges faced by those seeking to travel to the United States.[20]

The problem would only worsen as the months passed. In May 1909, the Ottoman consul in Marseille sent a report to the Foreign Ministry complaining about the large numbers of Ottoman migrants in that city who, like those in Liverpool, had been stranded after being denied steamship passage to the United States. While not 'holding back from discharging the legally mandated aid and assistance' to these migrants, the consul declared that the 25–30 liras it cost to purchase return tickets to the Ottoman Empire for such individuals was beginning to cause severe strain on his office's financial resources. He then questioned the efficacy of the revolutionary government's policy towards migration, stating:

> Before (the revolution) people, especially Armenians, were often denied permission to migrate from one place to another within the empire's borders to say nothing about their ability to travel abroad. If they wanted to seek their fortune overseas, they were forced to leave the empire clandestinely (*suret-i hafiyede*). Now following the reinstatement of the constitution, nothing is stopping them from just hopping on the next available ship and going wherever they wish. It is not appropriate for such individuals to migrate without a passport and without sufficient travel funds, and it is the primary reason why so many of them find themselves plunged into penury when they arrive here.[21]

As to what concrete steps the government should take to address this issue, the consul remained rather circumspect. He suggested only that the situation was untenable and requested information on how to handle the dozens of stranded migrants waiting outside his office hoping to receive assistance.[22] The consul would be much more direct in his recommendations the following year. In February 1910, he once again wrote to the Foreign Ministry complaining that his office was overwhelmed with 'Muslim villagers with minds filled with ridiculous dreams of wealth,' who after selling their lands in Anatolia to finance voyages to the United States had become stranded in Marseille. In the brief, tersely written note, the consul recommended that such individuals be restricted in their ability to travel abroad.[23] In a similarly sparse response, the Ministry of Interior reminded the consul that in the absence of a law prohibiting migration, there was nothing the ministry could do to prevent them from leaving the empire.[24]

The Ottoman consuls in Liverpool and Marseille had front row seats from which to observe the effects of the United States' harsher restrictionist policies. The passage of the Immigration Act of 1907 had led to a substantial increase in the number of migrants denied entry to the United States, or who found themselves unable to board steamships in European transit ports.[25] In 1910 alone, for example, agents of the British Cunard Line rejected nearly five thousand ticketed immigrant passengers attempting to depart the Hapsburg port of Fiume (today Rijeka in Croatia) after the American consul there warned that immigrants denied entry to the United States would be returned to Europe on the company's dime.[26] Doubtless many Ottoman migrants were among those denied passage. Indeed, in 1913, the Ottoman consul in Fiume sent a long report to the Foreign Ministry about the increasing challenges Ottoman immigrants were facing as a result of these restrictionist policies. The diplomat identified common medical conditions such as atherosclerosis and swelling of the lymph nodes as grounds for steamship companies to deny passage to Ottomans seeking to travel to the United States.[27] Consular officials were not the only ones to take note of the impact of these policies on Ottoman migrants en route to the United States. Sarkis Narzakian, who migrated from the Harput region to the United States in the late 1890s, transited through Marseille in 1910 on his way back home for a brief visit. While in the city, he encountered a significant number of Ottoman Armenians waiting to travel to the United States. In his memoir published nearly a half century later, he wrote:

> The immigrants going to America from Marseille had to pass a physical examination showing that they were physically fit and able to endure hard labor . . . Many had been waiting for this examination for days . . . Many had been totally

> rejected for immigration and had to return to their homes. Some having passed all difficulties did not have the required money for a ticket when a boat was available, the money having been spent during their prolonged stay. They were waiting for money from friends, sometimes waiting for weeks or months. And in the homeland, their loved ones were waiting for news from them, and along with the news perhaps some money to live on, while the poor immigrants were exhausted waiting for help. The longer these unfortunate ones stayed, the more profitable it was for the simsars (intermediaries), for when the expected money arrived, they, the simsars, collected their demands first. If the remaining money was still not enough for the boat ticket, they had to again ask for help from America, and it went on and on . . .[28]

Six months later, Narzakian would once again pass through Marseille on his way back to the United States. While there he encountered many of the same migrants still stranded in the city awaiting passage to the United States. Robert Mirak, meanwhile, notes that middlemen in Marseille were making a hefty profit off of selling forged bills of health to migrants desperate to escape the Kafkaesque transit port limbo that was becoming an increasingly common experience in the aftermath of the Immigration Act of 1907.[29] Ironically for the constitutional government – and tragically for Ottoman migrants – Istanbul was removing barriers to mobility just as the United States (along with many other immigrant receiving societies) was erecting and fortifying barriers of its own. During the nineteenth century the extent to which a government could be considered civilised was measured by the degree to which it viewed free mobility and commerce as a virtue. By the beginning of the second decade of the twentieth century, it was becoming increasingly clear that a new world order, one based more on the restriction and exclusion of certain migrating groups, was beginning to take shape. For the constitutional government and its commitment to freedom of mobility, this could not have come at a worse time. Meanwhile, other pressing issues were also beginning to test Istanbul's commitment to liberal migration policies.

Of Individual Liberties and Patriotic Duties

The victory of the more liberal voices in the parliamentary debate over the passport law hardly quieted those who advocated for a more restrictive approach to internal and international mobility. In fact, circumstances were adding grist to the mill for those within the Ottoman government who supported this position. A tension was beginning to emerge between constitutional guarantees of individual liberty and a growing sense that all Ottomans were duty bound to serve imperial society and the state that represented it. At the same time, in many sectors of Ottoman society, the initial wave of optimism that followed the revolution was beginning to give way to serious doubts about the empire's direction in the months and years that followed. After October 1909, non-Muslims could no longer pay an exemption tax (*bedel-i askeriye*) to avoid mandatory military service as they had been permitted to do since 1856. For those who had supported the legislation encoding this change into law, the argument in favour of it was self-evident: those who benefitted from the constitutional order that provided liberty to all citizens regardless of religious or ethnic background should be willing to defend it with their lives. Unbeknownst to the Ottoman Parliament, the bill passed on the eve of the most destructive, crisis-ridden decade in the history of the empire, one that would end in its demise. Meanwhile, Ottoman troops were already engaged in efforts to quell a bloody revolt led by Druze peasants in the province of Damascus, and several months later they would be called on to crush a rebellion in Albania. In 1911, Italy invaded Libya, triggering a war that lasted nearly a full year, and ended with the empire losing its final toehold on the African continent. The following year, after a humiliating defeat at the hands of its former provinces in the Balkans, the Ottomans were all but expelled from Europe. These catastrophic wars strained the empire's resources to the breaking point, hastening the end of the constitutional experiment. In January 1913, authoritarian-minded members of the Committee of Union and Progress (CUP), the political party that had spearheaded the revolution, seized control in a bloody coup.

These wars forced the Ottoman state to make extraordinary demands from a reluctant population of military-aged men, many of whom if given the choice would not have made the ultimate sacrifice for a government they did not fully trust.[30] For those who sought to avoid conscription in the years preceding World War I, Istanbul's relatively liberal migration policies presented them with an opportunity to do so. Draft dodging appears to have been a significant driver of emigration from the Ottoman Empire between 1910 and 1914, although it is not clear to what degree this was the case.[31] Both Ottoman and American archival sources attribute much of the spike in overseas migration in this period to the escape of military-aged men.[32] Meanwhile, figures provided by the United States Immigration Commission for the years following the 1908 revolution show a dramatic increase in Armenians entering the United States from a low of three thousand in 1911 to more than nine thousand in 1913, a jump that coincided with the disastrous Balkan Wars.[33] More tellingly, between 1909 and 1914, a greater percentage of Armenian migrants admitted to the United States were male when compared to the period preceding 1908.[34]

As the 1910s dawned, increasing rates of military desertion combined with the epidemic of Ottoman migrants stranded in European transit ports was increasingly tilting the intragovernmental debate in favour of tighter restrictions on mobility.

As early as the summer of 1910, just after the expansion of mandatory military service to include non-Muslims, officials in several Ottoman port cities were sounding alarms about the exodus of military-aged men.[35] In response, the Department of the Census, the government office responsible for military recruitment, recommended that those who requested the documents not be granted passports unless it was determined that they had completed their military service.[36] Apparently unsatisfied with such measures, voices from various corners of the Ottoman bureaucracy pressured the state to be more proactive in its efforts to prevent desertion and other problematic forms of mobility. In September 1910, the grand vizier responded to one such suggestion from the consul on Corfu who recommended that port city officials be required to issue a document (*pusula*) to all Ottoman subjects travelling within the empire by ship that indicated the bearer's final destination. Travellers would then be required to present the document to officials based in the indicated destination. The grand vizier's response to the consul reflected Istanbul's continued reluctance to adopt any measure that might limit the freedom of both domestic and international mobility. 'Your idea of tasking port city officials with issuing such documents to travelers,' he wrote, 'amounts to the reinstitution (*yeniden tatbik*) of the internal passport system, which the state has already abolished (*devletçe lağvedilmiştir*).' The grand vizier ended by reiterating Istanbul's opposition to any measures that might 'frustrate mobility and travel' (*tesib-i seyrüseyahat*).[37]

Yet as the epidemic of desertions worsened at the same time that military pressures on the empire were growing, cracks began to emerge within the highest echelons of the bureaucracy over the government's policies towards migration. In October 1911, officials within the Foreign Ministry and Ministry of War pressured the grand vizier to take more concrete action to prevent desertion, including tightening restrictions on travel. In response, he doubled down on his opposition to any effort to limit freedom of mobility. Nevertheless, he provided a series of recommendations for how to address the problem. In a long communiqué, the grand vizier stated:

> Any effort to prevent deserters from traveling to America or other foreign countries that also restricts freedom of mobility would not be viewed favourably by this office. When the annual call for conscripts begins, our foreign consulates should inform those individuals living in their consular districts

> who have yet to complete their service that they must do so. All necessary legal measures will be taken against those who refuse or ignore the call to serve. Steps must be taken to ensure that people, the peasantry in particular (*ahalinin bilhassa köylülerin*), are not seduced (*iğfalata kapılmamaları*) by those who seek to encourage migration. To achieve this, local governments should post written statements in the public areas of every town and village informing the public that those who are not in good health or do not have sufficient financial means will not be permitted into the United States. They must be aware of the challenges that they may face over the course of their journey that could render them penniless and desperate.[38]

In proposing the public information campaign outlined in his report, the grand vizier hoped to stem the twin epidemics of military desertion and migrant stranding without simultaneously impinging on the right to travel. It also revealed an emerging belief that a wide range of unscrupulous actors including travel agents, labour recruiters and shipping company representatives were responsible for much of the uptick in migration rates. The constitutional government was acutely aware of the important role such intermediaries played in the vast clandestine migration networks that emerged in response to the restrictionist policies of the Hamidian era. Indeed, this was used as an argument against adopting similar measures for fear that they might 'lead people to rely on exploitative informal channels' and 'open the door to corruption.'[39] Nevertheless, while the constitutional government's policies meant that migrants no longer had to rely on clandestine channels to leave and reenter the empire, they also provided opportunities for new (and less risky) ways to cash in on the migration business. In the Balkan port of Salonica alone, since 1908, twenty-five separate travel agencies had opened up shop in the city centre catering to prospective migrants from throughout the empire.[40] It was the grand vizier's hope that a public education campaign might prevent Ottoman subjects from falling victim to those trying to profit off of encouraging migration.

Concerns were indeed rife that the clandestine migration networks of the Hamidian era were giving way to a host of new intermediaries seeking to profit off of legal migration. The Foreign Ministry, citing a report from the consulate in Marseille, put the blame for the growing number of Ottoman nationals stranded in European transit ports squarely on the shoulders of those involved in the migration business, accusing them of encouraging overseas migration among those who lacked sufficient financial and physical means to do so. The ministry, quoting a government report that had pointedly accused such intermediaries of 'duping and swindling simpleminded folk (*sade-dilan ahaliyi teşvik ve iğfal*) for nothing but self gain and profit,' recommended that their operations 'either be stopped or brought under the strictest regulation as can be legally allowed.'[41] Meanwhile, the Ministry of Interior was bewildered that would-be migrants would turn to such 'exploitative channels' in an environment where 'freedom of mobility, labour and commerce' were guaranteed.[42] Their doing so raised questions as to whether these migrants were truly leaving of their own free will, or if these intermediaries were in fact compelling them to travel abroad. Similar questions had been central in the debate over immigrant restriction in other liberal polities such as the United States in the late nineteenth and early twentieth centuries. One of the key justifications for Chinese exclusion arose from the argument that Chinese migrants were not truly free, but were instead unwittingly fallen victim to unscrupulous labour recruiters who then forced them into indenture to pay for their travel debts. While the prevalence of this practice among Chinese migrants was grossly (and deliberately) exaggerated, as McKeown notes, this perception 'perpetuated an understanding of all Asian and especially Chinese migration as somehow illegitimate and unfree.'[43] In a similar vein, Ottoman officials at the highest levels of government were beginning to question whether 'simple minded folk,' when face-to-face with similarly unscrupulous, profit-driven travel agents, were truly migrating of their own free will.

By proposing a campaign to raise awareness about the dangers of overseas migration and of trusting those promoting it, the grand vizier hoped he had found a strategy to deal with military desertion and migrant strandings while at the same time preserving freedom of travel. Furthermore, a truly educated and informed population would no doubt understand the relative benefits of staying put and contributing to the maintenance and strengthening of the constitutional order. This logic underpinned a document titled 'An Announcement from the Provincial Governor Regarding Those Going to America,' circulated throughout the empire as part of this public awareness campaign.[44] It presented a particularly macabre picture of the dangers of migration, warning: 'the majority of Ottomans going to America are unable even to find a crumb to eat and are therefore left in a state of the most abject despair. The number of people who die, many by their own hand, because of their desperate situation outnumber those who return (to the empire) with money in their pockets more than a hundred to one.' It urged prospective migrants not to fall victim to 'those migration agents who tramp around . . . swindling ignorant folk and with no other goal in mind but making a buck.' Instead, it proclaimed: 'the factories need you, the Ottoman state's honourable military needs you . . . this government is nothing like its predecessor. It is . . . compassionate and just.'[45]

The language in the document reflected a broader change underway in the post-revolutionary regime's vision of constitutional government. In the euphoria that immediately followed the reinstatement of the constitution, the new government engaged in an ambitious effort to turn the lofty revolutionary slogans of liberty, equality, justice and brotherhood into a practical reality. Enshrining the principle of freedom to travel in Ottoman governance had been part and parcel of that broader effort. The ruling CUP, however, was a conservative organisation that, since its inception, was concerned first and foremost with safeguarding the stability of the empire and its territorial integrity.[46] By 1910, facing a series of internal and external challenges to its power, the CUP's attention increasingly turned towards issues of military and economic concern. Meanwhile, anxieties about upholding individual liberties, especially those concerning political expression and association, increasingly fell by the wayside.[47] This shift is on clear display in the document, which explicitly links factory work and military service to the defense of the constitutional order. Overseas migration, while legal, was not only dangerous but also fundamentally unpatriotic, marking a turning of one's back on the Ottoman nation.

This public awareness campaign was rooted in the assumption that people were being tricked into migrating. This view was certainly preferable to acknowledging that the phenomenon might be driven, at least in part, by the failures and shortcomings of the post-revolution government. But failure was exactly the message Istanbul was receiving on a regular basis from provincial officials stationed in migrant-sending regions throughout the empire. In September 1909, a Belgian newspaper published an article on the increase in the migration of Lebanese and Armenians from the empire. It blamed the constitutional government's inability to guarantee political and economic security as the primary driver behind the spiraling exodus.[48] Taken aback by the article's grim tone, the Ministry of Interior forwarded the article to the governors of the provinces of Mamuretülaziz and Aleppo to get their assessments of its claims.[49] In his response, the governor of Mamuretülaziz assured the ministry that the article had greatly exaggerated the rate of increase of Armenian migration from the province. Nevertheless, he continued: 'Armenian migration to America from this province is a longstanding phenomenon. The reasons for this are many. But the most important is simply that it is difficult to make a living here while it is easy to do so in America . . . local impoverished villagers, barely scraping by, see a significant number of Armenians who go to America become wealthy, take off for America the first chance they get, filled with dreams of greed and avarice.' The governor ended his report with a note of optimism, citing the large numbers of Armenians who were encouraged to return following the revolution and their significant contributions to the local economy.[50] This may have succeeded in easing some of the concerns triggered by the article's publication. At the same time, his characterisation of the situation hardly aligned with the image put forth by some in Istanbul that many if not most Ottoman migrants were not migrating of their own accord. Instead, the report made migrants look like rational actors *par excellence*.

Perhaps Mamuretülaziz could be dismissed as an outlier. After all, overseas migration from that province was a long-standing phenomenon. The following year, however, the grand vizier wrote to several provincial officials stationed in various parts of the empire to get their assessments of the migration crisis. The responses to his request could only have instilled further doubt in the minds of high-ranking bureaucrats in Istanbul that their existed either a cheap or easy solution to the problem. The governor of Aleppo's report echoed many of the claims made by his counterpart in Mamuretülaziz the previous year. He characterised overseas migration from the province as being a 'rather old thing' (*pek eski bir şey*) driven in large part by the by the promise of better economic opportunities in the United States. But he also pointedly criticised the post-revolution political order, citing problems that 'do not comport with a constitutional government' such as coerced taxation and uncontrolled brigandage as factors that contributed to the increasing rate of migration. 'The only way to prevent our people from migrating abroad' he wrote 'is to provide for them here the foundations for a better life and to find them work.' He concluded by claiming that monetary remittances and return migration had both proven to be great boons to the province's otherwise woeful economy. This fact, he continued, put him in no position to prevent locals from seeking economic opportunity abroad even if compelled to do so.[51]

While the other responses to the grand vizier's request did not contain the same degree of candour as the Aleppo governor's, they nonetheless contained similar themes. The governor of Beirut wrote:

> there are no legal means with which to put an end to this migration that is emptying this land (of its people) . . . There is no reason beyond desperation and the desire to make a decent living that someone would make the difficult decision to leave his home country for one whose language and culture are entirely strange to him.[52]

Reports from the Balkans contradicted the popular sense among bureaucrats in Istanbul that travel agents and other intermediaries were to blame for driving the increase in migration. Instead, they pointed to a sentiment prevailing among many in the region that better economic opportunities were to be found overseas. Like their colleagues in Mamuretülaziz and Aleppo, they too suggested that migration and return migration had an overall salubrious effect on local economies in the Balkans.[53] Only the local gendarmerie commander in Jerusalem's response to the grand vizier's request differed appreciably in content and tone. He did not dwell on the root causes of migration. Instead, he warned Istanbul that the exodus was 'inflicting major material and financial damage on the empire' and 'seriously imperilling our ability to fill the ranks of the military.' As the region's indigenous Muslim and Christian populations sought greener pastures overseas, the commander wrote, 'yet more of the lands of Palestine (*arz-i Filistin*) fall into the hands of the Zionist organisations (*Siyonist cemiyetleri*).'[54] He ended his missive arguing for the passage of a law against desertion (*firari men' edecek bir kanun*).

These reports coming in from all over the empire painted a more complicated picture of the dynamics driving Ottoman overseas migration than the assumptions underpinning Istanbul's response to the exodus. They threw cold water on the idea that migrants were mostly 'simple-minded folk' easily duped by intermediaries. Rather, whether driven by the hopes of finding more economic opportunity abroad or by seeking to avoid military service, the composite image of the average Ottoman migrant that these reports present is of someone not likely to be easily swayed in his or her decision merely by appeals to patriotism and civic duty. Of greater concern for Istanbul, however, was the fact that these reports made clear that the migration crisis could not be addressed on the cheap. Instead, they all seemed to point towards the pressing need for an ambitious project of economic development and political reform. By November 1911, however, with war in Libya intensifying, crisis brewing in the Balkans and political turmoil gripping Istanbul, the prospects of a major overhauling of the empire's economy seemed dim at best. Meanwhile, voices such as that of the Jerusalem gendarmerie commander calling for more proactive legal measures to limit the departures of military-aged men only grew louder.

As 1911 lurched to a close, the constitutional regime continued to insist that any effort to limit the ability of Ottomans to go overseas risked 'threatening the many benefits that result from the freedom to travel, work and engage in trade, and thus is to be viewed as fundamentally inappropriate (*esasen muvaffık görülemeyeceği*).'[55] Nevertheless, the dire condition of the Ottoman military did lead to one significant change in policy. In November 1911, acting on orders from Istanbul, port city officials began checking the state-issued identity cards (*nüfus tezkereleri*) of all Ottoman males departing the empire. Those found to be of military age and who were suspected of attempting to desert were to be denied authorisation to leave and promptly returned to their home communities or assigned regiments.[56] Just over a year earlier, Istanbul had rejected a proposal to institute a similar policy out of fear that doing so would effectively mean the resurrection of the hated internal passport. The pressing need for bodies to fill the ranks of the military had changed Istanbul's outlook on a number of issues. For some, this shift in policy was hardly sufficient. In a letter to the Ministry of Interior, officials in Beirut identified Istanbul's migration policies as being the primary reason for the desertion crisis.[57] The ministry responded by reminding Beirut that the government remained committed to upholding the freedom to travel. The governor wrote back lamenting the few tools available to him to prevent the departure of military age men, and bitterly decrying the fact that he and his counterparts were forced to combat the problem of desertion with 'one hand tied behind our backs.'[58] Beirut's complaints notwithstanding, however, the decision to task port city officials with checking identification documents marked the return of a degree of intrusive mobility control not seen since the end of the Hamidian era in 1908. In the following years, port city officials would come under even more pressure to interdict suspected deserters and to crack down on the growing number of hoteliers, shipping agents and boatmen assisting them in their efforts to escape.[59] Indeed, in September 1913, the governor of Beirut warned that efforts to put a stop to the exodus of military-aged men were contributing to the revival of the clandestine migration networks that had largely ceased to exist after the revolution. Once again 'brokers, smugglers, and agents in the interior and on the coasts are earning a handsome profit, and police officials have a reliable source of bribes.'[60]

For the most part, the documentary trail runs dry after 1913, perhaps the result of the successful coup in January of that year after which the Committee of Union and Progress fully cemented their hold on power and further marginalised sources of bureaucratic power not fully under its control. The exodus from the empire nonetheless continued largely unabated until the outbreak of the First World War, which brought about a sharp reduction in commercial steamship traffic through European transit ports. As was the case under the autocratic rule of Sultan Abdülhamid II, the constitutional government's migration policies largely fell victim to their own manifold internal contradictions. The regime could never adequately figure a way to prevent certain forms of mobility without violating its commitment to the principle that all Ottoman subjects should enjoy the right to travel freely within and outside the empire's borders.[61] The needs and desires of the individual did not always (or even often) align with those of the state, as much as itr tried to instill a sense of patriotic duty in those who entertained the idea of leaving. It would take Ottoman involvement in World War I for the authoritarian-minded triumvirate that ruled the empire after January 1913 to truly begin cracking down on the ability of imperial subjects to travel. The next four years would witness a dramatic effort to marshal the full resources of the state into the war effort by force if necessary. The pretense of a liberal constitutional order had been brought to a complete and decisive end. No group would suffer more as a result than the empire's Armenian populations.

War, Genocide and the End of Empire

Despite the archival record largely running dry after 1913, our story does not end there. Nor does it end two years later, when, in the midst of World War I, the Ottoman state oversaw the genocidal destruction of much of its Armenian population. Instead, the legacy of the sojourning Armenians of the Harput region survived long into the first decades of the Republic of Turkey, even as their physical presence became little more than an uncomfortable and inconvenient memory for the Turkish state and society alike. For although the region's once large and prosperous Armenian population had been almost entirely eradicated by the early 1920s, the property and capital they left behind helped to nourish the emergence of a new Muslim bourgeoisie that came to dominate its economic and political landscape. For this to happen, the government of the nascent Turkish Republic (founded 1923) first needed to construct a legal edifice to prevent survivors of the genocide and the families of its victims from successfully seeking the restoration of or reparations for lost properties. To do so, the new Republican government looked to the recent past where they found the tools and the means by which to restrict the ability of Armenians to return to their ruined homes and to limit their ability to obtain redress for the grave crimes that had been committed against them.

In 1914, more than five thousand Armenians left the empire for the United States, the most ever in a single year. The Ottoman state's efforts to contain the exodus proved to be largely ineffective. The volume of Armenians leaving was partially offset by the fact that in 1914, in excess of one thousand Armenians returned to the empire from the United States, more than in any other year. This fact may appear at first glance to be surprising given the catastrophe that would befall Ottoman Armenians the following year. Those who returned to the Harput region in 1914, however, had some reason to be optimistic. For the first time in several years, the Ottoman Empire was not at war. The Balkan Wars had ended in July 1913, with Istanbul recouping some of what it had lost in hostilities the previous year. More importantly, in February 1914, the Ottoman state and the Great Powers agreed in principle to a reform package that would give Armenians in the Ottoman east enhanced political representation in provincial governments; create a framework for addressing the still unresolved controversy surrounding the restoration of Armenian lands seized by Kurdish tribal groups during the final decades of the Hamidian era; and see the appointment of two European 'inspectors' to oversee the reforms. The reform package was a major victory for the Armenian political parties that had helped to spearhead the negotiations, and provided at least some hope that the empire was finally turning the page on the sordid legacy of anti-Armenian violence of the Hamidian era.[62] While the threat of war was rapidly increasing, this was a distant concern for most within Ottoman society. Few, if any, Armenians who returned to the Harput region in 1914 had any inkling of the disaster about to befall them.

Once war did break out in Europe at the end of July, it was not long before the Ottomans were pressured into taking sides. At the end of October 1914, the Ottoman navy launched a surprise attack on Russian forces in the Black Sea, marking the empire's official entrée into World War I as a member of the Central Powers. By early 1915, the empire was under siege on two fronts with the British attacking the Dardenelles in the west, hoping to advance towards Istanbul, and Russian forces invading from the east. In January, the Ottomans suffered a crushing defeat against Russian forces at the Battle of Sarıkamış, resulting in the loss of as many as sixty-five thousand soldiers.[63] In April, as Russian forces advanced from the Caucasus, Armenians in the city of Van (located near the Russian and Persian frontiers) staged a revolt against Ottoman forces in response to news of massacres against Armenian civilians in the city's hinterlands.[64] On 24 April, Armenian intellectuals in Istanbul were systematically arrested and deported into the Anatolian interior where many were eventually executed. Just over a month later, on 27 May, the Ottoman Parliament passed the Deportation Law (*Tehcir Kanunu*) authorising the forced removal of Armenian civilians from regions proximate to the Russian front, a broadly defined area that encompassed much of the Ottoman east. The genocide was officially underway.

A full discussion of the factors that led the Ottoman state to deport or exterminate much of its Armenian population during World War I is beyond the scope of this book.[65] A growing body of work, however, emphasises the radicalisation of Ottoman state policy towards non-Muslim groups in the aftermath of the Balkan Wars of 1912–1913.[66] The January 1913 coup empowered voices within the CUP that viewed the creation of a strong central state as paramount for ensuring the survival of the empire. Additionally, the post-coup Ottoman leadership increasingly emphasised the empire's Muslim and Turkish characteristics at the expense of the more cosmopolitan definition of Ottoman identity that prevailed in the initial years following the 1908 revolution. After 1913, as Fuat Dündar argues, the Ottoman state endeavoured to create a more ethnically and religiously homogenous population through a process of 'demographic engineering.' Beginning in 1913, non-Muslim communities in western Anatolia were targeted for forced resettlement or expulsion. Tens of thousands of Greek and Turkish-speaking Orthodox Christians were forced to leave their homes, with most fleeing to Greece. In their stead, the Ottoman state settled Muslim refugees fleeing violence and persecution in the Balkans.[67] The announcement of a new slate of Armenian reforms in February 1914 sparked concerns among many in Istanbul that they were merely a prelude to the creation of an independent Armenian state in the Ottoman east. The outbreak of World War I ensured that the reforms would never be implemented. Nevertheless, the defeat of Ottoman forces at Sarıkamiş followed several months later by the Armenian uprising in Van contributed to the further radicalisation of the CUP policy.[68] The passage of the Deportation Law in May 1915 marked the opening salvo in the demographic remaking of the Ottoman east. In the years immediately preceding World War I, most of the Orthodox Christian victims of Istanbul's ethnic cleansing campaign in western Anatolia had fled to the relative safety of Greece. For the primarily Armenian and Assyrian targets of the Deportation Law, there was nowhere to run. In the midst of a punishing war, 'demographic engineering' quickly took on murderous and genocidal dimensions.

By July 1915, deportations were in full swing in the Harput region. As Raymond Kevorkian notes: 'Relatively remote from the war zones, the vilayet of Mamuret ul-Aziz undermines (Ottoman) claims about security needs put forward elsewhere . . . (such justifications) do not suffice to mask the Young Turk's determination to 'homogenise' the population.'[69] In addition to its location far from the front, there is no evidence of a concerted effort by Armenians in the Harput region to rise up against the Ottoman government or to impede its war effort. In fact, as has already been shown, the region's urban Armenian elite were fully integrated into provincial and even imperial political networks. Nevertheless, economically powerful families such as the Fabrikatorians and the Harputlians were among the first to face either deportation or, as was the fate that befell most Armenian men, execution. By the end of the year, much of the Harput region's Armenian population had been either deported or killed.[70]

Leslie Davis, the US consul in Harput until 1917, is today known largely for a report he compiled for the State Department that chronicled the deportation and mass murder of the Armenians in his consular district. Armenian returnees and the families of migrants feature prominently in Davis' account, especially in the context of his efforts to protect the lives and property of those who claimed American citizenship.[71] These efforts were hamstrung not only by opposition from Ottoman officials, but also the policies of his own government that did not allow him to recognise the status of Armenian returnees who had naturalised. At one point, he claimed that he had been forced to surrender to the authorities fifty Armenians who sought his protection as American citizens.[72] Not least because of Washington's stance on the citizenship status of Armenian returnees residing in the Ottoman Empire, the evolution of which was described in the previous Chapter, Davis enjoyed greater success safeguarding Armenian property than he did Armenian lives.[73] When he was forced to leave his post in May 1917, after the United States entered the war in support of the Triple Entente, Davis estimated that more than $200,000 worth of gold and other moveable property had been left to him for safekeeping.[74] This was only a tiny fraction of the total value of property left behind by Armenians who were deported from the Harput region during the war. It was the fate of this property, much of it acquired with money earned over the course of sojourns in the United States, that would ensure that the legacy of overseas migration from Harput would survive Armenian presence in the region.

The socio-economic impact of overseas migration on the Harput region awaits a more systematic and detailed analysis. The evidence available for this project, however, hints at the scale of its effects on the region's political economy.[75] As early as 1898, one observer noted that money earned in North American was facilitating 'the acquirement of property upon the part of Armenians' in the Harput region.[76] In 1901, the American consul in Harput estimated that migrants in the United States remitted more than two hundred and fifty thousand dollars a year to the region, amounting to a significant percentage of the region's overall yearly economic output.[77] By 1911, more than six hundred thousand dollars were being remitted to the region each year. According to the consul, because of this influx of migrant money, Armenians in the region enjoyed a higher standard of living than their compatriots living in places 'where there had been no immigration comparatively to America.'[78] The lifting of restrictions on migration and return following the 1908 revolution only accelerated the process by which migrant money facilitated the acquisition of property and other trappings of wealth. For example, in his history of Parchanj, written several decades after the village's destruction, native Manoog Dzeron wrote that, 'by 1909, with the help of American dollars, three quarters of the land was in Armenian hands.'[79] In 1912, the US consul reported that,

> with the new regime . . . those who have lived from fifteen to twenty and twenty five years in America . . . have by industry and economy saved up several thousand dollars . . . (and) return(ed) to their homes (in order to) buy a little shop in the market or to purchase a little piece of ground to spend their remaining days in their native country.[80]

Meanwhile, Boghos Jafarian, who had returned to the Harput region in 1904 after a sojourn in the United States, fondly recalled putting the finishing touches to the silk factory he owned with his brother Nishan, also a returnee. He was especially proud of the factory's corrugated tin roof he had custom ordered from the United States. Indeed, the US consul reported a spike in orders for such luxury items as Armenian returnees sought to add a certain American aesthetic to their houses and shops.[81] As construction on his factory neared completion, Jafarian dreamt of the grand mansion he hoped to build once his silk business got off the ground, a plan he would never have the opportunity to realise.[82]

The fate of the property abandoned by victims of the Armenian genocide has become a major area of inquiry in the past decade. Scholars have argued that this confiscated wealth and property was essential to the creation of a national economy, a critical component of the broader Republican-era modernisation project.[83] Recent scholarship on the systematic dispossession and confiscation of the property of non-Muslims throughout the empire is especially important for what it shows about the connection between this process and the dynamics that have been at the front and centre of this book. In the immediate aftermath of World War I, the defeated Ottoman government, acceding to pressure from the victorious powers, permitted Armenians and other non-Muslims to return to the empire in order to seek the restoration of confiscated properties.[84] By 1920, however, the Istanbul-based Ottoman government was coming under increasing pressure from the movement led by Mustafa Kemal that sought to bring an end to the post-war European occupation of Anatolia, and bring the region under the control of an independent nationalist government. Over the next two years, the parallel government established by Mustafa Kemal in the city of Ankara increasingly eclipsed Istanbul's power. Continued political turmoil and instability, meanwhile, made it nearly impossible for Armenian survivors to return to their home communities in order to reclaim lost properties. Furthermore, beginning in the early 1920s, Ankara began implementing document-based internal mobility controls aimed at restricting the ability of non-Muslims in particular to travel within its growing zone of control. Mirroring the Hamidian-era, special measures were taken to restrict Armenian mobility above and beyond those targeting other groups, making it nearly impossible for survivors to return and reclaim property in territories administered by Ankara.[85]

The Treaty of Lausanne (1923) marked a major turning point in the fate of confiscated and abandoned Armenian properties. The treaty, negotiated between Ankara and several of the victorious powers from World War I, replaced the much more punishing Treaty of Sèvres (1919), which emerged out of the Paris Peace Conference and had been recognised by the now defunct Ottoman government. The Treaty of Lausanne recognised Ankara's control over the territory that would comprise the Republic of Turkey, officially declared several months after the signing in October 1923. Taner Akçam and Ümit Kurt argue that the parts of the treaty that dealt with the legal status of former Ottoman nationals living outside of the borders of the new republic allowed Turkey to ensure that the vast majority of Armenian genocide survivors would never be able to return or to seek restoration of lost properties.[86] For example, Article 30 of the treaty stipulated that erstwhile Ottoman nationals residing in former territories of the empire now under control of either Britain, France or Greece were to become 'nationals of the State to which such territory (was) transferred.' Articles 31 and 33, however, allowed those affected by Article 30 to opt for Turkish nationality within two years of the treaty coming into force provided that they relocate to Turkish territory.[87] These articles ostensibly afforded survivors the opportunity to return and to claim citizenship. By doing so, they then had the right under Turkish law to sue for restoration of lands that had been abandoned or confiscated during the war. However, for the vast majority of Armenian refugees, many of whom were living in orphanages and camps scattered throughout Syria and Iraq, returning to their homes within the two year window stipulated by the treaty was nearly impossible. Furthermore, the Turkish government instituted several measures to ensure that Armenians could not cross into its territory from the south. Among nineteen travel regulations issued in July 1924 were provisions that forbade individuals who did not possess a passport issued by the Ankara government from entering the country, and required former Ottoman nationals seeking to return to Anatolia to apply for permission a year in advance.[88] The combination of these factors meant that only a tiny fraction of the thousands of Armenian survivors stranded in former territories of the Ottoman Empire ever returned to Turkey, and even fewer succeeded in obtaining redress for lost property.

The United States government was not a signatory to the Treaty of Lausanne, and thus its citizens, including the many thousands of Armenians of Ottoman birth who had naturalised as US citizens, were exempted from its provisions. As a result, in the late 1920s and early 1930s, American citizens, including many Armenian Americans, with property claims in the former Ottoman Empire pressured the United States government to demand compensation from the Turkish government. This posed a major threat to the fledgling Turkish economy, which was in no position to handle a potentially significant monetary settlement. The Turkish government had an ace up its sleeve that it hoped might help it to avoid paying compensation to former subjects of the Ottoman Empire: the 1869 Nationality Law, which remained in force in effect in Turkey and elsewhere in the former Ottoman world. In negotiations with Washington in 1934, Ankara argued that the vast majority of Armenian citizens of the United States, representing the largest single bloc demanding compensation for lost property, had obtained US citizenship without the permission of the Ottoman state. As a result, under the Nationality Law they remained Turkish nationals and thus their claims could not be included under any agreement reached between the United States and Turkey.[89] Then, taking a page from the Hamidian-era playbook, Turkish negotiators maintained that Ankara had the right to debar any national who attempted to return to the country after illegally naturalising as a citizen of a foreign power. The Ottoman state had used similar arguments in the mid-1890s to justify its refusal to admit Armenian returnees who had naturalised as US citizens for fear they would seek extraterritorial protections under the Capitulations. Now, four decades later, with the Capitulations long ago abolished and with few Armenians left in what was now Turkey, the Republican government was repurposing the same tactics to prevent Armenian Americans of Ottoman birth from seeking the restoration of or compensation for their lost properties.

Despite initial American opposition, the agreement eventually reached between the two states largely reflected Turkey's position on the legal status of naturalised Armenian Americans of Ottoman birth, and exempted Ankara from responsibility for compensating them.[90] The United States may have been motivated in its decision by the desire to safeguard its budding commercial and political interests in Turkey by avoiding a clash with Ankara over this issue.[91] Once again, the United States government determined that Armenian migrants were not worthy of the full protections and privileges of citizenship.[92] The signing of the agreement firmly and finally foreclosed any opportunity for Armenians in the United States, who had escaped the destruction of the genocide, to seek compensation for lands and property lost during World War I. Meanwhile, most Armenians who had migrated to the United States before the fall of the Ottoman Empire would remain nationals of Turkey under Turkish law until the passage of a new nationality law in 1964.[93] By then, the vast majority had passed away without ever having the opportunity to return to the lands of their birth. For the Republican government, that defined itself primarily in opposition to the imperial past, Ottoman-era strategies to limit mobility, fortify borders and contest the legal status of migrants came in handy when once again it became imperative to contain the perceived threat of the Armenian migrant. In this way, the themes discussed in this book did not cease to be relevant with the collapse of the Ottoman Empire, but continued to shape the politics of migration well into the first decades of the republican era.

Conclusion

Contemporary Harput/Mezre, now called Elazığ (a shortened and altered version of the more regal sounding former provincial name of Mamuretülaziz), like many drab provincial Anatolian metropolises, bears few reminders of its imperial past. The ancient Urartu fortress, around which the bustling neighbourhoods of Harput once stood, now stands in splendid isolation perched high above the central city. The buildings that once comprised the campus of Euphrates College have long ago been demolished, along with the churches that were once an architectural mainstay of the hilltop city. The Armenian past of the once dual city has been methodically erased. Few reminders exist of the sojourners that regularly travelled between the villages that still dot the surrounding countryside and the factories of the American northeast. The Elazığ municipality website's page on the region's history ends abruptly in 1880, and makes no mention of its once substantial Armenian population.[1]

For those who know where to look, however, traces of Armenian existence remain. In the heart of the city, along a major thoroughfare, sits a nondescript ten-story office building of the variety that exists in every Turkish city. A sign with the building's name, The Five Brothers' Arcade (*Beşkardeşler Pasajı*), sits prominently above the entrance to a small cafe, flanked on one side by a pharmacy and on the other by a hair salon. It was on this spot more than one hundred years earlier that the Fabrikatorian brothers, the region's most prominent silk manufacturers, built five identical, connected row houses, one for the family of each brother. The wide, tree-lined boulevard in front of the marvellous edifice was evocative of the leafy suburbs of the American Northeast. The brothers' burgeoning manufacturing empire, and their growing economic and political clout in the region, was thanks in large part to the flood of migrant dollars coming in from the United States. With the outbreak of World War I, the brothers' world would come crashing down around them. A few short years after building their triumphant row houses in the heart of the bustling provincial capital, the five brothers were rounded up and shot – along with many other prominent local Armenians, including their hated rivals the Harputlians. The row houses would eventually be converted into a 'People's House' (*Halkevi*) dedicated to inculcating local residents in the guiding principles of the newly established Republic of Turkey. Following the building's destruction decades later, the name of the building erected in its place would carry on the legacy of the five brothers, even as the memory of the local Armenian community of which they were a part was consciously erased. As a memento of what once stood there, a chandelier that had once adorned the main room of one of the row houses hangs proudly in the building's pharmacy.

Like so many others from the Harput region in the late nineteenth and early twentieth centuries, migration was key to the brothers' success. Three of the brothers spent time in Britain and the United States acquiring the knowledge and machinery they needed to eventually open their silk factory, one that would grow to be among the largest in the Ottoman Empire. Like the Fabrikatorian brothers, the legacies of the sojourners that populate this book have been erased by genocide. The totality of the events of 1915 created a blank slate on which the globetrotting cosmopolitanism of the region's late Ottoman past was replaced by a deeply conservative provincialism. In stark contrast to Diyarbakir to its southeast and Dersim to its north, where support for Kurdish political organisations is strong, Elazığ is a firm stronghold of Turkey's conservative ruling Justice and Development Party (AKP). Although primarily Kurdish, Elazığ bears much greater resemblance economically and politically to the conservative boomtowns of central Anatolia such as Konya, Sivas and Kayseri. A century earlier, the region's Armenian political elite were similarly much more integrated into regional and imperial networks of political and economic power, and much less likely than their countrymen further south and east to support the activities of Armenian political organisations such as the Armenian Revolutionary Party and the Hunchakian Revolutionary Party. In this way, perhaps, some of the political dynamics of the late-Ottoman period have carried over to the present day.

This book has shed light on two fundamentally different yet linked phenomena at play in the final decades of the Ottoman Empire: mobility control and the anti-Armenian politics of the Hamidian era. Its findings complicate many of the narratives that continue to dominate the study of both late Ottoman history and global migration in the nineteenth and early twentieth centuries. The migration of tens of thousands of Armenians from the Harput region to North America between 1885 and 1915 was not *primarily* driven by fear of persecution and violence. For most of these sojourners, the relatively high wages that a labourer could earn in a factory in the northeastern United States or in other communities such as Brantford, Ontario, or Racine, Wisconsin, were worth the risks that came with travelling from the Ottoman east to these remote destinations. The historical experience of Armenian communities in the Ottoman east in the empire's final decades was hardly uniform. By the end of the nineteenth century, the threat of violence and massacre along and the necessity of organised armed resistance had increasingly become facts of life for Armenians in Sasun, Zeytun and elsewhere in the region. Given the political and economic instability that prevailed in these locations, migration to North America, particularly in the Hamidian era, was simply too expensive and risky an undertaking. Meanwhile, in the Harput region, generally more prosperous and politically stable than elsewhere in the Ottoman east, the potential benefits that came with overseas migration – the promise of higher wages to remit to families back home or to invest in land or a small shop upon return – outweighed the steep costs involved in leaving the empire and travelling abroad.

The news of the massacres of the mid-1890s doubtless led many to give up on their dreams of returning home to the Ottoman Empire. Many Armenian migrants upon naturalising as US citizens sought the assistance of the American consulate in Harput in reuniting with spouses and children in their adoptive land. Doing so came at a steep price. Istanbul would only consent to permitting such reunions if those seeking to leave renounced their Ottoman nationality and vowed never to return. Many others, meanwhile, made the harrowing journey back to their home communities, whether to marry and start families, assist with ageing parents, or to live out the rest of their days in the land of their birth. This book has revealed the surprising volume of return migration to the Ottoman Empire in the late nineteenth and early twentieth centuries, even when it was officially forbidden for Armenian returnees to reenter the empire. The rate of return may at first seem surprising given the deteriorating political environment in the Ottoman east in this period, and the fact that these communities would largely be destroyed in the Armenian genocide. It is important to bear in mind that those who made the return voyage could not foresee the disaster that would befall them during World War I. The massacres and violence of the mid-1890s terrified Armenian communities in the Harput region, and caused great consternation and anxiety among those residing in the United States. Over two decades later, news of the 1909 anti-Armenian pogrom in Adana shook the faith of many Armenians in the empire that the new constitutional regime could truly guarantee their safety. Nevertheless, few – if any – of the tens of thousands who sojourned between the Ottoman east and North America in this period or the family and friends they left behind interpreted these outbreaks of violence as preludes to the nearly complete annihilation of Armenian presence in their ancestral lands. The findings of this book are a reminder against letting the rupture of genocide eclipse the complexity and the vibrancy of the era that preceded it.

At the same time, it is undeniable that Armenians were the targets of systematic discrimination by the Ottoman state in the late nineteenth and early twentieth centuries. The onset of large-scale migration to North America in the late 1880s was for the Hamidian regime a phenomenon inextricably linked to the simultaneous emergence of several political organisations deeply critical of the Ottoman state's treatment of the empire's Armenian populations. By the early 1890s, Istanbul viewed parties such as the Armenian Revolutionary Federation and the Hunchakian Revolutionary Party as perhaps the greatest single threat to political stability in its vulnerable eastern periphery. It was feared that activities associated with these political parties would work to radicalise Armenian migrant workers in North America who would then return to sow the seeds of revolution throughout the Ottoman east. This belief fundamentally shaped Ottoman policy towards Armenian overseas migration until the 1908 constitutional revolution brought an end to Abdülhamid II's despotic rule. Migration to North America was by no means a solely Armenian phenomenon. Nevertheless, non-Armenian Ottoman migrants were not targeted with draconian restrictions on their overseas travel, nor did they face debarment or deportation if they returned to the empire after unlawful sojourns abroad. Although the Ottoman state was certainly concerned about the rise of separatist politics among its many constituent ethno-religious communities, by the end of the nineteenth century, Istanbul believed that Armenians posed a uniquely menacing threat to the empire's survival.

Ronald Grigor Suny has argued that this sentiment helped to give rise to a particularly virulent anti-Armenian 'affective disposition' among both the Ottoman bureaucracy and imperial society at large. What emerged by the beginning of the twentieth century was a certain 'mental universe' in which Armenianness was immediately associated with sedition, disloyalty and revolt.[2] Much more work is needed, especially studies that shed greater light on everyday life in the Ottoman east, to determine whether this concept of 'affective disposition' is useful for understanding this period.[3] It is nevertheless noteworthy that in the absence of any evidence that Armenian migrants and returnees were involved in any kind of concerted effort to undermine Ottoman authority in the region, these assumptions continued to colour Istanbul's response to overseas migration until the 1908 revolution. The story of returnees falsely denounced as revolutionaries by their fellow villagers, and the language used in some of the testimonies collected by the governor of Mamuretülaziz in his case against the prominent banker, Artin Harputlian, attests to the degree to which this 'mental universe' may have permeated beyond official circles. While the government's position on migration changed dramatically after 1908, these widely held perceptions certainly did not disappear.

This study has made a case for why the role of the state must not be overlooked when studying migration and mobility in the modern era. State power played a pivotal in shaping how Armenians both left and returned to the empire. Whether a migrant left out of Samsun or Beirut (or returned via Cyprus or Egypt), paid smugglers five or fifteen liras for their services, and left from a central port or from an informal pier was almost always determined by which provided the best opportunity to evade Istanbul's constantly evolving efforts to enforce the migration ban. At the same time, the clandestine migration networks that emerged to facilitate unauthorised migration could not have operated without the cooperation of state officials at every level of their operation. By painstakingly tracing the operations of these networks, this book has shed much needed light on the inner workings of the Ottoman state at the local and regional levels. State officials whether in Harput, Mersin, or Beirut were frequently more than willing to turn a blind eye to or even profit openly from the clandestine migration business. Certainly many officials were motivated by the opportunity to profit off of those seeking to travel abroad or to reenter the empire.

But this is much more than just a story of petty and endemic corruption. Even high-ranking officials such as provincial governors often found it difficult to enforce Istanbul's will on the ground, particularly when powerful local and regional interests had a stake in the migration economy. This dynamic is exemplified by the story of Artin Harputlian and his sprawling clandestine migration network. When in 1907, the newly appointed governor of Mamuretülaziz sought to put an end to Harputlian's vast operation, he quickly discovered that much of the province's political and economic elite had little interest in supporting his efforts to put a stop to migrant smuggling. Meanwhile, the banker was able to draw on his many connections to influential power brokers both in the Harput region and in Istanbul to protect himself from the governor's efforts. Even in the poisonous political environment of the late Hamidian-era, Armenians in the Ottoman east remained an integral and influential part of the Ottoman system capable of wielding extensive power at the local, regional and imperial levels. While on the surface, this is not particularly surprising, it is a dynamic that is often missed in the existing historiography on Ottoman Armenians that is focused to a much greater degree on questions of victimisation and disempowerment.

The Ottoman state's response to Armenian migration to North America in the late nineteenth and early twentieth centuries is just one chapter in a much larger, global history. Attending the Hamidian regime's (outsized) anxieties about Armenian migrants radicalising while overseas was a deep-seated concern about those who returned to the empire after having naturalised as United States citizens. Such individuals ostensibly could benefit from the Capitulations under which US citizens were granted extraterritorial protections while in the empire to engage in political activities otherwise forbidden by Ottoman law. In response to these concerns, Istanbul sanctioned the detention of several Armenian returnees suspected of having adopted US citizenship upon their arrival in the empire. This policy coincided with the public outcry in the United States concerning reports of anti-Armenian and anti-missionary violence in the Ottoman east, further exacerbating an already explosive public relations and diplomatic nightmare for Istanbul. In the hopes of blunting popular anger over the detention of American citizens, the empire's ambassador to Washington authorised the launching of a propaganda campaign intended to link Ottoman anxieties about Armenian migration to those driving growing anti-immigrant sentiments in the United States. As the violence in the Ottoman east subsided and faded from public consciousness, US State Department policy increasingly came into alignment with that of the Ottoman state regarding the status of Armenian returnees who had naturalised as American citizens. In the first years of the twentieth century, in the context of a crackdown on return migration following a brief period of lenience, Ottoman officials began a policy of debarring returnees upon their arrival in the empire and deporting those who had returned to their home communities in the preceding months and years. Those who attempted to claim protection as US citizens quickly discovered that by returning home, even if only for a temporary visit, they had involuntarily expatriated themselves and could expect no assistance from their adoptive government. The convergence of Ottoman and American policies on the status of Armenian returnees in the early years of the twentieth century reflected a global turn towards anti-migration and anti-migrant politics in this period. Meanwhile, Armenian returnees found themselves caught between two hostile governments in a perilous legal limbo of a sort that would become increasingly commonplace throughout the world as the twentieth century progressed. This study has argued for the fundamental comparability of Ottoman and US migration policies in the late nineteenth and early twentieth centuries. Such comparisons are important if the Ottoman Empire is to be better integrated into the study of modern world history. Furthermore, they help to illustrate the many ways in which the Ottoman experience sheds light on dynamics of global significance.

The lifting of the ban on Armenian overseas migration and return migration in the summer of 1908 very rapidly transformed the volume and geography of departures as migrants no longer needed to rely on clandestine channels in order to leave the empire. Furthermore, the available evidence suggests that return migration spiked in the aftermath of the 1908 revolution, reaching a peak in 1914, just one year before the Armenian genocide. In recent years, new scholarship has helped us to make sense of the post-1908 era, one that began with great optimism about the empire's future only to violently end a decade later following four years of warfare, mass violence and genocide.[4] As many historians of this period have noted, the new government's commitment to liberal constitutionalism was eventually overwhelmed by the desire of many within its ranks to strengthen the empire at all costs. The constitutional experiment did not only face challenges from conservative and revanchist elements within the empire. Supporters of the 1908 revolution viewed freedom to travel as a fundamental right. The despotic Hamidian regime's draconian restrictions on mobility were seen as further evidence of its inherent backwardness and hostility to liberty. Just as the newly empowered constitutional government began relaxing restrictions on the ability of Ottoman nationals to leave the empire, the United States government began redoubling its efforts to enforce new laws meant to limit immigration. As Ottomans began migrating abroad in unprecedented numbers, they found themselves the target of the increasingly restrictionist policies of the United States government. By 1910, Istanbul was dealing with an entirely new kind of migration crisis as hundreds of its own nationals became stranded in European transit ports unable to secure permission to continue their transatlantic voyages. Many of these hapless migrants sought financial assistance from Ottoman diplomatic officials in their efforts to return home, lending ammunition to voices in parliament calling for a return to Hamidian-era mobility controls. At the same time, growing numbers of Ottoman nationals migrating abroad in hopes of dodging military service at a time when the empire was facing a series of domestic and international crises further tested the governments commitment to upholding freedom of movement as a fundamental liberty. As World War I approached, Istanbul began re-introducing documentary controls on mobility in hopes of stemming the tide of desertions, signalling a pullback from the liberal policies on migration that it touted in the years immediately following the 1908 revolution.

The anecdote at the beginning of this conclusion is a reminder of the abruptness with which this story was ended in 1915. The many thousands of Armenian returnees and the families of migrants still residing abroad who were left in the Harput region, when the deportation orders inaugurating the genocide were issued in the late spring of 1915, mostly did not survive. This does not, however, mean that their experiences do not continue to be instructive in the contemporary period. After all, the backlash that their mobility generated, whether from the Ottoman state or the United States government, mirrors what would become the default response to migrants – especially those originating from the 'Global South' – throughout much of the twentieth century. Although the post-Cold War era has often been characterised as one of blurring borders and unparalleled interconnectivity, the globalised mobility control regime that underlies it in many ways resembles that of the Hamidian era. As anti-migrant discourse continues to dominate politics throughout much of the world, the experiences of Armenian sojourners at the end of the nineteenth century remain deeply relevant.

Notes

Introduction

1. Thomas Nail, *The Figure of the Migrant.*
2. Maurizio Albahari, *Crimes of Peace.*
3. Andersson, *Illegality, Inc.*, 5–6.
4. See: Ryan Gingeras, *Sorrowful Shores*; Vladimir Hamed-Troyansky, 'Circassian Refugees'.
5. See: Laura Robson, 'Refugees'; Keith Watenbaugh, *Bread from Stones.*
6. Aristide Zolberg, *A Nation By Design*, 199–242.
7. On the history of the 1924 Johnson-Reed Act and the immigration quotas that it introduced, see: Mae Ngai, *Impossible Subjects*, 21–55.
8. Chris Gratien, 'Ottoman Immigrants'.
9. Some representative examples that have been especially important for this study include: Grace Peña Delgado, *Making the Chinese Mexican*; Erica Lee, *At America's Gates*; Adam McKeown, *Melancholy Order*; Mae M. Ngai, *Impossible Subjects.*
10. See, for example: Eileen Kane, *Russian Hajj*; Michael Christopher Low, 'Empire and the Hajj'.
11. See, for example: James Meyer, *Turks Across Empire*; Lale Can, 'The Protection Question'.
12. The literature on Lebanese migration is especially well developed, but with few exceptions tends to focus on the importance of migration for the development of post-Ottoman Lebanon or on societies that received large numbers of Lebanese migrants. For example, see: Theresa Alfaro-Velcamp, *So Far from Allah*; Stacy Fahrenthold, *Between the Ottomans*; Akram Khater, *Inventing Home.*
13. This number is taken from Robert Mirak's estimate. See: Robert Mirak, *Torn Between Two Lands*, 71. Reliable statistics for Armenian migration to Canada are more difficult to come by. Isabel Kaprielian estimates that just over two thousand Ottoman Armenian migrants, overwhelmingly from

the district of Kiğı in Erzurum province, resided in Ontario. See: Isabel Kaprielian-Churchill, *Like Our Mountains*, 56.

14. Mae M. Ngai, *Impossible Subjects*, 10.
15. In addition to some of the works already cited, for the history of passports, see: John Torpey, *The Invention of the Passport*; Craig Robertson, *The Passport in America*. For a now classic history of the evolution of immigration policy in the United States, see: Aristide Zolberg, *A Nation by Design*.
16. Thomas Nail, *Figure of the Migrant*, 15.
17. Beth Lew-Williams, *The Chinese Must Go*, 10.
18. For a good, if dated, collection of essays on the contemporary phenomenon of people smuggling, see: David Kyle and Rey Koslowski (eds), *Global Human Smuggling*. For more on people smuggling on the Mediterranean, see: Albahari, *Crimes of Peace*; Theodore Baird, *Human Smuggling*.
19. Maurizio Albahari, *Crimes of Peace*, 95–6.
20. John Torpey, *Invention*, 57–92.
21. For more on the Armenian genocide in Ottoman historical writing, see: David Gutman, 'Ottoman Historiography'.
22. See, for example: Bedross Der Matossian, *Shattered Dreams of*; Lerna Ekmekçioğlu, *Recovering Armenia*; Richard Antaramian, 'In Subversive Service'.
23. See, for example: Janet Klein, *The Margins of Empire*; Sabri Ateş, *Ottoman–Iranian Borderlands*; Nilay Özok-Gündoğan, 'The Making of the Modern State', 238–40.
24. See, for example, Benjamin Braude's history of the millet system: Benjamin Braude, 'Foundation Myths'.
25. See, for example: Justin McCarthy et al., *Armenian Rebellion*.
26. 'Bana Gürcü, affedersin çok daha çirkin şeylerle Ermeni diyenler oldu', *Diken*, 6 August 2014, accessed 21 October 2017, http://www.diken.com.tr/afedersin-cok-daha-cirkin-seylerle-ermeni-diyen-oldu/.
27. 'Aysel Tuğluk'un annesinin saldırıya uğrayan cenazesi defnedildiği mezardan çıkarıldı', *BBC Türkçe*, 14 September 2017, accessed 21 October 2017, http://www.bbc.com/turkce/haberler-turkiye-41262278.
28. Late-Ottoman demography is a politically fraught topic, especially so when dealing with the empire's Armenian population. Depending on the source, the population of Mamuretülaziz Province in the late nineteenth and early twentieth centuries was anywhere between 450,000 (the estimate given by the Armenian Patriarchate in 1912) and 600,000 (historical demographer Justin McCarthy's figure). Of these totals, the patriarchate estimated 168,000 were Armenian (roughly 37% of the total population), while Justin McCarthy estimates the province's Armenian population was just over 110,000 (about 18% of the total population). These figures can be found in: Robert Hewson, 'Golden Plain', 41–2.
29. Manoog Dzeron, *Village of Parchanj*, 209.
30. I. Yildirim, 'Elazığ ve Çevresine', 280.

31. Vital Cuinet, *La Turquie D'Asie*, 229–30.
32. Parts of this chapter appear in: 'Agents of Mobility: Migrant Smuggling Networks, Transhemipsheric Migration, and Time–Space Compression in Ottoman Anatolia, 1888–1908', *Interdisciplines*, 1 (2012), 48–84.
33. Parts of this chapter appear in: 'Armenian Migration to North America, State Power, and Local Politics in the Late Ottoman Empire', *Comparative Studies of South Asia, Africa, and the Middle East*, 34:1 (Spring 2014), 176–90. Permission granted by Duke University Press.

Part I Introduction

1. The story of Hazar, Minas and Ahmed is based off of information found in the following document: BOA.ZB 459 66, Trabzon Police Commission of Investigation to Province of Trabzon (19 Temmuz 1320/2 August 1904).

Chapter 1

1. Musa Çadırcı, 'Tanzimat Döneminde', 178.
2. BOA.I.DH 1075/84332, Yıldız Palace, Office of the Chief Scribe (18 Ramazan 1305/30 March 1888). This is a modified translation of the same document that appears in: David Gutman, 'The Political Economy of Armenian Migration', 53.
3. M. Şükrü Hanioğlu, *A Brief History*, 74.
4. Ibid., 75.
5. For a detailed, if dated, discussion of the 1856 decree and its significance, see: Roderic Davison, *Reform in the Ottoman Empire*, 52–80.
6. Aylin Koçunyan, 'Long Live Sultan Abdülaziz', 199–200, 206. See, also: Ronald Grigor Suny, *History*, 59–61.
7. Richard Antaramian, 'In Subversive Service', 15.
8. Ibid., 206–7.
9. Ronald Grigor Suny, *History*, 69–70.
10. M. Şükrü Hanioğlu, *A Brief History*, 110–23.
11. For more on the ruling ideology of the Hamidian era, see: Selim Deringil, *The Well-Protected Domains*.
12. Sabri Ateş, *The Ottoman–Iranian Borderlands*, 38.
13. Ibid., 39.
14. Janet Klein, *The Margins of Empire*, 56–7.
15. Ali Sipahi, 'At Arm's Length', 26–36.
16. Janet Klein, *Margins of Empire*, 57.
17. Ali Sipahi, 'At Arm's Length', 26–110.
18. See, for example: Stephen Astourian, 'The Silence of the Land'; Owen Miller, 'Sasun 1894'; Mehmet Polatel, 'The Complete Ruin of a District'.
19. Owen Miller, 'Sasun 1894', 29–31; Nadir Özbek, 'The Politics of Taxation'.
20. Masayuki Ueno, 'For the Fatherland and the State', 94.

21. Nilay Özok-Gündoğan, 'Ruling the Periphery', 160–75.
22. Nilay Özok-Gündoğan, 'The Making of the Modern State, 238–40.
23. Nilay Özok-Gündoğan, 'Ruling the Periphery', 169.
24. Arsen Yarmen, *Palu-Harput 1878*, 179. This passage is also quoted in: Sipahi, 'At Arm's Length', 149.
25. Sipahi, 'At Arms Length', 92. See, also: Ali Sipahi, 'Suburbanization and Urban Duality, 247–67.
26. Sipahi, 'At Arm's Length', 144. As will become clearer later in this book, prominent Armenian manufactures and financiers based in Harput/Mezre would become critical players in the politics surrounding overseas migration from the region.
27. For more on the Harput region's economy, see: David Gutman, 'Political Economy'.
28. For a much more detailed discussion of the economic structure of the Harput region, see: David Gutman, 'Political Economy'.
29. Christopher Clay, 'Labour Migrations and Economic Conditions in Nineteenth Century Anatolia', *Middle East Studies* 34, No. 4 (October 1998), 20–1. See, also: Gutman, 'Political Economy'.
30. A prime example was the Kasap İlyas neighbourhood, popular with Muslim migrants from Arapgir, a town located ninety kilometres north and west of Harput/Mezre. See: Cem Behar, *A Neighborhood*, 97–8.
31. David Gutman, 'Political Economy', 50–2.
32. Hans-Lukas Kieser, *Nearest East: American Millennialism*, 2.
33. Katrine V. Walther, *Sacred Interests*, 1–2.
34. By 1856, the ABCFM had ended their missions to the Muslims and Jews of the empire. Hans-Lukas Kieser, *Der Verpasste Friede*, 57.
35. Ussama Makdisi, 'Reclaiming the Land', 712.
36. Selim Deringil, *The Well-Protected Domains*, 93–111, 125–32. See also: Hans Lukas Kieser, *Nearest East*, 34–62.
37. For information about the establishment and growth of the ABCFM presence in the Harput region, see: Hans Lukas-Kieser, *Der Verpasste Friede*, 86–93.
38. Hans-Lukas Kieser, *Nearest East*, 49.
39. Frank Andrews Stone, 'The Heritage of Armenia', 212–13. Euphrates College was known as Armenia College until 1888.
40. Robert Mirak, *Torn Between Two Lands*, 36–44.
41. Mirak, *Torn Between Two Lands*, 37.
42. For a good, if dated, analysis of this process, see: Reşat Kasaba, *The Ottoman Empire and the World Economy*.
43. On the survival of Ottoman manufacturing, see: Donald Quataert, *Ottoman Manufacturing*.
44. Vital Cuinet, *La Turquie D'Asie*, 229–30.
45. Philip Ernest Schoenberg, 'The Evolution of Transport', 360. According to one historian, between 1830 and 1896, cargo traffic through the port

of Istanbul alone went from approximately 400,000 tons to over thirteen million tons, an increase driven entirely by the arrival of the steamship. See: M. Emre Kılıçaslan, 'Avusurya Lloyd', 483.

46. For more information on the expansion of steam shipping in Mersin, see: Meltem Toksöz, 'Ottoman Mersin'. For Samsun, see: Ilhan Ekinci, '19. Yüzyıl'ın İkinci Yarısında'.
47. For more on boatmen operations in Ottoman port cities, see: Can Nacar, 'Yükselen bir Liman Kentinde'; Abidin Temizer, 'Karadeniz Ticaretinde Seyyar Iskeleler', 1077–84.
48. Donna Gabaccia and Franca Iacovetta, 'Women, Work, and Protest', 168.
49. Akram Khater, *Inventing Home*, 2001.
50. Janet Klein, *The Margins of Empire*, 21. See, also: Mehmet Fırat Kılıç, 'Between Empires'.
51. Özge Ertem, 'Considering Famine', 151–72.
52. Gerard Libaridian, 'What Was Revolutionary', 87.
53. For a useful, if dated history of these organizations, see: Louise Nalbandian, *Armenian Revolutionary Movement*. For a more recent study, see: Gerard Libaridian, 'What was Revolutionary', 84–109.
54. For a detailed discussion of the events leading to the protest at Kumkapı, see: Owen Miller, 'Sasun 1894', 97–116.
55. Janet Klein, *The Margins of Empire*, 4.
56. Ibid., 26.
57. Ibid., 14.
58. For a more detailed discussion of the Sasun uprising and massacre, see: Mehmet Polatel, 'The Complete Ruin of a District', 179–98; Owen Miller, Sasun 1894.
59. Owen Miller, Sasun 1894, 238–316.
60. Selim Deringil, 'The Armenian Question', 368.
61. Janet Klein, *The Margins of Empire*, 79–80.
62. Selim Deringil, 'The Armenian Question is Finally Closed', 344–71.
63. Richard Hovannisian, 'The Armenian Question', 223.
64. It is extremely difficult to estimate the total number of casualties that resulted from the anti-Armenian violence of the mid-1890s. The figure of 200,000 often cited in histories of the Armenian genocide is almost certainly too high. The number of deaths when combined with the number displaced or compelled to convert, however, may well exceed this number.
65. Edwin Munsell Bliss, *Turkey and the Armenian Atrocities*, 427–30. Much debate and uncertainty remains about the numbers of Armenians killed as a result of the pogroms and massacres of the mid-1890s. Missionary accounts of the violence almost certainly exaggerate the death toll. For example, in 1896, the American missionary, EM Bliss, claimed nearly 40,000 Armenians had been killed in the Harput region alone (See: Hans Lukas-Kieser, *Der Verpasste Friede*, 200). This many deaths, when combined

with the numbers of people displaced or compelled to convert to Islam, would have dealt an incredible blow to Armenian presence in the region from which it would have taken decades if not generations to recover. Meanwhile, Donald Quataert, in his work on the cloth manufacturing sector in Arapgir, a city located to the north and west of Harput/Mezre, notes that manusa cloth exports from the region were back to normal only one year after the violence had ended, speculating that the death and displacement of Armenians in and around the city may not have been as high as reported (See: Donald Quataert, *Ottoman Manufacturing*, 85–6). Given the dynamics discussed in this book, including the continued migration of single males to North America, and the relatively high rate of return in the years following the massacres, I would also argue that the scale of death and destruction was likely nowhere near some of the higher reports given primarily by foreign observers in the region, and nothing remotely close to the near total destruction of the Harput region's Armenian communities in the 1915 genocide. Indeed, the American missionary Henry Riggs, whose eyewitness account of the genocide in Harput provides a detailed account of the destruction of the region's Armenian communities, admitted 'so far as local conditions in Harpoot were concerned, the Armenian atrocities of 1915 had no historical setting' (Henry H. Riggs, *Days of Tragedy*, 45). Also quoted in: (Hans-Lukas Kieser, *Der Verpasste Friede*, 420). I believe many Armenians in the Harput region would have shared Riggs sentiment, and that as far as the Harput region is concerned, it is important not to read the pogrom of 1895 as any sort of precursor for or anywhere approaching the scale and horror of the events of 1915. Nevertheless, more work is desperately needed on the mid-1890s Armenian massacres, and their impacts on communities throughout the Ottoman east.

66. For a map of Hamidiye regiments, see: Janet Klein, *The Margins of Empire*, app.
67. See Chapters 2 and 3.
68. Robert Mirak, *Torn Between*, 206–7.
69. Ibid., 241–54.
70. David Gutman, 'Migrants, Revolutionaries, and Spies'.
71. Mirak, *Torn Between*, 254.
72. For a fuller discussion of the Ottoman state's policies on Armenian migration, see: Engin Deniz Akarlı, 'Ottoman Attitudes', 109–38; David Gutman, 'Travel Documents', 352–8.
73. For a more detailed discussion, see: David Gutman, 'Travel Documents', 362–3.
74. For examples, see: Despatches from the U.S. Consulate in Harput, 1904–1912. No. 84 350-10-7-3.
75. For more on Ottoman mobility control practices, see: David Gutman, 'Travel Documents'.
76. For more on Muslim and Assyrian migration in this period, see: A Deniz.

Balgamış and Kemal Karpat (eds), *Turkish Migration to the United States*. For Assyrian migration to the United States, see: Sargon Donabed, *Remnants of Heroes*.

77. BOA.HR.SYS 54 1, Ottoman Consul General in New York to Foreign Minister, Said Pasha (24 October 1894).
78. BOA.DH.MKT 107 35, Grand Vizier to Ministry of Interior (18 Muharrem 1311/1 August 1893).
79. See Chapter 5.

Chapter 2

1. See, for example: Ruben Andersson, *Illegality, Inc*; Maurizio Albahari, *Crimes of Peace*; Theodore Baird, *Human Smuggling*. The investigative journalism website, *The Intercept*'s, coverage of migrant smuggling in the Mediterranean and in the Americas has been especially strong. See, for example: Zach Campbell, 'Europe's Plan to Close Its Sea Borders Relies on Libya's Coast Guard Doing its Dirty Work, Abusing Migrants', *The Intercept*, 25 November 2017, https://theintercept.com/2017/11/25/libya-coast-guard-europe-refugees/.
2. On migrant smuggling during the era of Chinese exclusion, see: Erika Lee, *At America's Gates*; Grace Peña Delgado, *Making the Chinese Mexican*; Beth Lew-Williams, *The Chinese Must Go*. There has been comparatively little sustained scholarly attention on the historical role of smuggling in other contexts. For an exception to this, see: Libby Garland, *After They Closed the Gates*.
3. *Frontline*'s otherwise excellent documentary on the Mediterranean migrant and refugee crisis conveys this notion. See, James Bluemel, *Exodus* (Boston: Frontline, 27 December 2016) URL: https://www.pbs.org/wgbh/frontline/film/exodus/.
4. BOA.DH.MKT 99 40, Copy of the Liverpool Consul's report to the Foreign Ministry, 26 Haziran 1309/9 July 1893.
5. BEO.HR.SYS 2735 29, Report of the Ottoman Ambassador in Washington, Mavroyeni Bey to the Ottoman Foreign Ministry (6 February 1891).
6. BOA.BEO 45 3317, Office of the Grand Vizier to the Ministry of Police (6 Muharrem 1310/31 July 1892).
7. BOA.BEO 83 6197 Office of the Grand Vizier to Mamuretülaziz Province (10 Rabiulevvel 1310/1 October 1892). The relationship between Gaspar and Mardiros is ambiguous. The Ottoman ambassador's letter to the Ottoman Foreign Ministry in 1891 indentifies Mardiros as Gaspar's 'step son' (*fils adoptif*). Meanwhile an 1895 report by a Pinkerton agent claims Mardiros was fifty years old, and thus likely too old to be Gaspar's son, adoptive or otherwise. See: BOA.HR.SYS 2739 22, Report from John Cornish of the Pinkerton Detective Agency to Charles Iasigi, Ottoman Consul in Boston (25 January 1895).

8. BOA.BEO 83 6197, Office of the Grand Vizier to Mamuretülaziz Province (10 Rabiulevvel 1310/1 October 1892).
9. BEO.HR.SYS 2735 29, Mavroyeni Bey to the Foreign Ministry (6 February 1891). Mardiros Nahigian's appears in a book on the history of Armenians in the state of Rhode Island providing services to newly arrived Armenian migrants as early as 1888. See: Varoujan Karents. *Mitchanpert the Citadel*, 31.
10. BOA.DH.MKT 2063 83, Mehmed Fuad Bey to Grand Vizier (24 Ağustos 1309/6 September 1893).
11. BOA.HR.SYS 2739 22, Cornish to Iasigi (24 January 1895). Varoujan Karents' history of Armenians in Rhode Island suggests that Mardiros Nahigian may have been aiding Armenian migration as early as 1888. See: Varoujan Karents. *Mitchanpert the Citadel*, 31.
12. Gaspar Nahigian's links to Armenian political organisations was not entirely undisputed. In 1892, provincial officials in Mamuretülaziz strenuously denied that Nahigian's actions were motivated by anything except profit, and downplayed the scope of his smuggling operations. See: BOA. BEO 45 3317, Grand Vizier to Ministry of Police (6 Muharrem 1310/31 July 1892).
13. BOA.MKT.MHM 659 52, Office of the Grand Vizier to the Ministry of Interior (11 Şaban 1323/10 October 1905).
14. BOA.MKT.MHM 659 52, Grand Vizier to Ministry of Interior (11 Şaban 1323/10 October 1905).
15. BOA. DH.TMIK.M 249 56, Statement of Captain Riza Bey (3 Eylül 1323/16 September 1907).
16. Robert Mirak, Torn Between Two Lands, 150.
17. BOA.ZB 445 54, Ministry of Police to Mamuretülaziz (14 Eylül 1320/27 September 1904); BOA.ZB 446 24, Ministry of Police to Mamuretülaziz (27 Temmuz 1322/9 August 1906).
18. See, for example: Gunther Peck, 'Reinventing Free Labor', 848–71.
19. BOA.ZB 446 24, Ministry of Police to Mamuretülaziz (27 Temmuz 1322/9 August 1906).
20. BOA.ZB 446 150, Ministry of Police to Mamuretülaziz Province (17 Şubat 1323/1 March 1908).
21. BOA.DH.TMIK.M 134 13, Copy of telegram from the governor of Mamuretülaziz (29 Teşrinievvel 1318/19 December 1902). The set of documents in this file details more broadly the involvement of Muslims in the migration industry, and the need for harsher punitive measures to discourage this.
22. Mirak claims migrant parties on average numbered between forty and eighty people. See: Robert Mirak, *Torn Between Two Lands*, 60. Ottoman documents, meanwhile, discuss groups that ranged in size from three to fifty people.
23. Guiding was both lucrative and risky. Guides could expect to receive a

significant cut of the money paid by migrants to agents in the interior. See, for example: BOA.DH.TMIK.M 134 13, Telegram from Governor of Mamuretülaziz Province to Ministry of Interior (26 Teşrinievvel 1318/29 October 1902). Nevertheless, the state employed a number of strategies to dissuade guides from participating in migrant smuggling networks. In 1900, for example, the Ministry of Interior proposed requiring all muleteers turn their clients over to port city police upon arrival in order to determine whether or not they sought to travel abroad illegally. See: BOA. DH.TMIK.M 93 17, Ministry of Interior Reform Commission to the Provinces of Mamuretülaziz and Diyarbekir (11 Ağustos 1316/24 August 1900). In 1902, the Governor of Mamuretülaziz Province recommended that muleteer guides who abetted migrant smuggling be subject to internal exile, a suggestion ultimately rejected by the Ministry of Interior. See: BOA.DH.TMIK.M 134 13, Telegram from Governor of Mamuretülaziz Province to Ministry of Interior (26 Teşrinievvel 1318/29 October 1902); BOA.DH.TMIK.M 134 13, Ministry of Interior Reform Commission to Mamuretülaziz Province (28 Teşrinisani 1318/11 December 1902). For further references to muleteer guides in the source material, see: BOA. DH.TMIK.M 77 80, Telegram from the Governor of Mamuretülaziz Province to the Ministry of Interior (16 Recep 1317/7 August 1899); BOA. DH.TMIK.M 134 13, Copy of telegram from Mamuretülaziz Province to Ministry of Interior (17 Şubat 1319/1 March 1903); BOA.Y.MTV 308 108, Copy of telegram from the Representative of the Halep Extraordinary Commandant to the Office of the Commander-in-Chief of the Army (4 Nisan 1324/18 April 1908).

24. NARA-DC, Despatches from the United States consuls in Harput, 1895–1906, Thomas Norton, U.S. Consul to Department of State (22 January 1901).
25. The price of 20 liras is given in: BOA.DH.TMIK.M 134 13, Copy of Telegram from Governor of Mamuretülaziz Province (16 Teşrinievvel 1318/29 October 1902). The price of 19 liras is given in: BOA.DH.TMIK.M 121 23, Port Commission of Iskenderun to Ministry of Interior (2 Nisan 1318/13 April 1902). On the value of the US Dollar relative to the Ottoman Lira, see: Şevket Pamuk, *A Monetary History*, 209.
26. BOA.BEO 3136 235134, Testimony of Malatya Police Captain Riza Bey (3 Eylül 1323/16 September 1907).
27. One lira was worth one-hundred kuruş. According to Donald Quataert, the daily wage for Ottoman weavers in the Balkans and Anatolia in the 1890s was as little as 1.2 kuruş. See: İnalcık and Quataert, *Social and Economic History*, 923.
28. David Kyle and Rey Koslowski (eds), *Global Human Smuggling*, 1–31. Many of the essays in this volume also provide specific information about the cost of human smuggling in different regional contexts.
29. See also: Robert Mirak, *Torn Between Two Lands*: 51.

30. NARA, Despatches from the United States consuls in Harput, 1895–1906, Thomas Norten, U.S. Consul to Department of State, 22 January 1901; BOA.DH.TMIK.M 134 13 (16 Teşrinievvel 1318/29 October 1902).
31. Isabel Kaprielian similarly mentions the use of information networks among Armenian migrants from the district of Keghi (Kiğı) to inform potential migrants regarding the exploitative practices of middlemen. See: Isabel Kaprielian, 'Migratory Caravans', 20–38.
32. See for example: BOA.Y.PRK.DH 2 86, Copy of telegram from the Province of Mamuretülaziz to the Ministry of Interior (14 Temmuz 1304/27 July 1888); BOA ZB 588 1, Ministry of Police to Coastal Provinces (5 Rabiulahir 1310/27 October 1892).
33. BOA.DH.MKT 1554 16, Circular report from Ministry of Interior to all Provinces and Districts with the exception of the Province of Trabzon (8 Safer 1306/14 October 1888).
34. BOA ZB 588 1, Ministry of Police to Coastal Provinces (5 Rabiulahir 1310/27 October 1892).
35. Florien Riedler, 'Armenian Labour Migration', 163–6.
36. See: Donald Quataert, 'Labor Policies and Politics', 59–69.
37. BOA.DH.MKT 1743 81, Governor of Trabzon to Ministry of Interior (30 Zilkade 1307/17 July 1890).
38. BOA.DH.MKT 38 17, Trabzon to Ministry of Interior (11 Zilkade 1310/28 May 1893).
39. BOA.DH.MKT 1931 29, Ministry of Interior to Governor of Adana Province (10 Şaban 1309/10 March 1892).
40. For more on Mersin's emergence as a port see: Meltem Toksöz, *Nomads Migrants and Cotton*.
41. BOA.DH.MKT 367 33, Report of an informant provided to the Ministry of Police (11 Mart 1311/24 March 1895).
42. BOA.DH.MKT 139 19, Mersin Pier Commission to Ministry of Interior (13 Şevval 1320/12 January 1903).
43. See for example: BOA.ZB 426 59, Ministry of Police to Aydin, Mamuretülaziz, Trabzon, and Halep provinces (2 Teşrinievvel 1321/15 October 1905); BOA.DH.TMIK.M 251 11, The Province of Trabzon to Ministry of Interior (12 Temmuz 1323/25 July 1907).
44. BOA.Y.PRK.AZN 24 35 (2 Cemazeyilahir 1323/04 October 1905). This document consists of a journal containing numerous summaries of documents produced over a nearly six-year period. It is especially useful in demonstrating the emergence of eastern Mediterranean ports as exit points for Armenian migrations leaving for North America.
45. For more on Lebanese migrations to the Americas see: Akram Khater, *Inventing Home*.
46. Akarlı, 'Ottoman Attitudes Towards Lebanese Emigration', 123–4.
47. BOA. DH.MKT 2562 38, Ministry of Interior to the District Governor of Mount Lebanon (17 Şevval 1319/28 November 1901).

48. BOA ZB 709 29, Copy of report of the Beirut Pier Commission (21 Mayıs 1323/3 June 1907).
49. Yakub Karkar, *Railway Development*, 69–70.
50. A.E. Safarian, *Letters from Armenia*, 16–17. Safarian left Kiğı on 4 September 1907 and left Batumi on a ship bound for Marseille over four months later on 15 January 1908. Safarian identifies the two proprietors as Hagop and Zakar *Agha*. Ibid., 14.
51. Garabed Safarian to Israel Safarian (4 April 1909), Ibid., 32.
52. BOA.DH.TMIK.M 49 75, Iskenderun based Informant to the Ministry of Interior (7 Kanunisani 1313/20 January 1898).
53. DH.TMIK.M 99 17, Monthly Report of the Iskenderun Pier Commission, Teşrinisani 1316, marginal note 1 (23 Ramazan 1318/14 January 1901).
54. BOA.DH.TMIK.M 123 26, Province of Trabzon to Ministry of Interior (11 Zilkade 1321/29 January 1904).
55. BOA.ZB.401 102, Ministry of Police to the Province of Aydin and District of Canık (6 Temmuz 1321/19 July 1905).
56. BOA.DH.TMIK.M 123 26, Province of Trabzon to Ministry of Interior (11 Zilkade 1321/29 January 1904).
57. BOA.TMIK.M 120 37, Governor of Adana Province to Ministry of Interior (9 Zilhicce 1319/19 March 1902).
58. Ibid.
59. By the late nineteenth century, Ottoman law strictly limited the number of Ottoman subjects that foreign diplomats could employ and to whom they could extend these special privileges. M. Şükrü Hanioğlu, *A Brief History*, 47.
60. BOA.DH.MKT 1958 51, Ministry of Interior to the Province of Adana (25 Mayıs 1308/7 June 1892).
61. BOA.Y.PRK.AZN 24 35 (30 Ağustos 1316/12 September 1900).
62. BOA.DH.TMIK.M 139 19, Pier Commission of Mersin to Ministry of Interior (14 Şevval 1320/12 January 1903).
63. BOA.HR.SYS 2795 64, Copy of report from Province of Adana to Ottoman Foreign Ministry (22 Teşrinievvel 1319/4 November 1903). For the response of the Russian Ambassador see BOA.HR.SYS 2795 64, Embassy of Russia in Constantinople to Ottoman Foreign Ministry (12 December 1903).
64. BOA.BEO 2234 167477, Office of the Grand Vizier to the Ottoman Foreign Ministry (20 Ramazan 1321/12 December 1903).
65. NARA, Despatches from the United States consuls in Harput, 1895–1906 Thomas Norton, U.S. Consul to Department of State (22 January 1901).
66. BOA.DH.MKT 1743 81, Governor of Trabzon Province to Ministry of Interior (30 Zilkade 1307/17 July 1890).
67. Documents concerning boatmen involved in smuggling migrants tell very similar stories, suggesting a highly systematised and organised process. See, for example: BOA.DH.TMIK.M 93 32, Report of the Ministry of

Interior Reform Commission (13 Cemazeyilevvel 1318/8 September 1900); BOA.DH.TMIK.M 121 23, Iskenderun Pier Commission to Ministry of Interior (2 Nisan 1318/13 April 1902); BOA.Y.PRK.AZN 24 35.

68. BOA.MKT.MHM 545 7, Province of Adana to Ministry of Health (10 Haziran 1315/23 June 1899).
69. BOA.MKT.MHM 545 7, Copy of report of Mersin Vice Consulate (12 Haziran 1322/25 June 1899; BOA.MKT.MHM 545 7, Report of the District Governor of Mersin (12 Haziran 1322/25 June 1899).
70. See for example: BOA.DH.TMIK.M 90 26, Iskenderun Pier Commission to Ministry of Interior (30 Mayıs 1316/12 June 1900); BOA.DH.TMIK.M, Governor of Halep Province to Ministry of Interior (4 Rabiulevvel 1320/10 June 1902).
71. BOA.DH.TMIK.M 92 4 (16 Safer 1318/12 June 1900).
72. BOA.Y.PRK.AZN 24 35 (2 Cemazeyilevvel 1323/4 August 1905). In at least one instance, a boatman based in Latakia reportedly smuggled several Armenian migrants from Mersin to Cyprus. See: BOA.DH.TMIK.M 121 23, Ministry of Interior to Aleppo and Beirut (13 Safer 1320/22 May 1902).
73. One report lists the vessel of a Latakia-based boatman as having a twenty-ton cargo capacity. BOA.Y.PRK.AZN 24 35 (12 Mart 1320/25 March 1904); BOA.DH.TMIK.M 121 23, Iskenderun Pier Commission to Ministry of Interior (2 Nisan 1318/13 April 1902).
74. BOA.DH.TMIK.M 76 43, Monthly Report of the Iskenderun Pier Commission Ağustos 1315 (10 Cemazeyilahir 1317/16 September 1899).
75. BOA.DH.TMIK.M 90 26, Iskenderun Pier Commission to Ministry of Interior (13 Rabiulahir 1316/11 August 1900).
76. BOA.DH.TMIK.M 121 23, Iskenderun Pier Commission to Ministry of Interior (2 Nisan 1318/13 April 1902).
77. BOA.DH.TMIK.M 42 55, Ministry of Police to the Ministry of Interior (26 Cemazeyilevvel 1315/23 October 1897). Muhammad appears to have been involved in smuggling migrants as late as 1907. See: ZB 709 29, Copy of Report of Beirut Pier Commission (21 Mayıs 1323/3 June 1907).
78. I use the term 'internal passport' with some hesitation. A more accurate translation of *mürur tezkeresi* is 'document of passage'. The system of laws that governed this system is discussed in much greater detail in Chapter 3. Nevertheless, in many ways, these documents resembled passports in both form and function. See also: David Gutman, 'Travel Documents, Mobility Control, and the Ottoman State in an Age of Global Migration,1880–1915', *Journal of the Ottoman and Turkish Studies Association*, Vol. 3, No. 2 (November 2016) 347–68.
79. BOA.DH.MKT 1859 60, Ministry of Interior to Province of Sivas (10 Muharrem 1309/16 August 1891).
80. '*Ahali bu hâli gördükçe hükümet memurlarından nefret etmektedir*'. BOA. DH.TMIK.M 50 21, Ministry of Interior to Province of Mamuretülaziz (23 Şevval 1315/17 March 1898). The informant's statements on the civil

registrar's actions were part of a much longer missive directed at what he saw as rampant and destructive corruption by numerous officials in the district's bureaucracy.

81. BOA.DH.MKT 2094 46, Ministry of Interior to Province of Mamuretülaziz (4 Rabiulahir 1316/22 August 1898).
82. BOA.ZB 446 101, Ministry of Police, Council of Investigation to Province of Mamuretülaziz (8 Ağustos 1323/21 August 1907).
83. NARA, Despatches from the United States consuls in Harput, 1895–1906, Thomas Norton, U.S. Consul to John G. A. Leishman, Minister Plenipotentiary, Constantinople (5 November 1903).
84. BOA.DH.MKT 1976 17, Ministry of Interior to Coastal Provinces and the Ministry of Police (27 Zilhicce 1309/22 July 1892).
85. BOA.Y.PRK.AZN 24 35 (30 Ağustos 1316/12 September 1900).
86. BOA.TMIK.M 120 37, Ministry of Interior to Province of Adana (9 Zilhicce 1319/19 March 1902).
87. BOA.ZB 709 29, Report of Beirut Pier Commission (18 Ağustos 1323/31 August 1907).
88. See also: DH.TMIK.M 247 34, Coastal Inspector to the Office of the Commander of the Fifth Army (no date given).
89. See Chapters 4 and 5.
90. BOA.ZB 108 29, Province of Mamuretülaziz to Ministry of Police (2 Ağustos 1323/15 August 1907). Naturally, the operation did not come cheap. According to the governor's report, Artin Harputlian received at least one hundred liras from the two groups, a sum that appears not to have included monies paid out to the various officials involved in the plot.
91. BOA.MKT.MHM 659 52, Office of the Grand Vizier to Ministry of Interior (11 Şaban 323/10 October 1905).
92. BOA.DH.TMIK.M 249 56, Testimony of Hüseyin Farid Efendi (3 Eylül 1323/16 September 1907).
93. For more on Frontex' efforts, see: Maurizio Albahari, *Crimes of Peace*; Ruben Andersson, *Illegality, Inc.*

Chapter 3

1. In addition to the boatmen's fees, the letter states that the four had collectively paid thirty-two liras for passage to Marseille.
2. BOA.DH.MKT 38 17, Governor of Adana Province to Ministry of Interior (14 Rebiulevvel 1311/24 September 1893).
3. BOA.DH.MKT 38 17, Foreign Ministry Translation Office, Translation of Letter from the Embassy of France (28 October 1893).
4. BOA.DH.MKT 1511 119, Ministry of Interior to Grand Vizier (27 Ramazan 1305/7 June 1888).
5. BOA.DH.MKT 1549 75, Ministry of Interior to Ministry of Police (25 Muharrem 1306/3 October 1888).

6. Musa Çadırcı, 'Tanzimat döneminde', 169.
7. Ibid., 170.
8. Christoph Herzog, 'Migration and the State', 121.
9. Musa Çadırcı, 'Tanzimat döneminde', 174–8.
10. This is not to imply the existence of a linear transformation from a static pre-modern imperial economy to a dynamic and mobile one. As Reşat Kasaba (among others) has rightly pointed out, mobility of all sorts was a critical component of the empire's political economy from its inception (see, for example: Reşat Kasaba, *A Moveable Empire: Ottoman Nomads, Migrants, and Refugees* (Seattle: University of Washington Press, 2009). In addition, labour migration and trade had long been fixtures of the Ottoman economy. Overall, however, the nineteenth century did witness significant overall increases in the importance of both domestic and international trade (see: Donald Quataert, 'The Age of Reforms'.). Furthermore, labour migration from the eastern provinces of the Ottoman Empire to long-standing destinations such as Istanbul and Aleppo, as well as emerging economic nodes such as Adana increased greatly, especially in the second half of the nineteenth century (see: Christopher Clay, 'Migration and Economic Conditions'). The emergence in 1841 of the *Men'-i Mürur Nizamnamesi* to regulate such movements, which, unlike the mobility of nomadic groups or refugees that lent themselves to more individuated forms of regulation, should be understood as a reflection of these broader transformations in the empire's political economy.
11. As Cem Behar notes in his study of Istanbul's Kasap İlyas neighbourhood, local headmen were ill-equipped to monitor the constant flow of labour migrants in and out of the neighbourhood. According to his findings, residents regularly failed to register with the headman when they first arrived or when they departed, and were often not in possession of internal passports. Cem Behar, *A Neighborhood in Ottoman Istanbul*, 120.
12. Engin Akarli, 'Ottoman Attitudes'. By the first decade of the twentieth century, migrants from the empire's Balkan provinces were also using internal passports to facilitate illegal migration.
13. For a thorough comparison of the Lebanese and Armenian cases, see: David Gutman, *Travel Documents*.
14. BOA.DH.MKT 41 5, Ministry of Interior to Grand Vizier (25 Zilkade 1310/11 June 1893).
15. BOA.DH.MKT 19 34, Ministry of Interior to the Grand Vizier (8 Şevval 1310/26 April 1893).
16. BOA.DH.MKT 19 34, Province of Adana, Copy of report from the District Governor of Mersin (20 Kanunisani 1308/12 February 1893).
17. BOA.DH.MKT 41 5, Ministry of Interior to Grand Vizier (18 Zilhicce 1310/3 June 1893).
18. BOA.DH.MKT 16 4, Ministry of Interior to Grand Vizier (29 Şevval 1310/17 May 1893).

19. BOA.DH.TMIK.M 22 85, Iskenderun Pier Commission to Ministry of Interior (4 Teşrinisani 1312/16 November 1896).
20. BOA.DH.TMIK.M 22 85, Ministry of Interior to Iskenderun Pier Commission (6 Teşrinisani 1312/18 November 1896).
21. BOA.DH.TMIK.M 134 13, Copy of telegram from Province of Mamuretülaziz (13 Teşrinievvel 1318/26 October 1902).
22. BOA.MKT.MHM 654 11, Ministry of Interior to Grand Vizier (26 Muharrem 1320/29 April 1902).
23. BOA.DH.MKT 38 17, P.M Kourtzi & Co. to Ministry of Interior (14 Şevval 1310/1 May 1893).
24. BOA.DH.MKT 38 17, Ministry of Interior to Grand Vizier (1 Haziran 1309/14 June 1893).
25. BOA.DH.TMIK 38 17, Province of Trabzon to Ministry of Interior (11 Zilkade 1310/28 May 1893).
26. BOA.DH.MKT 38 17, Ministry of Police to Ministry of Interior. (19 Zilkade 1310/5 June 1893).
27. BOA.DH.MKT 38 17, Grand Vizier to Ministry of Interior (6 Zilhicce 1310/21 June 1893).
28. BOA.DH.TMIK.M 88 11, Ministry of Interior to Ministry of Police (16 Safer 1318/16 June 1900).
29. BOA.DH.MKT 288 78, Ministry of Interior to Grand Vizier (27 Rabiulevvel 1312/27 September 1894).
30. BOA.DH.TMIK.M 119 73, Province of Erzurum to Ministry of Interior (29 Şevval 1319/8 February 1902).
31. BOA.DH.TMIK.M 4 6, Ministry of Interior copy of telegram from Province of Diyarbekir (18 Nisan 1312/1 May 1896).
32. BOA.DH.TMIK.M 4 6, Ministry of Interior Reform Commission to Provinces of Adana, Aleppo, and Beirut, and the Sub-province of Jerusalem (29 Nisan 1316/11 May 1896).
33. BOA.DH.MKT 1743 81, Governor of Trabzon to Ministry of Interior (30 Zilkade 1307/17 July 1890).
34. Christopher Clay, 'Labour Migration', 10.
35. For example, Donald Quataert described Mersin at the turn of the twentieth century as 'an exposed roadstead: railroad cargoes were onloaded via long, unprotected piers equipped with a light tram and small cranes'. See: Quataert, 'Age of Reforms', 802.
36. Sibel Zandi-Sayek, 'Struggles Over the Shore'.
37. See for example: BOA.DH.MKT 1055 43 (10 Muharrem 1324/6 March 1906).
38. For further information about these documents and their usefulness in gauging passenger traffic through these ports, see Chapter 4.
39. BOA.DH.TMIK.M 72 12, Iskenderun Pier Commission to Ministry of Interior (3 Ağustos 1315/16 August 1899).
40. BOA.DH.TMIK.M 93 32, Office of the Military General Staff Branch

4- copy of telegram from Representative to the Adana High Commandant Farik Ali Muhas Paşa (8 Haziran 1316/21 June 1900).

41. BOA.DH.TMIK.M 93 32, Grand Vizier to Ministry of Interior (8 Rebiulevvel 1318/4 July 1900).
42. BOA.DH.TMIK.M 139 19, Council of the Mersin Pier Commission to Ministry of Interior (14 Şevval 1320/30 January 1903).
43. BOA.DH.TMIK.M 92 4, Province of Aleppo copy of response of the Council of the Iskenderun Pier Commission to the Office of the Governor of the sub-Province of Iskenderun (30 Mayis 1316/12 June 1900).
44. BOA.DH.TMIK.M 92 4, Ministry of Interior Reform Commission to Ministry of Police (15 Rabiulahir 1318/11 August 1900).
45. See for example: Donald Quataert, *Social Disintegration*, 95–120. Can Nacar's work also demonstrates the political and economic strength that boatmen in Mersin possessed. As he also shows, however, they came under increasing pressure in the late nineteenth and early twentieth centuries as large transport enterprises increasingly impinged on their economic livelihood. This may have been a factor leading many to participate in smuggling operations. See: Can Nacar, 'Yükselen Bir Liman Kentinde'.
46. BOA.DH.TMIK.M 127 14, Council of the Mersin Pier Commission to Ministry of Interior (25 Rabiulevvel 1320/7 July 1902).
47. BOA.DH.TMIK.M 92 4, Ministry of Interior Reform Commission to Ministry of Police (15 Rabiulahir 1318/11 August 1900).
48. See for example: BOA.DH.TMIK.M 72 12, Iskenderun Pier Commission to Ministry of Interior (3 Ağustos 1315/21 September 1899); BOA. DH.TMIK.M 125 41, Iskenderun Pier Commission to Ministry of Interior (29 Mart 1318/11 April 1902).
49. BOA.ZB 708 29, Copy of Report of Commission of the Beirut Pier Commission (21 Mayıs 1323/3 June 1907).
50. BOA.DH.TMIK.M 252 55, Report of the Beirut Pier Commission (2 Ağustos 323/15 August 1907).
51. BOA ZB 709 29, Police Directorate and Gendarmerie Commandant to Beirut Pier Commission (7 Cemazeyilevvel 1325/16 June 1907).
52. BOA.DH.TMIK.M 139 19, Committee of the Mersin Pier Commission to Ministry of Interior (14 Şevval 1320/12 January 1903).
53. BOA.DH.TMIK.M 139 19, Governor of Adana to Minister of Interior (18 Şevval 1320/17 January 1903).
54. BOA.DH.TMIK.M 139 19, Governor of Beirut to Ministry of Interior (20 Zilhicce 1320/20 March 1903).
55. BOA.DH.TMIK.M 139 19, Governor of Aleppo to Ministry of Interior (4 Muharrem 1321/2 April 1903).
56. BOA.DH.TMIK.M 150 54, Translated copy of letter from Agop Avadisiyan to İstepan Ağa Daldayan (22 Haziran 1319/5 July 1903).
57. BOA.DH.TMIK.M 150 54, Governor of Aleppo to Minister of Interior (9 Cemazeyilevvel 1321/2 August 1319).

58. BOA.DH.MKT 1914 103, Ministry of Interior to Mamuretülaziz and Aleppo Provinces (23 Cemazeyilevvel 1309/23 January 1892).
59. BOA.DH.MKT 1931 29, Ministry of Interior to Governor of Adana İzzet Efendi (10 Şaban 1309/9 March 1892).
60. See for example: BOA.BEO 45 3317, Office of the Grand Vizier to Ministry of Police (6 Muharrem 1310/31 July 1892) BOA.DH.TMIK.M 77 29, Governor of Diyarbekir to Ministry of Interior (26 Teşrinievvel 1315/7 November 1899).
61. See for example: BOA.DH.MKT 19 34, Governor of Adana province-copy of report from governor of Mersin sub-province (30 Kanunisani 1308/12 February 1893); BOA.DH.TMIK.M 68 72, Ministry of Police to Ministry of Interior (18 Zilhicce 1316/30 April 1899); BOA.DH.TMIK.M 88 11, Samsun Pier Commission to Ministry of Police (no date given).
62. BOA.DH.TMIK.M 76 2, Governor of Adana province to Ministry of Interior (11 Eylül 1315/24 September 1899).
63. BOA.DH.TMIK.M 89 55, Ministry of Interior-Reform Commission to Province of Mamuretülaziz (5 Temmuz 1316/18 July 1900).
64. Ibid.
65. BOA.DH.TMIK.M 89 55, Governor of Mamuretülaziz to Ministry of Interior (5 Temmuz 1316/18 July 1900).
66. BOA.DH.TMIK.M 132 6, Commission of the Iskenderun Pier Commission to Minister of Interior (4 Ağustos 1320/17 August 1902).
67. BOA.DH.TMIK.M 132 6, Governor of Mamuretülaziz Province to Ministry of Interior (25 Recep 1320/27 October 1902).
68. Reports of North America-bound migrants acquiring internal passports ostensibly for pilgrimage travel to Jerusalem abound in the documentation. See for example: BOA.ŞD 2224 7, Telegram from Aleppo Province to Ministry of Interior (1 Mart 1309/14 March 1893); BOA.DH.TMIK.M 4 6, Copy of Telegram from Diyarbekir Province to Ministry of Interior (18 Nisan 1312/1 May 1896); BOA.DH.TMIK.M 119 73, Governor of Adana to Ministry of Interior (23 Şubat 1317/8 March 1902).
69. In a similar case, officials in Trabzon complained that their counterparts in the province of Erzurum were failing to practice due diligence in vetting applicants for internal passports, leading to a spate of illegal embarkations. In an almost comically brief response to the accusation, the governor of Erzurum claimed no more than five internal passports had been given to provincial residents for travel to Trabzon in the past two years combined. See documents in: BOA.DH.TMIK.M 224 43.
70. BOA.DH.TMIK.M 141 31, Governor of Aleppo province to Ministry of Interior (12 Mart 1319/25 March 1903).
71. Nadir Özbek, 'Policing the Countryside', 55.
72. Rifa'at Abou-El-Haj, *Formation of the Modern State*, 61–72.
73. ZB 108 29, Province of Mamuretülaziz to Ministry of Police (6 Recep

1325/15 August 1907). The governor's letter cites a mix-up of documents related to two separate cases (including the case against Artin) along with accusations of torture by officials prosecuting the case against those implicated in the conspiracy as the primary reasons for the case's dismissal. His letter proceeds to challenge the validity of both pretexts, claiming all documents were supplied in a legal manner with all necessary signatures, and that claims of torture were unfounded.

74. BOA.DH.MKT 1075 19, Informant to Minister of Interior (24 Mart 1322/6 April 1906).
75. It is unclear at this point the circumstances under which Hasan Bey left his position. Interestingly, both he and Halid Bey were members of the powerful Council of State (Şura-yı Devlet). Upon leaving his position as governor, he was returned to a position on the Council of State. Further probing may reveal the extent to which the brevity of his tenure was related to his attempts to intervene in local politics.
76. BOA.DH.MKT 1075 19, Governor of Mamuretülaziz to Ministry of Interior (1 Rabiulahir 1324/25 May 1906).
77. NARA, Despatches from the United States consuls in Turkey, 1904–1912, Evan Young, U.S. Consul, Harput, to HM. Smith-Lyle Esquire, American Vice Consul General, Constantinople (10 May 1907).
78. BOA.DH.TMIK.M 252 61, Statement of Fabrikatorian Minas Efendi (Minas Fabrikatorian) (10 Temmuz 324/23 July 1907).
79. This feud would continue well into the Second Constitutional Era, including a major dispute between the two families over a proposal by the Fabrikatorian family to widen a roadway in the city of Harput near a business owned by the Fabrikatorian family. See: BOA.DH.TMIK.M 56 13 (16 Muharrem 1329/17 January 1911).
80. BOA.DH.TMIK.M 252 61, Statement of Hüseyin Farid Efendi (3 Eylül 1323/16 September 1907).
81. Harputlian Artin would retain his position on the powerful Provincial Executive Council well into the Young Turk Era. See: BOA.MTV 62 53 (30 Muharrem 1332/29 December 1913).
82. BOA.ZB 156 152 (12 Ağustos 1322/25 August 1906).

Part II Introduction

1. NARA, Despatches from the U.S. Consuls in Sivas, 1895–1906, Milo Jewett, U.S. Consul to J. G. A. Leishman, Minister Plenipotentiary, Constantinople (12 April 1906). Copies of Topalian's naturalisation papers and military service records can be found in a communiqué sent to Istanbul a few months later. See: NARA, Despatches from the U.S. Consuls in Sivas, 1895–1906, Milo Jewett, U.S. Consul to J. G. A. Leishman, Minister Plenipotentiary, Constantinople (27 September 1906).
2. NARA, Despatches from the U.S. Consuls in Sivas, 1895–1906, P. A. Jay,

American Chargé d'Affaires, Constantinople to Milo Jewett, U.S. Consul (24 April 1906).

3. NARA, Despatches from the U.S. Consuls in Sivas, 1895–1906, Lewis Iddings, U.S. Consul General, Cairo to J. G. A Leishman, U.S. Ambassador, Constantinople (16 March 1907).

Chapter 4

1. Garabed Safarian to Israel Safarian (18 June 1909). In A. E. Safarian, *Letters from Armenia*, 34–6.
2. Hagop Kevorkian to Israel Safarian (18 January 1911). In, ibid., 45–8.
3. NARA, Despatches from the United States consuls in Harput, 1895–1906, Thomas Norton, U.S. Consul to David J. Hill, Assistant Secretary of State, Washington, DC (17 May 1901).
4. For the contemporary period, Anthropologist Ruben Andersson argues that the European Union's frenzied efforts to strengthen its mobility control efforts over the Mediterranean and to outsource its enforcement of migration policies to various countries in North and Sub-Saharan Africa are wholly out of proportion to the rather tiny percentage of irregular migrants who attempt to enter Europe by sea. According to Andersson, this outsized response is fuelled by the widespread perception in Europe that the continent risks 'invasion' by migrants entering from the south. Ruben Andersson: *Illegality, Inc.*, 4–8.
5. The United States government did not keep regular statistics on return migration until 1908.
6. Isabel Kaprielian's work is an exception to this. See: Isabel Kaprielian, 'Sojourners from Keghi'.
7. These numbers are taken from Robert Mirak's work in the Commission's records. See: Robert Mirak, *Torn Between Two Lands*, 265. Commission numbers released in 1911 are slightly higher than Mirak's, citing 234 Armenians departing the United States in 1908, 561 in 1909, and 521 in 1910. See: William Dillingham, *Reports of Immigration Commission: Statistical Review of Immigration, 1820–1910* (Washington, D.C.: Government Printing Office, 1911), 373.
8. Robert Mirak, *Torn Between Two Lands*, 265.
9. For statistics on Lebanese return migration, see: Akram Khater, *Inventing Home*, 110–14. In order to produce a very rough and conservative estimate of a rate of Lebanese return migration in this period of twenty-five percent, Khater also uses the Immigration Commission records that provide an average annual rate of Lebanese arrivals to the United States between 1899 and 1914 of nearly 5200 per annum, and an annual average of Lebanese departing the country between 1908 and 1910 of approximately 1300. Khater is tentative enough about these statistics to title this section of the book, 'Ambiguous Numbers'. For a detailed analysis of return migration in

the Italian case, see: Dino Cinel, *The National*. For a more general discussion of the phenomenon of return migration in the late nineteenth and early twentieth centuries, including detailed statistics, see: Mark Wyman, *Return Trip to America*.

10. Manoog Dzeron, *Village of Parchanj*, 209. For more on Armenian responses to the 1908 revolution, see: see: Bedross Der Matossian, *Shattered Dreams of Revolution*.
11. Robert Mirak, *Torn Between Two Lands*, 1983: 77. Isabel Kaprielian, while echoing Mirak's claims that return migration was a rarity before 1908 (p. 122), provides some anecdotal evidence that would suggest otherwise. Isabel Kaprielian, 'Sojourners from Keghi', 228–9; 250.
12. This issue will be discussed in greater depth below and in Chapter 5. Documents abound in both United States and Ottoman sources on the issue of Armenian return in the mid-1890s. For example, documents in the file BOA.HR.SYS 2827 contain correspondences and summaries of correspondences between the two governments on this matter.
13. Whereas the reports for March–October include numerous pages of information and provide detailed quantitative and qualitative information on the numbers of Armenians arriving to Samsun from North America, the report for the month of Teşrinievvel 1314 (October–November 1898) consists of only one page. Armenians returning from North America are not specifically enumerated but rather are included in a vague category dubbed 'miscellaneous foreign arrivals' (*memalik-i ecnebiyye-i saireden gelen*).
14. BOA.DH.TMIK.M 52 1 (24 Zilkade 1315/16 April 1898); BOA.DH.TMIK.M 53 16 (25 Zilhicce 1315/17 May 1898); BOA.DH.TMIK.M 54 51 (1 Safer 1316/ 21 June 1898); BOA.DH.TMIK.M 56 39 (28 Safer 1316/18 July 1898); BOA.DH.TMIK.M 58 57 (5 Rabiulahir 1316/22 August 1898); BOA.DH.TMIK.M 62 41 (5 Cemazeyilahir 1316/21 October 1898).
15. BOA.DH.TMIK.M 72 60, Samsun Pier Commission to Ministry of Interior (30 Safer 1317/8 July 1899); BOA.DH.TMIK.M BOA.DH.TMIK.M 78 46, Samsun Pier Commission to Ministry of Interior (8 Recep 1317/12 November 1899); BOA.DH.TMIK.M 79 29, Samsun Pier Commission to Ministry of Interior (29 Recep 1317/3 December 1899); BOA.DH.TMIK.M 79 14, Samsun Port Commission to Ministry of Interior (6 Şaban 1317/10 December 1899).
16. Leo Bergholz, U.S. Consul at Erzurum to David Hill, Assistant Secretary of State, Washington, DC (19 September 1899); Norton (Harput) to David Hill, Assistant Secretary of State (16 April 1901). In a report sent to the United States Secretary of State in April 1901, the United States consul in Harput estimated that nearly three hundred Armenian naturalised citizens (of the United States) of 'native birth' were residing in his consular district (comprised of the provinces of Mamuretülaziz and Diyarbekir). These figures, presumably provided to the consul by local contacts in the

Armenian community, only represent returnees known or suspected to be naturalised citizens of the United States, and thus represent only a portion of the returnee population in the region.

17. BOA.MKT.MHM 550 1, Ministry of Interior to Office of the Grand Vizier (27 Şaban 1323/26 October 1905).
18. BOA.I.DH 1075 84332, Yıldız Palace Office of the Chief Scribe (18 Recep 1305/31 March 1888).
19. BOA.Y.A.RES 55 53, Sublime Port Council of Ministers (2 Zilhicce 1308/6 July 1891); BOA.I.HUS 3 1310 S/114, Yıldız Palace Office of the Chief Scribe (21 Safer 1310/13 September 1892).
20. BOA.I.DH 1075 84332, Yıldız Palace Office of the Chief Scribe (18 Recep 1305/31 March 1888).
21. For more on Hagop Bogigian, see: David Gutman, 'Migrants, Revolutionaries, and Spies, 284–96; Hagop Martin Deranian, *Hagop Bogigian*.
22. Musa Çadırcı, 'Tanzimat Döneminde, 178–81.
23. This policy is discussed in greater detail in Chapter 5.
24. Y.PRK.BSK 31 101 (29 Zilhicce 1310/14 July 1893).
25. BOA.DH.MKT 2063 83, Ottoman Consul in New York Mehmet Fuat Bey to Office of the Grand Vizier (22 Safer 1311/6 September 1893). Although dated September, the document references correspondences dating back to July 1893.
26. BOA.Y.PRK.ZB 12 17, Yıldız Palace Office of the Office of the Chief Scribe of the Grand Vizier (3 Safer 1311/16 August 1893).
27. Ibid.
28. BOA.Y.PRK.ZB 12 17, Yıldız to Grand Vizier (3 Safer 1311/16 August 1893).
29. BOA.Y.MTV 111 10, Armenian Patriarchate in Istanbul to the Chief Secretary of Yıldız Palace (20 Cemaziyelahir 1312/19 December 1894).
30. MKT.MHM 533 41, Grand Vizier to Province of Trabzon (13Kanunievvel 1310/25 December 1894).
31. MKT.MHM 533 41, Ministry of Police to Grand Vizier (16 Recep 1321/22 December 1894).
32. HR.SYS 2782 2, Foreign Ministry Office of Legal Counsel (26 Rabiulevvel 1313/16 September 1895).
33. BOA.HR.SYS 2742 9, Copy of Report sent from the New York Consulate to the Ottoman Embassy in Washington (24 Teşrinievvel 1898/24 October 1898).
34. BOA.HR.SYS 2739 24, Copy of report from Ministry of Interior to Foreign Ministry (24 Recep 1312/20 January 1895).
35. BOA.TMIK.M 45 24, Ministry of Interior to Office of the Grand Vizier (20 Cemazeyilahir 1315/16 November 1897).
36. BOA.DH.TMIK.M 41 13, Province of Beirut to Ministry of Interior (29 Eylül 1313/12 October 1897).
37. I have not been able to locate the original decree, which is referenced in:

BOA.DH.TMIK.M 32 64, Ministry of Interior to Province of Aleppo (29 Haziran 1313/11 July 1897).

38. BOA.DH.TMIK.M 46 5 (5 Cemazeyilevvel 1315/1 November 1897). The document contains profiles of thirteen Armenian migrants; however, only twelve are confirmed as having migrated to America.
39. DH.TMIK.M 46 5, Governor of Mamuretülaziz Province to Ministry of Interior (5 Cemaziyülahir 1315/1 November 1897).
40. BOA.46 26, Governor of Trabzon Province to Ministry of Interior (27 Şaban 1313/21 January 1898).
41. MKT.MHM 542 19, Province of Trabzon to Ministry of Interior (17 Kanunievvel 1313/30 December 1897).
42. BOA.MV 94 24, Decision of the Council of Ministers (16 Şaban 1315/5 January 1898).
43. NARA, Despatches from the U.S. Consuls in Sivas, 1895–1906, Milo. A Jewett, U.S. Consul to David Hill, Assistant Secretary of State, Washington, DC (25 March 1899).
44. BOA.MV 94 24, Decision of the Council of Ministers (16 Şaban 1315/5 January 1898).
45. BOA.MV 94 24, Ottoman Council of Ministers (16 Şaban 1315/5 January 1898).
46. Aristide Zolberg, *A Nation by Design*, 229.
47. BOA.DH.TMİK.M 73 60, Decision of Ministry of Interior Reform Commission (7 Rabiulahir 1317/14 August 1899).
48. BOA.DH.TMIK.M 52 93, Province of Mamuretülaziz to Ministry of Interior (22 Zilkade 1315/14 April 1898).
49. BOA.DH.TMIK.M 52 93, Ministry of Interior Reform Commission to Ministry of Police (24 Safer 1316/12 July 1898).
50. BOA.DH.TMIK.M 55 30, Ministry of Interior to the Province of Trabzon (23 Safer 1316/13 July 1898). For their part, local officials vigorously denied that returnees were being escorted to the interior in chains.
51. BOA.DH.TMIK.M 61 78, Petition sent to Armenian Patriarchate in Istanbul (2 Teşrinievvel 1314/15 October 1899).
52. BOA.DH.TMIK.M 105 13, Ministry of Interior to the Province of Trabzon (11 Mayis 1317/24 May 1901). Unfortunately, the outcome of both petitions is unclear from the available documentation.
53. See for example: Profiles of Asadeer der Bogosian, Mardross Garabedian, and Sarkis der Garabedian in NARA, Despatches from the U.S. Consuls in Harput, 1895–1906, Thomas Norton U.S. Consul to John G. A. Leishman, Minister Plenipotenitiary, Constantinople (23 November 1903).
54. BOA.DH.TMIK.M 79 17, Mersin Pier Commission to Ministry of Interior (20 Recep 1318/14 November 1899); BOA.DH.TMIK.M 81 21, Ministry of Police to Ministry of Interior (1 Şevval 1317/4 January 1900).
55. DH.TMIK.M 76 77, Ministry of Interior to Ministry of Police (18 Cemazeyilahir 1317/24 October 1899).

56. BOA.DH.TMIK.M 52 110, Iskenderun Pier commission to Ministry of Interior (17 Teşrinievvel 1315/29 August 1899).
57. Ibid., Iskenderun Pier commission to Ministry of Interior (6 Şubat 1315/18 February 1900).
58. BOA.DH.TMIK.M 78 28, Ministry of Interior to Province of Adana (4 Cemaziyilevvel 1318/30 August 1900).
59. BOA.MV 102 30, Decision of the Ottoman Council of Ministers (1 Safer 1319/19 May 1901).
60. BOA.Y.PRK.ZB 26 92, Assistant Police Inspector for Beyoğlu to Yıldız Palace (13 Mart 1317/26 March 1901).
61. See for example: BOA.DH.TMIK.M 81 21, Governor of Jerusalem to Ministry of Interior (11 Mart 1316/24 March 1900); HR.SYS 2863 46, Ottoman Embassy in Paris to Ministry of Interior (28 Teşrinisani 1901/28 November 1901).
62. BOA.Y.EE.KP 22 2116, 28 Haziran 1320/10 July 1904.
63. BOA.ZB 400 104, Ministry of Police to Province of Aydın (2 Eylül 1320/15 September 1904).
64. Boghos Jafarian, *Farewell Kharpert*, 59–60.
65. BOA.ZB 320 4, Ministry of Police to Ministry of Interior (21 Kanunievvel 1322/3 January 1907).
66. BOA.MKT.MHM 659 47, Ministry of Interior to Office of Grand Vizier (14 Rabiulahir 1322/28 June 1904).
67. BOA.ZB 446 37, Ministry of Police to Mamuretülaziz Province (15 Eylül 1322/28 September 1906).
68. BOA.ZB 709 29, Copy of report from Pier Commission of Beirut (31 Mayis 1323/13 June 1907).
69. See for example: BOA.DH.TMIK.M 246 33, Mersin Customs Office to Ministry of Interior (23 Rabiulahir 1325/25 May 1907); BOA.DH.TMIK.M 265 49, Cyprus Saltworks Directorate to Beirut Customs Office (8 Şubat 1323/21 February 1908).
70. See for example: BOA.HR.SYS 2863 46, Ottoman Consulate in Paris to Foreign Ministry (26 Teşrinisani 1901/26 November 1901).
71. BOA.DH.TMIK.M 200 86, Province of Mamuretülaziz to Ministry of Interior (25 Cemazeyilevvel 1323/28 July 1905).
72. For a description of the events surrounding the assassination attempt, see: Gaidz Minassian, 'The Armenian Revolutionary Federation'.
73. Toygun Altıntaş, 'The Ottoman War', 115.
74. BOA.DH.TMIK.M 232 6, Province of Mamuretülaziz to Ministry of Interior (5 Teşrinievvel 1322/18 October 1906).
75. BOA.DH.TMIK.M 236 14, District of İçil to Ministry of Interior (16 Kanunievel 1322/29 December 1906).
76. BOA.ZB 476 111, Ministry of Police to the Mersin Inspectorate for Volatile and Flammable Materials (31 May 1323/13 June 1907).
77. DH.TMIK.M 243 55, Copy of Report from Adana Province (10 Kanunisani 1322/23 January 1907).

78. DH.TMIK.M 243 55, Ministry of Police to Ministry of Interior (23 Rabiulahir 1325/5 June 1907).
79. DH.TMIK.M 243 55, Ministry of the Navy to Ministry of Interior (22 Muharrem 1323/25 February 1908).
80. BOA.DH.TMIK.M 267 35, Province of Adana to Ministry of Interior (3 Nisan 1324/17 April 1908).
81. BOA.DH.TMIK.M 267 35, Ministry of Interior to Office of Grand Vizier (10 Nisan 1324/23 April 1908).
82. Mostafa Minawi, *The Ottoman Scramble for Africa*, 122.
83. BOA.DH.TMIK.M 259 48, Tuzla Telegraph Clerk to the Postal and Telegraph Ministry (15 Teşrinisani 1323/28 November 1907). With the Ottoman line out of service, Ottoman telegraph clerks were likely forced to rely on infrastructure controlled by the British, and thus were entirely at their mercy as to when their messages were sent out. For more on the imperial politics of Ottoman telegraph infrastructure, see: Minawi, *Ottoman Scramble*, 99–115.
84. BOA.DH.TMIK.M 259 48, Ministry of Interior to the provinces of Adana, Aleppo, Beirut, Aydin and Konya (12 Kanunievvel 1323/25 January 1908).
85. For more on Cyprus' status as a British protectorate, see: Andrekos Varnova, *British Imperialism in Cyprus*.
86. Aimee M. Genell, 'Empire by Law', 12.
87. BOA.DH.TMIK.M 259 48, Tuzla Telegraph Clerk to the Postal and Telegraph Ministry (15 Teşrinisani 1323/28 November 1907).
88. Exceptions to this include: Sabri Ateş. See: Sabri Ateş, The *Ottoman Iranian Borderlands*; Matthew Ellis, *Desert Borderland*.
89. Beth Lew-Williams, *The Chinese Must Go*, 88.
90. See: ibid., 53–88.
91. See, for example: BOA.DH.TMIK.M 269 19, Governor of Trabzon Province to Ministry of Interior (28 Rabiulevvel 1326/25 April 1908).
92. Case in point, two returnees who were caught attempting to enter the empire at Tripoli on the Levantine coast dressed as Bedouins. BOA.DH.TMIK.M 268 5, Tripoli Pier Commission to Ministry of Interior (17 Mart 1324/30 March 1908).
93. BOA.DH.TMIK.M 266 35, Yıldız Palace Decree (1 Rabiulevvel 1326/4 April 1908).

Chapter 5

1. Irene Bloemraad, 'Citizenship Lessons', 930.
2. Ibid.
3. Kemal Karpat, 'The Ottoman Emigration', 185.
4. Akram Khater, *Inventing Home*, 108–45.
5. Torrie Hester, *Deportation*, 49–50.
6. Selim Deringil, *Conversion and Apostacy*, 182.

7. Will Hanley, 'What Ottoman Nationality', 277–98.
8. Ibid., 284.
9. Alexander De Groot, 'The Historical Development', 575–604.
10. Umut Özsu, 'The Ottoman Empire', 129.
11. Lale Can, 'The Protection Question', 681.
12. Will Hanley, 'What Ottoman Nationality Was', 284.
13. Quoted in: Ibid., 287.
14. Karpat, 'Ottoman Emigration', 190. British passports specifically stated that the bearer, if a naturalised citizen of Britain, would not be recognised as such if his naturalisation had taken place in contravention of the laws of his natal country. The Ottoman government would later pressure the United States to adopt similar language.
15. Ibid.,190.
16. Leland Gordon, 'Turkish–American Treaty Relations', 716.
17. According to Patrick Weil, the United States government signed more than three dozen such treaties and agreements following 1868, the year it signed the treaty with Prussia that served as the model for the US–Ottoman agreement. See: Patrick Weil, *The Sovereign Citizen*, 4.
18. BOA.Y.A RES 55 53, Governor of Mamuretülaziz Province to Ministry of Interior (19 Şevval 1308/28 May 1901).
19. BOA.Y.A RES 55 53, Ottoman Council of Ministers (2 Zilhicce 1308/6 July 1891). The council had made a similar recommendation the previous year. See: BOA.Y.A RES 51 20, Ottoman Council of Ministers (15 Zilkade 1307/3 July 1890). According to Craig Robertson, the United States State Department recognised the renewal of a passport, which the bearer of the document was required to perform every two years, as a satisfactory method by which an individual could avoid the presumption that he had denaturalised through 'silent withdrawal'. See: Craig Robertson, *The Passport in America*, 152.
20. BOA.MV 76 123, Decision of the Ottoman Council of Ministers (8 Recep 1311/19 October 1893).
21. See Chapter 4.
22. Dorothee Schneider, *Crossing Borders*, 196.
23. Patrick Weil, *The Sovereign Citizen*, 17. One important exception to this concerned Chinese migrants who, after the passage of the Chinese Exclusion Act of 1882, were legally barred from naturalising as US citizens. See: Lucy Salyer, *Laws as Harsh as Tigers*, 17–18.
24. Aristide Zolberg, *A Nation by Design*, 80–1.
25. Patrick Weil, *The Sovereign Citizen*, 15.
26. Dorothee Schneider, *Crossing Borders*, 204.
27. BOA.Y.A. RES 68 49, Foreign Minister to Grand Vizier (9 Cemaziyelahir 1311/18 December 1893).
28. Craig Robertson, *The Passport in America*, 151–8.
29. BOA.HR.SYS 2782 2, Mavroyeni to Foreign Minister, Said Pasha (4 August

1893). This document is the summary of Mavroyeni's letter to Gresham he forwarded to his superiors in Istanbul. The original document is unavailable.

30. BOA.HR.SYS 2782 2, Gresham to Mavroyeni (24 August 1893).
31. BOA.HR.SYS 2782 2, Secretary of State Walter Gresham to Mavroyeni (24 August 1893).
32. Adam McKeown, *Melancholy Order*, 94.
33. Beth Lew-Williams, *The Chinese Must Go*, 178–85.
34. Ibid., 189.
35. Quoted in ibid., 189.
36. Grover Cleveland, First Annual Address (second term), 4 December 1893.
37. Grover Cleveland, quoted in: Adam McKeown, *Melancholy Order*, 171.
38. Grover Cleveland, First Annual Address (second term), 4 December 1893.
39. 'Outrages on American Citizens', *New York Times*, 12 February 1894.
40. 'The Sultan Need Not Tremble Yet', *New York Times*, 11 February 1894.
41. BOA.HR.SYS 2782 2, Minister Plenipotentiary A. W. Terrell to Ottoman Foreign Minister (3 October 1894).
42. For more on Mavroyeni and his ties to American high society, see: David Gutman, 'Migrants, Revolutionaries, and Spies'.
43 'Defends the Sultan', *The Chicago Herald*, 1894.
44. For more on the life of Alexander Russell Webb, see: Umar F. Abd-Allah, *A Muslim in Victorian America*.
45. Umar F. Abd-Allah, *A Muslim in Victorian America*, 245–9.
46. *A Few Facts About Turkey*, 65. The following pamphlet, published anonymously but also attributed to Alexander Russell Webb, includes many of the same arguments concerning Armenians who naturalised as United States citizens: *The Armenian Troubles and Where the Responsibility Lies*.
47. See: BOA.HR.SYS 2782 2, Mavroyeni to Gresham (22 October 1894).
48. 'As to Naturalized Armenians', *Washington Post*, 1894.
49. BOA.HR.SYS 2782 2, Mavroyeni Bey to Said Pasha (5 December 1894).
50. Grover Cleveland, Fourth Annual Address (second term), 7 December 1896.
51. *S. Doc. No. 33*, 54th Cong., 1st Sess. (1895): 1–5.
52. Ibid., 5.
53. Ibid., 5.
54. Ibid., 6.
55. Ibid., 6.
56. Ibid., 6.
57. Ibid., 6–7.
58. BOA.MKT.MHM 652 5, Province of Aleppo to Office of the Grand Vizier (29 Temmuz 1312/11 August 1896).
59. BOA.MKT.MHM 652 5, United States Diplomatic Legation to Foreign Ministry (4 Ağustos 1896/4 August 1896).
60. BOA.MKT.MHM 652 5, Office of the Grand Vizier to Ministry of Interior (18 Recep 1314/23 December 1896).

61. NARA, Despatches from the United States consuls in Harput, 1895–1906, Thomas H Norton, U.S. Consul to David Hill, Assistant Secretary of State, Washington, DC (13 April 1901).
62. BOA.DH.TMIK.M 60 74, Province of Trabzon to Ministry of Interior (20 Rabiulahir 1316/7 September 1898).
63. BOA.Y.PRK.HR 27 7, Report of the Ottoman Foreign Minister (20 Zilkade 1316/1 April 1899).
64. Y.PRK.ZB 23 43, Report of the District Governor of Beyoğlu (5 Ağustos 315/17 August 1899).
65. U.S. Department of State, 'Notice to American Citizens Formerly Subjects of Turkey Who Contemplate Returning to that Country', 4 January 1901, in *Papers Relating to the Foreign Relations of the United States 1901*, Washington, DC: GPO, 1901, 513–14.
66. BOA.Y.PRK.ZB 26 92, Report of the Beyoğlu Assistant for Documentary Affairs and Censor (14 Mart 1317/27 March 1901).
67. NARA, Despatches from the United States consuls in Harput, 1895–1906, Charles Dickinson, U.S. Consul General, Constantinople to Thomas H. Norton, U.S. Consul (1 May 1901).
68. Ibid.
69. NARA, Despatches from the United States consuls in Harput, 1895–1906, Thomas H. Norton, U.S. Consul to David J. Hill, Assistant Secretary of State (17 May 1901).
70. Robertson, *The Passport in America*, 125–26.
71. Ibid. 153–55.
72. Neil Larry Shumsky, 'American Hostility to Return Migration'.
73. Aristide Zolberg, *A Nation By Design*, 210.
74. 'The Troubles in Constantinople: the Last Attempt of the Armenian Conspirators to Produce Revolution in the Turkish Empire', *The New York Herald*, 27 August 1896. A copy of the article can be found in: HR.SYS 2872 2 (27 August 1896).
75. Aristide Zolberg, *A Nation by Design*, 228–30.
76. NARA, Despatches from the United States consuls in Harput, 1895–1906, Thomas H. Norton, U.S. Consul to David J. Hill, Assistant Secretary of State, Washington, DC (17 May 1901).
77. See, for example: NARA, Despatches from the United States consuls in Harput, 1895–1906, Thomas Norton, U.S. Consul to Department of State, Washington, DC (14 April 1903).
78. BOA.MV 102 30, Decision of the Ottoman Council of Ministers (1 Safer 1319/19 May 1901).
79. BOA.DH.TMIK.M 32 64, Ministry of Interior to Province of Aleppo (29 Haziran 1313/11 July 1897).
80. See: for example: BOA.DH.TMIK.M 168 1, Province of Mamuretülaziz to Ministry of Interior (7 Ramazan 1321/14 November 1904).
81. See, for example: BOA.DH.TMIK.M 166 16, Province of Mamuretülaziz

to Ministry of Interior (4 Safer 1322/20 April 1904); BOA.DH.TMIK.M 168 1, Province of Mamuretülaziz to Ministry of Interior (10 Safer 1322/26 April 1904); BOA.MKT.MHM 659 47, Ministry of Interior to Grand Vizier (14 Rabiulahir 1322/28 June 1904).

82. BOA.DH.TMIK.M 140 43, Kervan, Kevork, Dikran, Serkis, and Bagdasar to Grand Vizier (8 Mart 1319/21 March 1903).
83. BOA.DH.TMIK.M 140 43, Mamuretülaziz to Ministry of Interior (10 Mart 1319/23 March 1903).
84. BOA.DH.TMIK.M 140 43, Ministry of Interior to Mamuretülaziz (24 Mayis 1319/6 June 1903).
85. See: BOA.DH.TMIK.M 153 15, Ministry of Police to Ministry of Interior (21 Recep 1321/13 October 1903); BOA DH.TMIK.M 161 38, Telegram from Aleppo Province (19 Kanunievvel 1319/1 January 1904).
86. BOA.DH.TMIK.M 144 31, Province of Adana to Ministry of Interior (19 Mayis 1319/1 June 1903).
87. BOA.DH.TMIK.M 201 56, Province of Mamuretülaziz to Ministry of Interior (7 Rabiülahir 1322/9 June 1905).
88. BOA.DH.TMIK.M 201 37, Armenian Prelacy to Ministry of Interior (11 Haziran 1321/24 June 1905); BOA.MKT.MHM 659 51, Grand Vizier to Province of Mamuretülaziz (16 Cemazeyilahir 1323/17 August 1905).
89. BOA.DH.TMIK.M 659 51, Governor of Mamuretülaziz to Grand Vizier (8 Recep 1323/07 September 1905).
90. BOA.DH.TMIK.M 208 51, Mamuretülaziz to Ministry of Interior (29 Eylül 1321/11 October 1905).
91. BOA.DH.TMIK.M 208 51, Ministry of Interior to Mamuretülaziz (8 Şevval 1323/5 December 1905).
92. Torrie Hester, *Deportation*, 1.
93. Ibid., 50–1.
94. BOA.I.HUS 133 B/8, Order of the Ottoman Cabinet (26 Cemazeyilahir 1323/27 August 1905).
95. NARA, Despatches from the United States consuls in Turkey, 1904–1912, Evan Young, United States Consul, Harput, to J. R. G. Leishman, American Ambassador Extraordinary and Chief Plenipotentiary, Constantinople (1 June 1907).
96. NARA, Despatches from the United States consuls in Turkey, 1904–1912, Evan Young, United States Consul, Harput, to J. R. G. Leishman, American Ambassador Extraordinary and Chief Plenipotentiary, Constantinople (29 August 1907).
97. For example, a group of eleven returnees were deported in October 1906, see: DH.TMIK.M 232 51, Mamuretülaziz to Ministry of Interior (9 Ramazan 1323/27 October 1906). As many as twenty were deported shortly after their arrival at Adana in March 1908, see: DH.TMIK.M 266 13, Telegram from Adana to Ministry of Interior (9 Mart 1324/26 March 1908).

98. See, for example: DH.TMIK.M 208 31 Mamuretülaziz to Ministry of Interior (27 Recep 1323/26 September 1906), DH.TMIK.M 237 74, Mamuretülaziz to Ministry of Interior (11 Şubat 1322/24 February 1907).
99. BOA.DH.TMIK.M 204 9, Ministry of Police to Ministry of Interior (1 Cemaziyelevvel 1323/3 August 1905).
100. BOA.DH.TMIK.M 204 9, Ministry of Interior to Police Ministry and Province of Mamuretülaziz (19 Cemaziyelevvel 1323/17 August 1905).
101. BOA.DH.TMIK.M 226 80, Ministry of Police to Ministry of Interior (13 Rabiulahir 1324/16 June 1906).
102. BOA.DH.TMIK.M 226 80, Ministry of Interior to Ministry of Police (6 Temmuz 1322/19 July 1906).
103. BOA.DH.TMIK.M 239 16, Governor Mamuretülaziz to Ministry of Interior (22 Şubat 1322/7 February 1907).
104. BOA.DH.TMIK.M 239 16, Ministry of Interior to Mamuretülaziz (11 Mart 1323/24 March 1906).
105. BOA.DH.TMIK.M 239 16, Ministry of Interior to Mamuretülaziz (18 Temmuz 1323/1 August 1907).
106. See below. Also: BOA.DH.TMIK.M 157 65, Mersin Pier Commission to Ministry of Interior.
107. Kent Schull, *Prisons*, 91–101.
108. BOA.DH.TMIK.M 225 33, Mamuretülaziz Catholic Parish to Ministry of Interior (28 Nisan 1322/11 May 1906).
109. BOA.DH.TMIK.M 225 33, Governor of Mamuretülaziz to Ministry of Interior (14 Cemaziyelahir 1323/2 August 1906).
110. BOA.DH.TMIK.M 225 33, Ministry of Interior to Mamuretülaziz (3 Teşrinievvel 1322/16 October 1906).
111. BOA.DH.TMIK.M 209 21, Ministry of Police to Ministry of Interior (23 Teşrinisani 1321/6 October 1905).
112. NARA, Despatches from the United States consuls in Turkey, 1904–1912, Jesse Jackson, U.S. Consul, Alexandretta, to Philip Brown, U.S. Chargé d'Affaires, Constantinople (7 February 1908).
113. NARA, Despatches from the United States consuls in Turkey, 1904–1912, Jesse Jackson, U.S. Consul, Alexandretta, to John G. A. Leishman. Alexandria, 7 March 1908. This document is an acknowledgment of Leishman's order to refuse Demirjian official protection.
114. BOA.DH.TMIK.M 232 6, Governor of Mamuretülaziz to Ministry of Interior (5 Teşrinievvel 1322/18 October 1906).
115 NARA, Despatches from the United States consuls in Turkey, 1904–1912, Evan Young, United States Consul, Harput, to J. R. G. Leishman, American Ambassador Extraordinary and Chief Plenipotentiary, Constantinople (15 August 1907).
116. In his refutation of the informant's accusations, the governor of Mamuretülaziz suggests that Ziya Bey's activities involved 'concealing' (*ifha eylemek*) those who had returned. See: BOA.DH.MKT 1075 19,

Mamuretülaziz Province to the Ministry of Interior (1 Rabiulahir 1324/25 May 1906).

117. BOA.ZB 108 29, Copy of Report from the Iskenderun Pier Commission (6 Recep 1325/15 August 1907).
118. BOA.DH.TMIK.M, Governor of Erzurum to Ministry of Interior (20 Nisan 1324/3 May 1908).
119. BOA.DH.TMIK.M, Armenian Patriarchate to Ministry of Justice (27 Rabiulahir 1326/28 May 1908).
120. BOA.DH.TMIK.M 273 101, Ministry of Interior to Mamuretülaziz (27 Temmuz 1324/9 August 1908).

Part III Introduction

1. This may be a misspelling of a more common Armenian name.
2. BOA.DH.TMIK.M 273 101, Kirkor, Giragos, and Yankob to Sadrazam (16 Temmuz 1324/29 July 1906).
3. BOA.DH.TMIK.M 273 101, Sadrazam to Mamuretülaziz (27 Temmuz 1324/9 August 1908).

Chapter 6

1. BOA.DH.TMIK.M 274 23, General Telegram from the Ministry of Interior (17 Temmuz 1324/30 July 1908).
2. See: Musa Çadırcı, 'Tanzımat Döneminde Çıkarılan Men'-i Mürur ve Pasaport Nizamnameleri', *Belgeler*, Vol. 15, No. 19, 169–181. While the text of the mobility and passport law does not outright outlaw domestic or international migration, as is discussed in Chapter Three, it was promulgated in order to allow the Ottoman state to more easily distinguish between what it saw as legitimate and illegitimate forms of mobility by requiring imperial subjects to obtain documentary permissions before moving within or outside the empire's borders. Reflecting the constitutional regime's commitment to a more liberal and relaxed interpretation of the law, the documents from the post-revolutionary period refer to the law as the 'Mobility and Passport Law' (Mürur ve Pasaport Nizamnamesi), while in the pre-revolutionary period it was referred to as the 'Prevention of Mobility and Passport Law' (Men'-i Mürur ve Pasaport Nizamnamesi).
3. BOA.DH.TMIK.M 274 23, Letter of the Minister of War (31 Recep 1326/11 August 1908).
4. BOA.DH.TMIK.M 274 23, Ministry of Interior to Province of Trabzon (2 Ağustos 1324/15 August 1908); BOA.DH.TMIK.M 274 23, Ministry of Interior to Aleppo Province (5 Ağustos 1324/18 August 1908).
5. BOA.DH.MKT 2622 62, Province of Beirut to Ministry of Interior (18 Eylül 1324/2 October 1908).

6. Erik Jan Zürcher, 'The Ottoman Conscription System, 1844–1914', *International Journal of Social History*, 43 (1998), 447.
7. Ibid., 121.
8. BOA.DH.MKT 2679 33, Ministry of Interior to all provinces and districts, the office of the prefect of Istanbul, and Ministry of Police (11 Teşrinisani 1324/24 November 1908).
9. Statement of Rıza Tevfik, *Meclisi Mebusan Zabıt Ceridesi*, Kırkaltıncı İnikad, Devre 1, Cilt 2, İçtima Senesi 2 (13 Şubat 1325/26 February 1910), 510.
10. Statement of Mehmet Talat Bey, in ibid., 507.
11. Statement of Artas Yorgaki Efendi, in ibid., 507.
12. *Meclisi Mebusan Zabıt Ceridesi*, Üçüncü İnikad, Devre 1, Cilt 1 İçtima Senesi 3 (4 Teşrinisani 1326/17 November 1910), 33–44.
13. Christoph Herzog, 'Migration and the State', 129.
14. John Torpey, *Invention of the Passport*, 91–2.
15. Adam McKeown, *Melancholy Order*, 66–89. For an analysis of how concepts such as 'civilised' and 'uncivilised' and 'free' and 'unfree' continue to shape the image of the migrant in the contemporary period, see: Hagar Kotef, *Movement and the Ordering of Freedom.*
16. Russia's internal mobility controls, for instance, is one reason that in McKeown's words, it was 'held up as the epitome of despotic surveillance'. Adam McKeown, *Melancholy Order*, 42.
17. For more on the evolution of United States immigration policies in the first decade of the twentieth century, see: see: Aristide Zolberg, *A Nation by Design*, 199–242.
18. Robert DeC. Ward, 'The New Immigration Act', 590.
19. BOA.DH.MKT 2672 25, Foreign Ministry to Ministry of Interior (2 Teşrinisani 1324/15 November 1908).
20. BOA.DH.MKT 2731 51, Ministry of Interior to all provinces (15 Muharrem 1327/6 February 1909).
21. BOA.DH.MKT 2818 4, Copy of Report sent by Marseille Consulate (16 Mart 1325/28 March 1909).
22. Ibid.
23. BOA.DH.MUI 71 25, Office of Overseas Consuls to Ministry of Interior (12 Safer 1328/27 February 1910).
24. BOA.DH.MUI 71 25, Ministry of Interior to Foreign Ministry (18 Safer 1328/4 March 1910).
25. Dorothy Schneider, 'The United States Government', 198–201.
26. Ibid., 204
27. BOA.DH.MB.HPS.M 9 34, Copy of report from the Fiume Consul (5 Muharrem 1332/4 December 1913). This date is for the entire document set; no date is given for the actual report which probably dates to earlier in 1913.
28. Sarkiz Narzakian, *Memoirs of Sarkiz Narzakian*, 133–4.

29. Robert Mirak, *Torn Between Two Lands*, 65.
30. As Eyal Ginio notes, the (real and perceived) widespread desertion rates of non-Muslim soldiers during the Balkan Wars became a rallying cry for voices within Ottoman society and politics who pointed to non-Muslim perfidy as a central factor in the empire's defeat at the hands of its former Christian subject populations. See: Eyal Ginio, *The Ottoman Culture of Defeat*, 105–7.
31. For example, Michelle Campos states that 'dozens of Jewish and Christian youth were leaving Palestine weekly, with hundreds leaving Greater Syria', after the Ottoman state began inducting non-Muslims from the region into the military. See: Michelle Campos, *Ottoman Brothers*, 154–5. Meanwhile, Devi Mays notes that the 1911 war with Italy and the Balkan Wars 'propelled an increasing number of Sephardi Jews – conscriptable into the Ottoman military since 1909 – to seek new shores'. See: Devi Mays, 'I Killed Her', 7.
32. For Ottoman reports touching on this issue see: BOA.DH.MUI 18-2 37, Cemaziyülevvel 1328/26.05.1910; BOA.DH.SN-THR 41 86, Telegram from the Governor of Mamuretülaziz Province to Ministry of Interior (19 Eylül 1327/2 October 1911) – also other documents in this document set; BOA.DH.EUM.EMN 60 10, Trabzon Province to Interior Minister (5 Mart 1330/18 March 1914). For American reports see especially: William Masterson, U.S. Consul, Mamouret-ul-Aziz to John Ridgley Carter, American Minister, Constantinople (22 February 1911); William Masterson, U.S. Consul, Mamouret-ul-Aziz to John Ridgley Carter, American Minister, Constantinople (15 February 1912). Both are annual reports on the political, social and economic status of Mamuretülaziz Province, and surrounding areas. Each also contains detailed reports on migration from the region to the United States.
33. Statistics reproduced in: Robert Mirak, *Between Two Lands*, 292. According to these figures, migration from the Levant similarly spiked in 1913.
34. Before 1908, just under 25% of migrants classified as Armenian who were admitted to the United States were women. Between 1908 and 1914, this number declined to just under 16% of Armenian migrants. Imre Ferenczi and Walter Willcox, *International Migrations*, 433–9.
35. BOA.DH.SN-THR 45 28, Pier Commission of Yafa to Yafa Police Commissioner (26 Temmuz 1326/8 August 1910); BOA.DH.SN-THR 45 28, Province of Salonica to Ministry of Interior (26 Temmuz 1326/8 August 1910).
36. BOA.DH.SN-THR 45 28, Census Department Bureau of Trade to all Provinces and Districts (31 Temmuz 1326/13 August 1910).
37. BOA.SN-THR 45 28, Office of the Grand Vizier (24 Ramazan 1328/28 September 1910).
38. BOA.DH.SN-THR 45 28, Office of the Grand Vizier (14 Şevval 1328/18 October 1911).
39. BEO 2743 280651, Office of the Grand Vizier (21 Rabiulevvel 1328/8

March 1910); BOA.DH.SN-THR 45 28, Copy of report from the Ministry of Interior to the Directorate of General Security (24 Nisan 1326/10 May 1910).

40. BOA.DH.MUI 18-2 37, Ministry of Interior to Sublime Porte (5 Teşrinisani 1315/18 November 1909). According to a report by the governor of Mamuretülaziz, increasing numbers of Armenians from the Harput region were transiting through Salonica in the aftermath of the revolution. See: BOA.DH.MUI 8-3 12, Governor of Mamuretülaziz to the Ministry of Interior (3 Eylül 1326/16 September 1909).
41. Document from Foreign Ministry is quoted in the following: BEO 2743 280651, Office of the Grand Vizier (21 Rabiulevvel 1328/8 March 1910).
42. DH.MUI 18-2 37, Ministry of Interior to all Provinces and Districts (10 Kanunisani 1325/23 January 1910).
43. McKeown, *Melancholy Order*, 85.
44. BOA.DH.SN-THR 45 28 (No date given). The document is not dated, and it is not entirely clear where it was circulated and whether it was published in languages other than Turkish.
45. BOA.DH.SN-THR 45 28 (No date given).
46. Şükrü Hanioğlu, *A Brief History*, 150–1.
47. Ibid., 153–4.
48. BOA.DH.MUI 8-3 12, Copy of Article Published in the newspaper *Independence Belge* on 1 September 1909 (23 Ağostos 1325/4 September 1909).
49. BOA.DH.MUI 8-3 12, Ministry of Interior to Mamuretülaziz and Aleppo (29 Ağustos 1325/11 September 1909).
50. BOA.DH.MUI 8-3 12, Copy of telegram from Mamuretülaziz (3 Eylül 1325/16 September 1909).
51. BOA.DH.SN-THR 45 28, Governor of Aleppo to Ministry of Interior (14 Şevval 1328/17 October 1910).
52. BOA.DH.SN-THR 45 28, Governor of Beirut to Ministry of Interior (18 Şevval 1328/21 October 1910).
53. BOA.DH.SN-THR 45 28, Governor of Kosova Province to Ministry of Interior (no date given); BOA.DH.SN-THR 45 28, Governor of Manastir Province to Ministry of Interior (3 Muharram 1329/4 January 1911); BOA.DH.SN-THR 45 28, Governor of the Province of the Archipelago to Ministry of Interior (9 Mart 1327/22 March 1911).
54. BOA.DH.SN-THR 45 28, Gendarmerie Commander of Jerusalem to Governor of the District of Jerusalem (26 Şubat 1326/11 March 1911).
55. See for example: BOA.DH.SN-THR 41 86, Census Office to Province of Beirut (1 Teşrinisani 1327/14 November 1911).
56. The governor of Salonica province dates the central government order to mid-October. The original order is not available. BOA.DH.SN.-THR 45 28, Province of Salonika to Ministry of Interior (8 Zilhicce 1329/30 November

1911). Officials in Beirut and Istanbul were executing the policy by mid-October. See: BOA.DH.SN-THR 41 86, Istanbul Police Directorate to Ministry of Interior (8 Teşrinievvel 1327/21 October 1911); BOA.DH.SN-THR 41 86, Province of Beirut to Ministry of Interior (15 Teşrinievvel 1327/28 October 1911).

57. BOA.DH.SN-THR 41 86, Province of Beirut to Ministry of Interior (10 Zilkade 1329/14 November 1911).
58. BOA.DH.SN-THR 41 86, Governor of Beirut to Ministry of Interior (18 Zilhicce 1329/11 December 1911).
59. See, for example: BOA.DH.EUM.EMN 60 10, District Governor of Canık to Ministry of Interior (1 Şubat 1329/14 March 1913); BOA.DH.EUM. EMN 60 10, Governor of Trabzon Province to Ministry of Interior (no date provided).
60. BOA.DH.EUM.EMN 60 10, Governor of Beirut Province to Ministry of Interior (29 Ağustos 1329/11 September 1913).
61. Freedom of mobility remained the stated position of the Ottoman state at least until the 1913 coup, despite the crackdown on draft dodgers. Those not suspected of avoiding military service remained free to leave. To prevent stranding, migrants departing the empire were encouraged to submit to a full medical examination and review of their finances. Migrants were also told that they would receive no assistance from the Ottoman government to return to the empire if denied entry to the United States. See: DH.MB. HPS.M 9 34, Report of the Ministry of Interior (13 Teşrinievvel 1328/26 October 1912).
62. Yiğit Akın, *When the War Came Home*, 46–50; Raymond Kevorkian, *The Armenian Genocide*, 158–65, 171. For more on the 'agrarian question' that drove major demands for reform, see: Janet Klein, *The Margins of Empire*, 128–69.
63. Yiğit Akın, *When the War Came Home*, 87.
64. Raymond Kevorkian, *The Armenian Genocide*, 319–33.
65. For a detailed discussion of this debate, see: David Gutman, 'Ottoman Historiography', 167–83.
66. See, for example: Donald Bloxham, 'The Armenian Genocide'; Eyal Ginio, *The Ottoman Culture of Defeat*; M. Hakan Yavuz, 'Warfare and Nationalism'; Taner Akçam, *The Young Turks*.
67. See: Fuat Dündar, *Modern Türkiye'nin Şifresi*; Fuat Dündar, *İttihat ve Terakki'nin*.
68. Ronald Grigor Suny, *A History*, 281–2.
69. Raymond Kevorkian, *The Armenian Genocide*, 382.
70. Ibid., 381–427.
71. Leslie A. Davis, *The Slaughterhouse Province*, 55–6.
72. In one instance, he was forced to surrender to Ottoman authorities fifty Armenians he claimed (apparently in contravention of both Ottoman and United States law) were legally American citizens. Ibid., 121–2. The

Committee of Union and Progress government officially abrogated the Capitulations in 1914.

73. In a June 1915 report, Davis informed his superiors that the governor of Mamuretülaziz was permitting his office to accept the moveable property of local Armenians who sought to safeguard what wealth they could. See: Raymond Kevorkian, *The Armenian Genocide*, 391.
74. Leslie Davis, *The Slaughterhouse Province*, 57.
75. For more on this, see: David Gutman, 'Political Economy'.
76. Ohan Gaidzakian, *Illustrated Armenia*, 42–3.
77. NARA, Despatches from the United States consuls in Harput, 1895–1906, Thomas H. Norton, Consul in Harput to the Department of State, Washington, DC (22 January 1901).
78. NARA, Despatches from the United States consuls in Turkey, 1904–1912, William Masterson, U.S. Consul, Harput, to John Ridgley Carter, American Minister Plenipotentiary, Constantinople (22 February 1911).
79. Manoog Dzeron, *Village of Parchanj*, 164.
80. NARA, Despatches from the United States consuls in Turkey, 1904–1912, William Masterson, U.S. Consul, Harput to John Ridgley Carter, American Minister Plenipotentiary, Constantinople (22 February 1911).
81. NARA, Despatches from the United States consuls in Turkey, 1904–1912, William Masterson, U.S. Consul, Harput to John Ridgley Carter, American Minister Plenipotentiary, Constantinople (15 February 1912).
82. Boghos Jafarian, *Farewell Kharpert*, 73–4.
83. See, for example: Taner Akçam and Ümit Kurt, *Kanunların Ruhu*; Uğur Ümit Üngör and Mehmet Polatel, *Confiscation and Destruction*; Bedross Der Matossian, 'The Taboo within the Taboo'.
84. See: Taner Akçam and Ümit Kurt, *Kanunların Ruhu*, 49–59; Uğur Ümit Üngör and Mehmet Polatel, *Confiscation and Destruction*, 48–9.
85. Taner Akçam and Ümit Kurt, *Kanunların Ruhu*, 73–7.
86. Ibid., 108.
87. 'Treaty of Peace with Turkey Signed At Lausanne, 24 July 1923', *The Treaties of Peace 1919–1923, Vol. II* (New York: Carnegie Endowment for International Peace, 1924), https://wwi.lib.byu.edu/index.php/Treaty_of_Lausanne.
88. Ibid., 197–209.
89. Akçam and Kurt, *Kanunların Ruhu*, 163–4.
90. Ibid., 164–5.
91. Under Mark Bristol, American High Commissioner to Turkey, 1919–1927, US foreign policy in the region was reoriented away from its earlier focus on missionary work to a focus primarily on a combination of strengthening economic ties between Turkey and the United States and cultivating Turkey as a bulwark against the spread of Communism. See: Thomas A. Bryson, 'Admiral Mark L. Bristol', 450–67.
92. As early as 1931, Leland Gordon recognised the link between

Ottoman–United States nationality agreements before World War I and those being negotiated between Washington and Ankara nationality negotiations after World War I, see: Leland J. Gordon, 'The Turkish American Controversy'.

93. Akçam and Kurt, *Kanunların Ruhu*, 237.

Conclusion

1. 'Tarih', https://www.elazig.bel.tr/icerik.php?id=216 (Accessed 1 November 2017).
2. Ronald Grigor Suny, *They Can Live in the Desert*, 134.
3. The work of İlkay Yılmaz demonstrates the pervasive use of terms such as anarchism, sedition, and anarchy to characterise the threat posed by uncontrolled mobility in the Hamidian era. See: İlkay Yılmaz, *Serseri*.
4. See, for example: Bedross Der Matossian, *Shattered Dreams*; Hans-Lukas Kieser, *Talaat Pasha*.

Bibliography

Archival Sources

Başbakanlık Osmanlı Arşivi (BOA) Istanbul, Turkey

Bab-ı Ali Evrak Odası (BEO)
Dahiliye Nezareti, Mektubi Kalemi (DH.MKT)
Dahiliye Nezareti, Meban-i Emiriye ve Hapishaneler Müdiriyet Belgeleri (DH.MB.HPS.M)
Dahiliye Nezareti, Muhaberat-ı Umumiye İdaresi Belgeleri (DH.MUI)
Dahiliye Nezareti, Sicill-i Nüfus İdare-i Umumiyesi Belgeleri (DH.SN-THR)
Dahiliye Nezareti, Tesri-i Muamelat ve Islahat Komisyonu Muamelat (DH.TMIK.M)
Hariciye Nezareti, Siyasi Kısmı Belgeleri (HR.SYS)
İrade-Dahilye (I.DH)
İrade-Hususi (I.HUS)
Sadaret Mektubi Mühimme Kalemi Evrakı (MKT.MHM)
Meclis-i Vükela Mazbataları (MV)
Sadaret Resmi Maruzat Evrakı (Y.A.RES)
Sadrıazam Kamil Paşa Evrak-ı – Yıldız Esas Evrak'ına Ek (Y.EE.KP)
Sadaret Resmi Maruzat Evrakı (Y.MTV)
Yıldız Perakende Evrakı Adliye ve Mezahib Nezareti Maruzatı (Y.PRK.AZN)
Yıldız Perakende Evrakı Başkitabet Dairesi Maruzatı (Y.PRK.BSK)
Yıldız Perakende Evrakı Dahiliye Nezareti Maruzatı (Y.PRK.DH)
Yıldız Perakende Evrakı Hariciye Nezareti (Y.PRK.HR)
Yıldız Perakende Evrakı Zaptiye Nezareti (Y.PRK.ZB)
Zaptiye Nezareti Evrakı (ZB)

National Archives and Records Administration, Washington, DC

Despatches from the US Consulate in Harput, 1895. Microfilm publications microcopy no. T-579
Despatches from the US Consulate in Harput, 1904–1912. No. 84 350-10-7-3
Despatches from the US Consulate in Sivas, 1896–1906. Microfilms publications microcopy
no. T-681

Official Published Primary Sources

Congressional Record
Meclis-i Mebusan Zabit Ceridesi
Papers Relating to the Foreign Relations of the United States

News Media

BBC Türkçe, London, United Kingdom
Chicago Herald, Chicago, IL, United States
Frontline, Boston, MA, United States
The Intercept, New York, NY, United States
New York Herald, New York, NY, United States
New York Times, New York, NY, United States
Washington Post, Washington, DC, United States

Other Published Primary Sources

A Few Facts About Turkey under the Reign of Abdul Hamid II (New York: J. J. Little & Co., 1895).

The Armenian Troubles and Where the Responsibility Lies (New York: J. J. Little & Co., 1895).

Davis, Leslie A., *The Slaughterhouse Province: An American Diplomat's Report on the Armenian Genocide, 1915–1917* (New Rochelle, NY: Aristide Caratzas, 1990).

Dzeron, Manoog, *Village of Parchanj: General History 1600–1937*, trans. Arra S. Avakian (Fresno: Panorama West Books, 1984).

Gaidzakian, Ohan, *Illustrated Armenia and the Armenians* (Boston: B. H. Aznive, 1898).

Jafarian, Boghos, *Farewell Kharpert: The Autobiography of Boghos Jafarian* (Madison: C. Mangasarian, 1989).

Sarkiz Narzakian, *Memoirs of Sarkiz Narzakian*, trans. Garine Narzakian (Ann Arbor: Gomidas Institute, 1995).

Safarian, A. E., *Letters from Armenia to Israel Safarian* (Toronto: 632083 Ontario Ltd, 2002)

Bibliography

Secondary Sources

Abd-Allah, Umar F., *A Muslim in Victorian America: The Life of Alexander Russell Webb* (Oxford: Oxford University Press, 2006).

Abou-El-Haj, Rifaʾat, *Formation of the Modern State: The Ottoman Empire Sixteenth to Eighteenth Centuries, Second Edition* (Syracuse, NY: Syracuse University Press, 2005).

Akarlı, Engin Deniz, 'Ottoman Attitudes Towards Lebanese Emigration, 1885–1910', in Albert Hourani et al. (ed.), *The Lebanese in the World: A Century of Emigration* (London: I. B. Tauris, 1991), 109–38.

Akçam, Taner, *The Young Turks' Crime Against Humanity: The Armenian Genocide and Ethnic Cleansing in the Ottoman Empire* (Princeton: Princeton University Press, 2012).

Akçam, Taner and Ümit Kurt, *Kanunların Ruhu: Emval-i Metruke Kanunlarında Soykırımın İzini Sürmek* (Istanbul: İletişim, 2012).

Akın, Yiğit, *When the War Came Home: The Ottomans' Great War and the Devastation of an Empire* (Stanford: Stanford University Press, 2018).

Albahari, Maurizio, *Crimes of Peace: Mediterranean Migrations at the World's Deadliest Border* (Philadelphia: University of Pennsylvania Press, 2015).

Alfaro-Velcamp, Theresa, *So Far from Allah, So Close to Mexico: Middle Eastern Immigrants in Modern Mexico* (Austin: University of Texas Press, 2007).

Altıntaş, Toygun, 'The Ottoman War on "Anarchism" and Revolutionary Violence', in Houssine Alloul et al. (eds), *To Kill a Sultan: A Transnational History of the Attempt on Abdülhamid II (1905)* (London: Palgrave Macmillan, 2017), 99–128.

Andersson, Ruben, *Illegality, Inc.: Clandestine Migration and the Business of Bordering Europe* (Oakland, CA: University of California Press, 2014).

Antaramian, Richard, 'In Subversive Service of the Sublime State: Armenians and Ottoman State Power, 1844–1896' (Unpublished PhD Dissertation, University of Michigan, 2014).

Astourian, Steven, 'The Silence of the Land: Agrarian Relations, Ethnicity, and Power', in Ronald Grigor Suny et al. (eds), *A Question of Genocide: Armenians and Turks at the End of the Ottoman Empire* (Oxford: Oxford University Press, 2011), 55–81.

Ateş, Sabri, *The Ottoman–Iranian Borderlands: Making a Boundary, 1843–1914* (Cambridge: Cambridge University Press, 2013).

Baird, Theodore, *Human Smuggling in the Eastern Mediterranean* (London: Routledge Press, 2016).

Balgamış, A. Deniz. and Kemal Karpat (eds), *Turkish Migration to the United States: From Ottoman Times to the Present* (Madison: University of Wisconsin Press, 2008).

Behar, Cem, *A Neighborhood in Ottoman Istanbul: Fruit Vendors and Civil Servants in the Kasap İlyas Mahalle* (Albany: State University of New York Press, 2003).

Bliss, Edwin Munsell, *Turkey and the Armenian Atrocities: A Graphic and Thrilling History of Turkey, the Armenians, and the events that have led up to the terrible Massacres in Armenia* (New York: Hibbard and Young, 1896).

Bloemraad, Irene, 'Citizenship Lessons from the Past: Contours of Immigrant Naturalization in the Early 20th Century, *Social Science Quarterly*, Vol. 85, No. 5 (December 2006), 847–950.

Bloxham, Donald, 'The Armenian Genocide of 1915–1916: Cumulative Radicalization and the Development of a Destruction Policy', *Past and Present*, No. 81 (Nov. 2003) 141–91.

Benjamin Braude, 'The Foundation Myths of the Millet System', in Benjamin Braude (ed.), *Christians and Jews in the Ottoman Empire* (Boulder: Lynne Rienner Publishers, 2014), 65–86.

Bryson, Thomas A., 'Admiral Mark L. Bristol, An Open-Door Diplomat in Turkey', *International Journal of Middle East Studies*, Vol. 5, No. 4 (September 1974), 450–67.

Çadırcı, Musa, 'Tanzimat döneminde çıkarılan Men-i Mürur ve Pasaport Nizamnameleri', *Belgeler*, Vol. 15, No. 19 (1993), 169–82.

Campos, Michelle, *Ottoman Brothers: Muslims, Christians, and Jews in Early Twentieth-Century Palestine* (Stanford: Stanford University Press, 2011).

Can, Lale, 'The Protection Question: Central Asians and Extraterritoriality in the Late Ottoman Empire', *International Journal of Middle East Studies*, Vol. 48, No. 4 (November 2016), 679–99.

Cinel, Dino, *The National Integration of Italian Return Migration, 1870–1929* (Cambridge: Cambridge University Press, 2001).

Clay, Christopher, 'Labour Migrations and Economic Conditions in Nineteenth Century Anatolia', *Middle East Studies*, Vol. 34, No. 4 (October 1998), 1–32.

Cora, Yaşar Tolga, Dzovinar Derderian, Ali Sipahi (eds), *The Ottoman East in the Nineteenth Century: Societies, Identities and Politics* (London: I. B. Tauris, 2016).

Cuinet, Vital, *La Turquie D'Asie: Geographie Administrative, Statistique Descriptive et Raisonee de Chaque Province de L'Asie-Mineur: L'Anatolie centrale Angora et Adana, Mamouret-ul-Aziz, Sivas* (Istanbul: Les Editions Isis, 2001).

Davison, Roderic, *Reform in the Ottoman Empire* (Princeton: Princeton University Press, 1963).

De Groot, Alexander, 'The Historical Development of the Capitulatory Regime in the Ottoman Middle East from the Fifteenth to the Nineteenth Century', *Oriente Moderne*, 83, 3 (2003): 575–604.

Der Matossian, Bedross, *Shattered Dreams of Revolution: From Liberty to Violence in the Late Ottoman Empire* (Stanford: Stanford University Press, 2014).

Der Matossian, Bedross, 'The Taboo within the Taboo: The Fate of 'Armenian Capital' at the End of the Ottoman Empire', *European Journal of Turkish Studies*, Available online: http://ejts.revues.org/index4411.html.

Deranian, Hagop Martin, *Hagop Bogigian: Armenian American Pioneer & Philanthropist* (Arlington: Armenian Cultural Foundation, 2016).

Deringil, Selim, 'The Armenian Question is Finally Closed': Mass Conversions of Armenians in Anatolia during the Hamidian Massacres of 1895–1897', *Comparative Studies in Society and History*, Vol. 51, No. 2 (2009), 344–71.

Deringil, Selim, *Conversion and Apostacy in the Late Ottoman Empire* (Cambridge: Cambridge University Press, 2012).

Deringil, Selim, *The Well-Protected Domains: Ideology and the Legitimation of Power in the Ottoman Empire 1876–1909* (London: I. B. Tauris, 2011).

Donabed, Sargon *Remnants of Heroes: The Assyrian Experience: The Continuity of the Assyrian Heritage from Kharput to New England* (Chicago: Assyrian Academic Society Press, 2003).

Dündar, Fuat, *İttihat ve Terakki'nin Müslüman iskan politikası, 1913–1918* (Istanbul: İletişim Yayınları, 2001).

Dündar, Fuat, *Modern Türkiye'nin Şifresi: İttihat ve Terakki'nin Etnisite Mühendisliği (1913–1918)* (Istanbul: İletişim Yayınları, 2008).

Ekinci, Ilham, '19. Yüzyıl'ın İkinci Yarısında Samsun'da Deniz Ulaşımı', in *Geçmişten Geleçeğe Samsun*' (Samsun: Samsun Büyükşehir Belediyesi, 2007), 113–31.

Ekmekçioğlu, Lerna, *Recovering Armenia: The Limits of Belonging in Post-Genocide Turkey* (Stanford: Stanford University Press, 2016).

Ellis, Matthew, *Desert Borderland: The Making of Modern Egypt and Libya* (Stanford, CA: Stanford University Press, 2018).

Ertem, Özge, 'Considering Famine in the Late Nineteenth Century Ottoman Empire: A Comparative Framework and Overview', *Studies Across Disciplines in the Humanities and Social Sciences*, Vol. 22 (2017), 164–5.

Fahrenthold, Stacy, *Between the Ottomans and the Entente: The First World War in the Syrian and Lebanese Diaspora, 1908–1925* (Oxford: Oxford University Press, forthcoming 2019).

Ferenczi, Imre and Walter Willcox, *International Migrations: Vol. 1 Statistics* (Boston: National Bureau of Economic Research, 1929).

Gabaccia, Donna and Franca Iacovetta, 'Women, Work, and Protest in the Italian Diaspora: An International Research Agenda', *Labour/Le Travail*, Vol. 42 (1998), 161–81.

Garland, Libby, *After They Closed the Gates: Jewish Illegal Immigration to the United States, 1921–1965* (Chicago: University of Chicago Press, 2014).

Genell, Aimee M., 'Empire by Law: Ottoman Sovereignty and the British Occupation of Egypt, 1882–1923' (New York: Columbia University, unpublished PhD dissertation, 2013).

Gingeras, Ryan, *Sorrowful Shores: Violence, Ethnicity, and the End of the Ottoman Empire, 1912–1923* (Oxford: Oxford University Press, 2009).

Ginio, Eyal, *The Ottoman Culture of Defeat: The Balkan Wars and Their Aftermath* (Oxford: Oxford University Press, 2016).

Gordon, Leland, 'Turkish–American Treaty Relations', *The American Political Science Review*, Vol. 22, No. 3 (1928), 711–21.

Gordon, Leland J., 'The Turkish American Controversy over Nationality', *The American Journal of International Law*, Vol. 25, No. 4 (October 1931), 658–69.

Gutman, David, 'Migrants, Revolutionaries, and Spies: Surveillance, Politics, and Ottoman Identity in the United States', in Christine Isom-Verhaaren and Kent Schull (eds), *Living in the Ottoman Realm: Empire and Identity, 13th to 20th Centuries* (Bloomington: Indiana Univerity Press, 2016), 284–96.

Gutman, David, 'Ottoman Historiography and the End of the Genocide Taboo: Writing the Armenian Genocide into Late Ottoman History', *Journal of the Ottoman and Turkish Studies Association*, Vol. 2, No. 1 (2015), 167–83.

Gutman, David, 'The Political Economy of Armenian Migration from the Harput Region to North America in the Hamidian Era, 1885–1908', in Yaşar Tolga Cora et al. (eds), *The Ottoman East in the Nineteenth Century: Societies, Identities and Politics* (London: I. B. Tauris, 2016), 42–61.

Gutman, David, 'Travel Documents, Mobility Control, and the Ottoman State in an Age of Global Migration, 1880–1915', *Journal of the Ottoman and Turkish Studies Association*, Vol. 3, No. 2 (November 2016), 352–8.

Hamed-Troyansky, Vladimir, 'Circassian Refugees and the Making of Amman, 1878–1914', *International Journal of Middle East History*, Vol. 49, No. 4 (November 2017), 605–23.

Hanioğlu, M. Şükrü, *A Brief History of the Ottoman Empire* (Princeton: Princeton University Press, 2008).

Hanley, Will, *Identifying with Nationality: Europeans, Ottomans, and Egyptians in Alexandria* (New York: Columbia University Press, 2017).

Hanley, Will, 'What Ottoman Nationality Was and Was Not', *Journal of the Ottoman and Turkish Studies Association*, Vol. 3, No. 2 (Nov. 2016), 277–98.

Herzog, Christoph, 'Migration and the State: On Ottoman regulations concerning migration since the age of Mahmud II', in Ulrika Freitag et al. (eds), *The City in the Ottoman Empire: Migration and the Making of Urban Modernity* (New York: Routledge, 2012), 117–34.

Hester, Torrie, *Deportation: The Origins of U.S. Policy* (Philadelphia: University of Pennsylvania Press, 2017).

Hewson, Robert H., 'The Five 'Peoples' of Tsopk/Sophene', in Richard Hovannisian (ed.), *Armenian Tsopk/Kharpert* (Costa Mesa: Mazda Publishers Inc., 2002), 123–36.

Hovannisian, Richard, 'The Armenian Question in the Ottoman Empire', *East European Quarterly*, Vol. 6, No. 1 (March 1972), 1–26.

Kane, Eileen, *Russian Hajj: Empire and the Pilgrimage to Mecca* (Ithaca: Cornell University Press, 2015).

Kaprielian-Churcill, Isabel, *Like Our Mountains:A History of Armenians in Canada* (Montreal: McGill-Queen's University Press, 2005).

Kaprielian, Isabel, 'Migratory Caravans: Armenian Sojourners in Canada', in *Journal of American Ethnic History*, Vol. 6, No. 2. (Spring 1987), 34–5.

Kaprielian, Isabel, 'Sojourners from Keghi: Armenians in Ontario to 1915' (Unpublished PhD Dissertation, University of Toronto, 1984).

Karents, Varoujan, *Mitchanpert the Citadel: A History of Armenians in Rhode Island*. (Lincoln, NE: iUniverse, Inc, 2004).

Karkar, Yakub, *Railway Development in the Ottoman Empmire, 1856–1914* (New York: Vantage Press, 1972).

Kasaba, Reşat, *The Ottoman Empire and the World Economy, The Nineteenth Century* (Albany: SUNY Press, 1988).

Kevorkian, Raymond, *The Armenian Genocide: A Complete History* (London: I. B. Tauris, 2013).

Khater, Akram, *Inventing Home: Emigration, Gender, and the Middle Class in Lebanon, 1870–1920* (Berkeley: University of California Press, 2001).

Kieser, Hans-Lukas, *Der Verpasste Friede: Mission, Ethnie, un Staat in der Ostprovinzen der Türkei, 1839–1938* (Zürich: Chronos Verlag, 2000), 57.

Kieser, Hans-Lukas, *Nearest East: American Millenialism and Mission to the Middle East* (Philadelphia: Temple University Press, 2010).

Kieser, Hans-Lukas, *Talaat Pasha: Father of Modern Turkey, Architect of Genocide* (Princeton: Princeton University Press, 2018).

Kılıç, Mehmet Fırat 'Between Empires: the Movement of Sheikh Ubeydullah', *The International Journal of Kurdish Studies*, Vol. 20, No. 1/2 (2006), 57–121.

Kılıçaslan, M. Emre, 'Avusturya Lloyd Vapur Şirketi'nin İstanbul'un Yolcu ve Eşya Taşımacılığındaki Yeri' in Coşkun Yılmaz ed., *Büyük İstanbul Tarihi, İktisat: Ulaşım ve Haberleşme* (Istanbul: İSAM, 2016), 480–90.

Klein, Janet, *The Margins of Empire: Kurdish Militias in the Ottoman Tribal Zone* (Stanford, CA: Stanford University Press, 2011).

Koçunyan, Aylin, 'Long Live Sultan Abdülaziz, Long Live the Constitution', in Kelly Grotke et al. (eds), *Constitutionalism, Legitimacy, and Power: Nineteenth-Century Experiences* (Oxford: Oxford University Press, 2014), 189–210.

Kotef, Hagar, *Movement and the Ordering of Freedom: On Liberal Governances of Mobility*, Durham, NC: Duke University Press, 2015.

Kyle, David and Rey Koslowski (eds), *Global Human Smuggling: Comparative Perspectives* (Baltimore: The Johns Hopkins University Press, 2011).

Lee, Erika, *At America's Gates: Chinese Immigration during the Exclusion Era* (Chapel Hill: University of North Carolina Press, 1998).

Lew-Williams, Beth, *The Chinese Must Go: Violence, Exclusion, and the Making of the Alien in America* (Cambridge, MA: Harvard University Press, 2018).

Libaridian, Gerard, 'What Was Revolutionary about Armenian Revolutionary Parties in the Ottoman Empire?', in Ronald Grigor Suny, et al. (eds), *A Question of Genocide: Armenians and Turks at the End of the Ottoman Empire* (Oxford: Oxford University Press, 2011), 82–112.

Low, Michael Christopher, 'Empire and the Hajj: Pilgrims, Plagues, and Pan-Islam under British Surveillance, 1865–1908', *International Journal of Middle East Studies*, Vol. 40, No. 2 (May 2008): 269–90.

Mays, Devi, '"I Killed Her Because I loved Her Too Much": Gender and Violence in the 20th Century Sephardi Diaspora', *Mashriq and Mahjar*, Vol. 2, No. 1 (2014), 4–28.

Makdisi, Ussama, 'Reclaiming the Land of the Bible: Missionaries, Secularism, and Evangelical Modernity', *The American Historical Review*, Vol. 102, No. 3 (June 1997), 680–713.

McCarthy, Justin, Esat Arslan, Cemalettin Taşkıran, Ömer Turan, *The Armenian Rebellion at Van* (Salt Lake City: University of Utah Press, 2006).

McKeown, Adam, *Melancholy Order: Asian Migration and the Globalization of Borders* (New York: Columbia University Press, 2008).

Meyer, James, *Turks Across Empire: Marketing Muslim Identity in the Russian–Ottoman Borderlands, 1856–1914* (Oxford: Oxford University Press, 2014).

Miller, Owen, 'Sasun 1894: Mountains, Missionaries and Massacres at the End of the Ottoman Empire' (PhD Dissertation, Columbia University, 2015).

Minassian, Gaidz, 'The Armenian Revolutionary Federation and Operation "Nejuik", in Houssine Alloul et al. (eds), *To Kill a Sultan: A Transnational History of the Attempt on Abdülhamid II (1905)* (London: Palgrave Macmillan, 2017), 35–65.

Minawi, Mostafa, *The Ottoman Scramble for Africa: Empire and Diplomacy in the Sahara and the Hijaz* (Stanford: Stanford University Press, 2016).

Mirak, Robert, *Torn Between Two Lands: Armenians in America 1890 to World War I* (Boston: Harvard University Press, 1983).

Nacar, Can, 'Yükselen bir Liman Kentinde Ekonomik Pastayı Paylaşmak: 20. Yüzyılın Başında Mersin'de Rekabet, Çatışma, ve İttifaklar', *Cihannuma Tarih ve Coğrafya Dergisi*, Vol. 3, No. 1 (July 2017), 71–94.

Ngai, Mae M., *Impossible Subjects: Illegal Aliens and the Making of Modern America* (Princeton: Princeton University Press, 2004).

Nail, Thomas, *The Figure of the Migrant* (Stanford: Stanford University Press, 2015).

Nalbandian, Louise, *The Armenian Revolutionary Movement* (Berkeley: University of California Press, 1963).

Özbek, Nadir, 'Policing the Countryside: Gendarmes of the Late 19th-Century Ottoman Empire (1876–1908)', in: *International Journal of Middle East Studies*, Vol. 40, No. 1 (February 2008), 47–67.

Özbek, Nadir, 'The Politics of Taxation and the "Armenian Question" during the Late Ottoman Empire, 1876–1908', *Comparative Studies in Society and History*, 54, No. 4 (October 2012), 770–97.

Özok-Gündoğan, Nilay, 'The Making of the Modern State in the Kurdish Periphery: The Politics of Land and Taxation, 1840–1870' (PhD Dissertation, Binghamton University, 2011).

Özok-Gündoğan, Nilay, 'Ruling the Periphery, Governing the Land: The Making of the Modern Ottoman State in Kurdistan, 1840–70', *Comparative Studies of South Asia, Africa, and the Middle East*, Vol. 34, No. 1 (2014), 160–75.

Özsu, Umut, 'The Ottoman Empire, the Origins of Extraterritoriality, and

International Legal Theory', in Florian Hoffman and Anne Orford (eds), *The Oxford Handbook of the Theory of International Law* (Oxford: Oxford University Press, 2016), 123–37.

Pamuk, Şevket, *A Monetary History of the Ottoman Empire* (Cambridge: Cambridge University Press, 2000), 209.

Peck, Gunther, 'Reinventing Free Labor: Immigrant Padrones and Contract Laborers in North America, 1885–1925', *Journal of American History*, Vol. 83, No. 3 (December 1996), 848–71.

Peña Delgado, Grace, *Making the Chinese Mexican: Global Migration, Localism, and Exclusion in the U.S.–Mexico Borderlands* (Stanford: Stanford University Press, 2012).

Polatel, Mehmet, 'The Complete Ruin of a District: The Sasun Massacre of 1894', in Yaşar Tolga Cora et al. (eds), *The Ottoman East in the Nineteenth Century: Societies, Identities and Politics* (London: I. B. Tauris, 2016), 179–98.

Quataert, Donald, 'The Age of Reforms', in Halil İnalcık and Donald Quataert (eds), *An Economic and Social History of the Ottoman Empire 1300–1914* (Cambridge: Cambridge University Press, 1994), 824–42.

Quataert, Donald, 'Labor Policies and Politics in the Ottoman Empire: Porters and the Sublime Port, 1826–1896', in Heath Lowry and Donald Quataert (eds), *Humanist and Scholar: Essays in Honour of Andreas Tietze* (Istanbul: Isis Press, 1993), 59–69.

Quataert, Donald, *Ottoman Manufacturing in the Age of the Industrial Revolution* Cambridge: Cambridge University Press, 1993).

Quataert, Donald, *Social Disintegration and Popular Resistance in the Ottoman Empire 1881–1908* (New York: New York University Press, 1983).

Riedler, Florien, 'Armenian Labour Migration to Istanbul and the Migration crises of the 1890s', in Ulrike Freitag et al (ed.), *The City in the Ottoman Empire: Migration and the Making of Urban Modernity* (London: Routledge Press, 2011), 160–76.

Riggs, Henry H., *Days of Tragedy in Armenia: Personal Experiences in Harpoot, 1915–1917* (Ann Arbor: Gomidas Institute Press, 1997).

Robertson, Craig, *The Passport in America: The History of a Document* (Oxford: Oxford University Press, 2010).

Robson, Laura, 'Refugees and the Case for International Authority in the Middle East: The League of Nations and the United Nations and Works Agency for Palestinian Refugees in the Near East Compared', *International Journal of Middle East Studies*, Vol. 49, No. 4 (November 2017), 625–44.

Salyer, Lucy, *Laws as Harsh as Tigers: Chinese Immigrants and the Shaping of Modern Immigrant Law* (Chapel Hill: University of North Carolina Press, 1995).

Schneider, Dorothee, *Crossing Borders: Migration and Citizenship in the Twentieth Century United States* (Cambridge, MA: Harvard University Press, 2011).

Schneider, Dorothee, 'The United States Government and the Investigation of

European Emigration in the Open Door Era', in Nancy Green and François Weil (eds), *Citizenship and Those Who Leave: The Politics of Emigration and Expatriation* (Urbana, IL: University of Illinois Press, 2007), 195–210.

Schoenberg, Philip Ernest, 'The Evolution of Transport in Turkey (Eastern Thrace and Asia Minor) under Ottoman Rule, 1856–1918', *Middle Eastern Studies,* Vol. 13, No. 3 (Oct. 1977), 359–72.

Schull, Kent, *Prisons in the Late Ottoman Empire: Microcosms of Modernity* (Edinburgh: Edinburgh University Press, 2014).

Shumsky, Neil Larry, 'American Hostility to Return Migration, 1890–1924, *Journal of American Ethnic History*, Vol.11, No. 2 (Winter 1992), 56–75.

Sipahi, Ali, 'At Arm's Length: Historical Ethnography of Proximity in Harput' (PhD Dissertation, University of Michigan, 2015).

Sipahi, Ali, 'Suburbanization and Urban Duality in the Harput Area', in Yaşar Tolga Cora et al. (eds), *The Ottoman East in the Nineteenth Century: Societies, Identities and Politics* (London: I. B. Tauris, 2016), 247–67.

Stone, Frank Andrews, 'The Heritage of Armenia or Euphrates College', in Richard Hovannisian (ed.), *Armenian Tsopk/Kharpert* (Costa Mesa: Mazda Publishers Inc., 2002), 209–238.

Suny, Ronald Grigor, *'They Can Live in the Desert but Nowhere Else': A History of the Armenian Genocide* (Princeton: Princeton University Press, 2015).

Suny, Ronald Grigor, Fatma Müge Göçek, and Norman Naimark (eds), *A Question of Genocide: Armenians and Turks at the End of the Ottoman Empire* (Oxford: Oxford University Press, 2011).

Temizer, Abidin, 'Karadeniz Ticaretinde Seyyar Iskeleler: Kayıkçılar', in Osman Köse (ed.), *Tarih Boyunca Karadeniz Ticareti ve Canık* (Samsun: Canık Belediyesi Kültür Yayınları, 2013), 1077–84.

Toksöz, Meltem, *Nomads Migrants and Cotton in the Eastern Mediterranean: The Making of the Adana-Mersin Region, 1850–1908* (Leiden: Brill, 2010).

Toksöz, Meltem, 'Ottoman Mersin: The Making of an Eastern Mediterranean Port-town', *New Perspectives on Turkey*, Vol. 31 (Fall 2010), 83–134.

Torpey, John, *Invention of the Passport: Surveillance, Citizenship, and the State* (Cambridge: Cambridge University Press, 2000).

Ueno, Masayuki, ''For the Fatherland and the State': Armenians Negotiate the Tanzimat Reforms', *International Journal of Middle East Studies*, Vol. 45, No. 1 (2013), 93–109.

Üngör, Uğur Ümit and Mehmet Polatel, *Confiscatıon and Destruction: The Young Turk Seizure of Armenian Property* (London: Bloomsbury, 2011).

Varnova, Andrekos, *British Imperialism in Cyprus, 1878–1915: The Inconsequential Possession* (Manchester: Manchester University Press, 2005).

Walther, Katrine V., *Sacred Interests: The United States and the Islamic World, 1821–1921* (Chapel Hill: University of North Carolina Press, 2015).

Ward, Robert DeC., 'The New Immigration Act', *The North American Review*, Vol. 185, No. 619 (July 1907), 587–93.

Watenpaugh, Keith, *Bread from Stones: The Middle East and the Making of Modern Humanitarianism* (Oakland: University of California Press, 2015).

Weil, Patrick, *The Sovereign Citizen: Denaturalization and the Origins of the American Republic* (Philadelphia: University of Pennsylvania Press, 2013).

Wyman, Mark, *Return Trip to America: The Immigrants Return to Europe, 1880–1930* (Ithaca:Cornell University Press, 1996).

Yarmen, Arsen, *Palu-Harput 1878: Çarsancak, Çemişgezek, Çapakçur, Erzincan, Hizan ve Civar Bölgeler, Volume II* (Istanbul: Derlem Press, 2010).

Yavuz, M. Hakan, 'Warfare and Nationalism: The Balkan Wars as a Catalyst for Homogenization', in M. Hakan Yavuz and Isa Blumi (eds), *War and Nationalism: The Balkan Wars, 1912–1913, and Their Sociopolitical Implications* (Salt Lake City: University of Utah Press, 2013), 31–84.

Yildirim, I, 'Elazığ ve Çevresine Demiryollarının Gelişi', in Fikret Karaman, *Dünü ve Bügünüyle Harput* (Elazığ, Turkey: Türkiye Diyanet Vakfı Elazığ Şubesi Yayınları, 1999).

Yılmaz, İlkay, *Serseri Anarşist ve Fesadın Peşinde: II. Abdülhamid Dönemi Güvenlik Politakaları Ekseninde Mürur Tezkereleri, Pasaportlar ve Otel Kayıtları* (Ankara: Türk Tarih Kurumu Yayınları, 2014).

Zandi-Sayek, Sibel, 'Struggles Over the Shore: Building the Quay of Izmir, 1867–1875', *City & Society*, Vol. 7, No. 1 (June 2000): 55–78.

Zolberg, Aristide, *A Nation by Design: Immigration Policy in the Fashioning of America* (Cambridge, MA: Harvard University Press, 2008).

Index

Index

THE POLITICS OF ARMENIAN MIGRATION TO NORTH AMERICA, 1885–1915

Edinburgh Studies on the Ottoman Empire
Series Editor: Kent F. Schull

Published and forthcoming titles

Migrating Texts: Circulating Translations around the Ottoman Mediterranean
Edited by Marilyn Booth

Ottoman Sunnism: New Perspectives
Edited by Vefa Erginbaş

Jews and Palestinians in the Late Ottoman Era, 1908–1914: Claiming the Homeland
Louis A. Fishman

The Politics of Armenian Migration to North America, 1885–1915: Sojourners, Smugglers and Dubious Citizens
David Gutman

The Kizilbash-Alevis in Ottoman Anatolia: Sufism, Politics and Community
Ayfer Karakaya-Stump

Çemberlitaş Hamami in Istanbul: The Biographical Memoir of a Turkish Bath
Nina Macaraig

Nineteenth-Century Local Governance in Ottoman Bulgaria: Politics in Provincial Councils
Safa Saraçoğlu

Prisons in the Late Ottoman Empire: Microcosms of Modernity
Kent F. Schull

Ruler Visibility and Popular Belonging in the Ottoman Empire
Darin Stephanov

Children and Childhood in the Ottoman Empire: From the Fourteenth to the Twentieth Centuries
Edited by Gulay Yilmaz and Fruma Zachs

euppublishing.com/series/esoe